Enriching Mind & Spirit

A History of Higher Education in the Church of God (Anderson)

BARRY L. CALLEN

Additional copies of this book may be secured from Warner Press, the distributor of Anderson University Press books. To order, call toll free: 1-877-346-3974 or email to wporders@warnerpress.org

ISBN 0-9646682-9-7
Printed in the United States of America

Arthur M. Kelly, Editorial Assistant
Jan R. Callen, Editorial Assistant
Vivian H. Nieman, Church Archivist
David Liverett, Cover Design
Tamara Burrell, Copy Layout
Nancy's Photography (p.3)

Dedication

To the memory of Robert H. Reardon, leader in Church of God higher education, a special brother who went to be with the Lord as this book was being completed. The whole church is deeply in debt to Dr. Reardon, and to hundreds of his colleagues who have given their lives to enhance the minds and spirits of generations of young people. May these pages help to keep alive an awareness of their great sacrifices and accomplishments.

A Core Commitment

A central commitment of John Wesley and his brother Charles Wesley in their eighteenth-century church reform movement in England was:

> "Unite the pair so long disjoined,
> knowledge and vital piety—
> learning and holiness combined."

Such a commitment is an appropriate characterization of the Church of God movement as it has sought to bring fresh reform to the church since the 1880s—first without institutions of higher education, and then proudly through the ones now born into its midst. The goal has been the enhancing of both mind and spirit in the image of Jesus Christ and for the sake of God's ongoing mission in this world.

Acknowledgements

An undertaking of this magnitude could not have been completed without the cooperation of many persons. Dozens have shared from their personal records and memories, often through taped interviews for this book. Quotations in the text not otherwise identified are from such interviews.

Current leaders of the institutions represented in these pages, whenever possible, have assisted with research activities and read carefully the chapters on their respective campuses to help insure proper perspective and accuracy of detail. The financial support and personal encouragement from the office of Ronald V. Duncan, General Director of Church of God Ministries, were crucial in making this publication possible.

I express my gratitude to all who have shared with me in this review of the past and look to the future. To become acquainted in detail with the histories of these institutions of Christian higher education is to come to love them and be deeply grateful for the vision of their founders and the faithfulness of those who have followed.

Barry L. Callen
Anderson, Indiana
May, 2007

Table of Contents

Introduction

The year 1917 saw the launching of the first of the higher educational institutions still in existence in the Church of God movement (Anderson). In effect, that year was the beginning of higher education in the movement. Thus, the year 2007 is the 90th year, a pivotal anniversary of what has evolved into a diverse and distinguished educational enterprise in the service of the church. This is an appropriate time to publish a history of this major enterprise, one into which so much of the church's resources have been invested. The preliminary work for this present history was done by Barry L. Callen in the book *Preparing for Service* (Warner Press, 1988). Much has happened in the decades since that book was released.

From the very beginning of the Church of God movement in the final quarter of the nineteenth century, there was a sense of divine vision and urgency among its people. They wanted to do the will of God for their times. Many felt that the "evening time" of the gospel age was at hand and a bright new day was dawning. Robert H. Reardon titled his 1979 book on the first fifty years of the movement's life *The Early Morning Light*. Time was thought to be short, workers were few, and it was important to get out the news! The result? There was a boldness among the gospel messengers; there also was a humbleness. They believed that God would give freely of divine grace and the special gifts necessary for the expansion and nurturing of the true church. This gave considerable motivation and confidence. But these excited disciples were well aware of their own limitations in the face of human frailties and the immensity of the task. Thus, in their idealism, and despite the time urgency, they desired to prepare for their service in the best way possible.

This present volume is the story of their journey to discover the most appropriate and effective ways to become better prepared to fulfill their high calling from God. In particular, it recalls the issues, attitudes, experiments, and institutions of higher education that emerged along the way. While eventually this movement of the Church of God spread across the world and

Total Years of Educational Service to the Church of God Movement, as of 2007

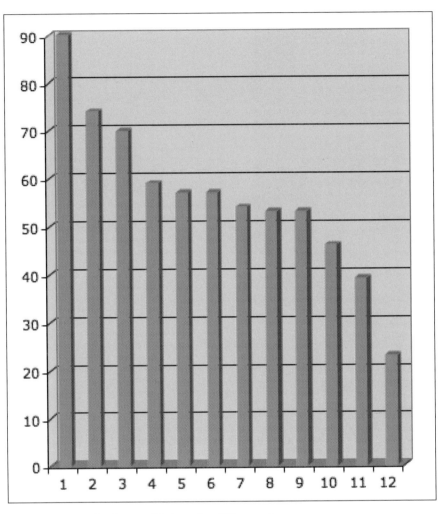

1. Anderson University (90 years)
2. Gardner College (74 years)
3. Warner Pacific College (70 years)
4. Fritzlar Bible College (59 years)
5. Anderson School of Theology (57 years)
6. West Indies Theological College (57 years)
7. Mid-America Christian University (54 years)
8. Arlington/Azusa Pacific University (53 years)
9. Kima International School of Theology (53 years)
10. Bay Ridge Christian College (46 years)
11. Warner Southern College (39 years)
12. Mediterranean Bible College (23 years)

developed various educational programs in many countries, the following study is limited primarily to a consideration of events and institutions in the United States, Canada, and the Caribbean (chapter twelve is the exception). It is further limited to institutions that continue to exist today, including Arlington College that continues through merger with another institution. Other educational programs, such as Berean Bible College, Kansas City Bible Training School, and the Southern Bible Institute, have been excluded from extended consideration because of their relatively brief existence and/or restricted scope of program. The histories of Gordon Bible College and Warner Memorial University are treated fully because of their relatedness to the eventual founding of the school that grew into the present Mid-America Christian University.

God calls all of his children to serve. Institutions of higher education have become a major means by which the Church of God has sought to assist persons to prepare for that service. Higher education has attracted much attention and required many dollars. The colleges, universities, and seminary have become very influential in the life of the church, and sometimes controversial. They have been significant cohesive forces, as well as centers of activity, creativity, and relationship building. They have helped a loosely organized church fellowship to focus its identity, extend its borders, and both conserve and rethink its history, teaching, and traditions. Their stories must be known if the history of the Church of God movement itself is ever to be understood.

Higher education in the Church of God movement has come to rest in part on a conviction that was stated this way in the 1920-1921 catalog of Anderson Bible Training School (now Anderson University): "Though many have seemed to decrease in spirituality while increasing in knowledge, the reverse should be the case—better qualified men should be more spiritual men."

But informed spirituality has not been the only goal in the church's higher education. Personal maturity and professional preparation and effectiveness also have been essential concerns over the years. So has the need to be free and able to think for oneself in the service of God, the church, and humankind.

Two outstanding men have embodied well the addressing of this latter goal during the formative decades of higher education of the Church of God. One, Russell R. Byrum, has been described by Robert H. Reardon as the man who "threw open the windows and doors of learning." He was a teacher-scholar who "encouraged his students to explore frontiers and to drink at the great fountain of historic thought." According to Reardon, "It was largely through the breadth and vision of this man that we were saved as a movement from theological rigidity and the same kind of closed-mindedness our movement had come into being to oppose" (in *Vital Christianity*, May 4, 1980, 5). The other, Otto F. Linn, was one of those people who has been, in the words of church historian Merle D. Strege, "captured by our notion that the truth may be pursued more than possessed. He firmly opposed authoritarian control of some minds by other minds" (in *Vital Christianity*, Dec. 7, 1986, 18-19). Linn, Byrum, and other educational pioneers who appear in the following pages highlighted scholarship as a valuable companion to Christian spirituality.

This pair, Christian faith and honest academic pursuit, has led to a range of institutions of higher education in the life of the Church of God movement. Thousands upon thousands now have benefited. It is quite a story! And the story goes on and offers to the emerging leadership of today's generation a great resource. So, one will find here an important history recounted, a present admired, and a future that appears to be crucial for the health and ministries of the church. For today's church youth, the colleges, universities, and seminary of the Church of God offer almost anything needed, and with high quality. The hope is that, through these pages, the church's institutions of higher education will become better known, appreciated, and supported.

CHAPTER 1

Higher Education in the New World

The colleges associated with the Church of God movement (Anderson, Indiana) are the inheritors of a long tradition of higher education in the United States. Knowing at least the highlights and trends of this new-world tradition is essential to understanding what has developed within the Church of God movement.

The American Tradition of Higher Education

As early as 1619, when 10,000 acres of land were granted by the Virginia Company for America's first university, the goal was to combine classical learning and the Christian faith for the sake of cultivating "the humane person." Clearly in the tradition of England's seventeenth-century colleges at Oxford and Cambridge and the Scottish universities, this new school in the American colonies sought to provide a general education which emphasized the arts of clear thinking and effective communication and the principles which ought to direct all personal and public affairs. Unfortunately, malaria and an Indian massacre ended this initial venture by 1622.

Very soon, however, learning and religion joined forces again. This time it was the Puritans. They established Harvard College in 1636, patterning it after Emmanuel College of Cambridge University in England.

This new school became the first of a series of colonial institutions which lifted high the banner of Christ in the context of serious academic study. The central purpose of these new schools was represented well by Harvard's famous statement of beginning:

> After God had carried us safe to New England, and we had builded our houses, provided necessaries for our livelihood, rear'd convenient places for God's worship, and settled the Civil Government: One of the next things we longed for, and looked after was to advance Learning, and perpetuate it to Posterity, dreading to leave an illiterate ministry to the churches, when our present Ministers shall lie in the Dust.

The charter of William and Mary, the next American college, declared that it was to exist so that "the church of Virginia may be furnished with a seminary for Ministers of the Gospel, and that the youth may be piously educated in good letters and manners, and that the Christian faith may be propagated amongst the Western Indians to the glory of Almighty God." The next school, Yale, was founded in 1701 by a group of ministers as a school "wherein youth may be instructed in the arts & sciences, who through the blessing of Almighty God may be fitted for public employment, both in church and civil state."

In general, collegiate education in the new world found its parent and main sponsor in the Christian churches. Religion was unashamedly recognized as the keystone of the educational arch. The Christian faith in particular was the determining factor in educational theory and practice. This is exactly how most Americans wanted it and how it had been for centuries before the birth of Harvard. The God worshipped by Christians was recognized as the ground of truth and, therefore, the guiding light and ruling principle in the education of the young.

Such a central place for the Christian faith was really a continuance of the medieval university tradition in a new world setting. The medieval mind had tended to conceive the whole of human society as unified in Christ through his royal, priestly, and prophetic roles. These roles were understood to be embodied in the three major earthly institutions, namely the state, based on law, the church, founded on revelation, and the university, upheld by reason. Even today, the relatedness of these institutions is preserved by the symbolism of the gowns worn by the justices in court, the ministers in church, and the professors and graduates in college commencements.

This European heritage of higher learning did not perish in the American wilderness as many assumed it would. Its beginnings in the new world may have been fragile, more promise than performance at first, and certainly affected by the practical needs and limitations of a young nation. But higher learning was planted securely on American shores and it did survive.

The nature of this higher learning was more deeply concerned with forming character than with fostering pure academic research. It placed great value on a controlled residential pattern of life for students. It oriented itself primarily toward the training of a special elite for community leadership. Early American higher education was intended to educate gentlemen and professionals. At first, it concentrated on preparing ministers, but soon lawyers, doctors, and teachers were included. Hebrew, Greek, Latin, and classical history and literature were basic to the curriculum. The whole frame of reference for this curriculum was dominated by the assumptions and goals of Christian faith.

During the nineteenth century, Americans tended to group themselves by occupation, social class, religion, gender, locality, and ethnic background. Almost all of these groups found adequate reason to set up their own colleges, both to perpetuate their own sub-cultures and to give themselves legitimacy in the larger society. Hundreds of colleges owed their entire existence to the vision and energy of a single person, often a clergyperson. When schools began to emerge in the Church of God movement, the circumstance would be similar. Pioneers of higher education would come to include Harry Gardner, Horace Germany, Albert Gray, John Morrison, Nellie Olson, and Joseph Wilson. But this is getting ahead of our story.

The numerous Christian denominations in the United States, themselves significant sub-cultures, provided a tremendous impulse for college founding. They were motivated by the need for an educated ministry and by a missionary spirit that sought to establish new and vital centers of Christian education and living. They also were motivated by the concerns of strengthening denominational loyalty, competing with denominational rivals, and off-setting the "secularistic" influences spreading throughout the culture.

Particularly after 1819, when the Supreme Court's decision in the Dartmouth College case essentially assured private institutions freedom from state interference, private liberal arts colleges multiplied. By 1860 over five hundred new colleges had been founded in the United States, most of them under church sponsorship. Although many of these did not survive beyond the Civil War years (particularly those in the South), and although they were very weak institutions by modern standards, the American "hill-top" colleges were a major shaping force in the society. So it remained in the United States without significant change for generations. Faith and learning went hand-in-hand. Together, they were an essential part of the backbone of a young nation.

Almost from the beginning, however, there were contrary forces. Some of them caused many Christian people to distrust higher education. Is cultivating the mind dangerous to the life of faith and a direct threat to the health of the church? Or is higher education essential to the integrity, maturity, and effectiveness of church life and mission? These had become questions for debate.

Challenges to Faith and Learning

The claims of the Christian faith may have enjoyed great prestige and have influenced the basic nature of higher education in America even before the nation's beginning. But faith claims came to face decades of change and turmoil. Traditional piety began to be pitched out many windows. Theological and political assumptions, virtually unquestioned for centuries, came under attack—and much of the action inevitably came to focus on college campuses.

By the end of the eighteenth century, the dominant beliefs and values of the early colonial period were being challenged directly. Critical winds were blowing vigorously in some quarters. Orthodox Christianity was beginning to struggle to hold its own against the "Enlightenment" mentality that was taking hold in intellectual circles. New approaches and names filled the air, approaches like rationalism, deism, naturalism, and empiricism, and names like Descartes, Bacon, Hobbes, Locke, and Rousseau. In America, the bitter writings of Thomas Paine and the milder ones of Thomas Jefferson tended to encourage a style of religious unbelief typical of the European skeptics and political radicals of the time. From a Christian perspective, therefore, by the late eighteenth century there was a general decline in the American public's commitment to traditional religion and morals.

Timothy Dwight, who became president of Yale in 1795, described increasing numbers of college students of the day: "Youths. . .with strong passions and feeble principles. . . delighted in the prospect of unrestrained gratification. . . and became enamored with the new doctrines. . . . Striplings scarcely fledged suddenly found that the world had been enveloped in general darkness through the long succession of preceding ages, and that the light of human wisdom had just begun to dawn upon the human race" (C. Robert Pace, *Education and Evangelism*, 1972, 10). An anti-church play was staged at Dartmouth. When the dean of Princeton opened the chapel Bible to read, a pack of playing cards fell out. Someone had carved a rectangle out of each page to accommodate the pack—and to infuriate the school!

In the decades that followed, there were times of dramatic spiritual awakening on the nation's campuses that brought back some of the mutual supportiveness between learning and religious faith. But society-wide trends were pointed the other way. Interest in the natural sciences was rising. Pressure was increasing for higher education to be freed from the control of religious bodies. It was argued that the mind must be unfettered, loosed to reason boldly and act revolutionarily on behalf of human happiness. The industrial progress of the nation was developing a need for persons with specialized training not available in most church-related schools.

With the emergence of a more open society during the early decades of the nineteenth century, the inherited educational system began to be challenged. American society was too democratic to be satisfied with the idea of a gentleman's education, and too practical and competitive to accept indefinitely the static character of many classical and church views. Something very new was bound to come along. That something would be more "secular" and practical, more "scientific" and specifically related to the materialistic needs and desires of a changing society. No longer would higher education be designed to convey the body of Christian truth to undergraduate students. Rather, it would view knowledge more as a progressive field of inquiry freed from religious presuppositions and restrictions.

In 1862, the Congress of the United States passed and Abraham Lincoln signed the Morrill Act endowing new colleges of agriculture and mechanical arts. These land-grant colleges broke radically with the historic pattern of liberal education (the Ivy League classical ideal) by emphasizing the "practical" branches of knowledge so necessary for an expanding young nation. They also separated their educational work from church control. Cornell University, founded in 1865, was the earliest example of a frankly secular university established to meet the needs of an emerging industrial society. Its charter stated clearly that "persons of every religious denomination or of no religious denomination shall be equally eligible to all offices and appointments." It was to be a new day that saw the money to finance a rapidly expanding academic community coming not from Christian bodies, which had been the financial foundation of the past, but from the federal government and industrialists.

Another development equally abhorred by most church-related educators of the day was the importation of the German university model of higher education. It was dramatized by the founding of Johns Hopkins University in 1876. Defenders of traditional church-related colleges spared little in denouncing this major development. John Blanchard wrote: "German universities have done more to make the Bible contemptible than have all other causes since Luther rescued it from the convent of Erfort" (in *Congregational News*, Jan., 1892). Between 1815 and World War I, more than ten thousand American students journeyed to Germany to secure their Ph.D. degrees from prestigious universities like Heidelberg, Leipzig, and Berlin. In those settings they learned a new model of education and picked up viewpoints about the Christian faith that were considered heretical at home. The new model gave priority to studies at the doctoral level, stressed faculty research, and degraded undergraduate education (the typical college years) to little more than preparation for postgraduate specialization. Heavy emphasis was placed on freedom—freedom for students to elect their own courses of study and for faculty members to teach subjects of their choice and to pursue sophisticated research.

Here was a far more scientific, technical, and specialized notion of scholarship. The spirit of critical inquiry was fostered. Nothing, including the Bible, was to be immune from the severest of rational investigation. No longer was there to be any orthodoxy except belief in the right to pursue truth in a setting freed from artificial restraints on the scholarly process. Emphasis was usually placed on factual knowledge rather than on meaning and morals. The prime goal was the acquiring of relevant data and not the nurturing of persons. These were a few of the key building blocks for what later would be a network of state universities in which most American youth would be educated. They would be very different from the classic church-related college.

The new approach to higher education, whether carried on in Germany or by its many American imitators, became infamous in the eyes of much of the nineteenth-century Christian community. It was especially objectionable when such "enlightened" persons joined the faculties of church-related colleges. In some institutions, the educational process deteriorated into bitter battles for control. In others the new trends were decried and every attempt was made to continue business as usual in isolation from such unwelcome developments. Reaction to the encroachment of this "modernism" was so severe in some quarters that many traditional and especially church-related colleges found themselves alienated from the culture around them. The reaction often was one of anger and a pulling away from what was judged to be the increasingly corrupted scene of higher education.

Social and educational trends were multiplying against the church-related college. By 1900 many persons had concluded that the small Christian college was living on borrowed time. The trend away from a narrow sectarian spirit in religion, coupled with the growing strength and vocational versatility of the state-supported institutions, all suggested difficulty if not doom for the small church college that championed traditional assumptions and was desperate for dollars. As the twentieth century dawned, it was common in evangelical Christian pulpits and holiness camp meetings to hear tirades against formal learning, almost as if such learning were little more than a cunning wile of the devil designed to draw a person away from dependence on the grace of God. Seminaries were condemned as "cemeteries." Many unlettered spokespersons for "the old-time religion" were given enthusiastic hearings on almost any subject they cared to address. Higher education had fallen under the cloud of a haughty attempt to lean on one's own understanding.

By 1900, conservative Christianity in the United States had reacted dramatically. The resurgence of "holiness" teaching had brought with it a considerable isolation from "the world," including the world of learning. It had led to a lack of interest in art, literature, science, and general culture. Christians by the thousands had retired from the mainstream of society and placed their faith squarely in the authority of their personal experiences with Christ. While the "modernists" were undercutting the public's traditional confidence in the Bible, many conservative Christians had become rigid in their views, sometimes blindly defending the faith against all comers. In their view, human learning and Christian faith were at odds. It was a troubled time, the time of the emergence of the Church of God movement.

A Reformation Movement Emerges

The Church of God movement made its modest appearance on the American scene in the late nineteenth century. By then, church-related higher education already had known its day of glory and was living through a controversial and chaotic period. This new Christian movement was in strong reaction to the turmoil of rampant denominationalism. The focus of its reform vision was that the church is the spiritual body of Christ and denominations are only religious organizations brought about by Christian people, not churches in the New Testament sense. The ideal is that all Christians should abide in Christ alone, the only road to oneness in the church. Feeling strongly that ecclesiastical organizations erode the leadership of the Holy Spirit in the church, these Christians "came out" of all denominational entanglements. They sought to accept the apostolic faith as defined in the New Testament and fulfill its mission in an open and free fellowship of sanctified and unified believers.

The pioneers of this movement were heavily experience-oriented (in common with many conservative Christians of the time). They also were quite anti-institutional in general outlook. They were disgusted with denominational rivalries and less than impressed with the tendency of denominations to found colleges as part of that competitive process. The emphasis on spiritual experience and away from institutions, plus the general tenor of the times, led to considerable caution about the appropriateness of actually establishing "Church of God" institutions for the purpose of fostering the life of the mind. Quite understandably, then, higher education got off to a very slow start in the Church of God movement.

CHAPTER 2

Giving First Place to The Spirit of God

I t happened in the earliest decades of the history of the Church of God movement. It was just about the way one would have expected. The movement was experience oriented, anti-institutionally minded, and a generally rural body of Christian people who were full of zeal and urgency for a gospel cause. They were living in the middle of revolutionary changes in American higher education that rarely were friendly to the Christian faith. Therefore, founding colleges was not a high priority. To the contrary, formal learning and evangelistic believing tended to be seen more as competitors than companions. Education typically was identified as part of the sectarian scene that God was calling to an end.

Beware of Formal Education!

Soon after his conversion experience in 1865, Daniel S. Warner attended Oberlin College in Ohio, enrolling for an English preparatory course. There he was exposed to persons of learning and refinement. At the time, the president of the college was Charles Finney, the nation's foremost preacher of holiness. Later, Warner attended Vermillion College where he studied Greek and New Testament. In 1876, when Warner was a Winebrennerian minister, the West Ohio Eldership met in Findlay, Ohio, and expressed its belief "that in no other way can we so effectually build up the Church and retain the children of our brotherhood than by establishing an institution of learning to be owned and controlled by the Church" (C. Forney, *History of the Churches of God*, 1914, 566). Warner was one of three ministers appointed to plan a way to bring such a thing about (the resulting institution continues to this day as the University of Findlay).

But the presumed significance of such an educational institution was not high on Warner's agenda in the years that followed, even though he was himself a highly motivated reader, researcher, poet, and writer-editor. As a mature minister later separated from the Winebrennerian brotherhood, starting institutions of any kind (especially ones such as colleges intended in part to solidify denominational loyalty) was seen as far from acceptable. He once wrote in the *Gospel Trumpet* that the only credentials required for ministry were "to be filled with the Holy Spirit and have a reasonable knowledge of the English language." On another occasion, he expressed his attitude toward much in the world of higher education: "Colleges are necessary to fit men for the work of the devil and the business of the world.... They are but devil's playhouses" (*Gospel Trumpet*, Oct. 15, 1884, 2).

A major manuscript of Warner's was revised and completed by H. M. Riggle after Warner's death in 1895. It was an extensive critique of the "sects" based on their reading of biblical prophecy. Particularly criticized as a "mark of the Beast" was the denominational practice of instilling particular sectarian doctrines in the minds of adherents. Warner and Riggle pictured education as a tool to solidify the disastrous dis-unity of God's church. How should it be instead? According to these prominent Church of God leaders:

> God's ministers received the everlasting gospel which they
> preach from the Lord. They receive it free. The anointing
> teaches them. They are "taught of God." . . . But all sects have
> their peculiar mark or doctrine with which they mark their
> subjects. They have erected preacher factories for the express

purpose of marking their ministers with their particular mark (*The Cleansing of the Sanctuary*, 1903, 379-380).

Being formally trained was announced as merely the process of a person being boxed in a human institution and tied by human thinking. It was understood to be a key element of the diseased backbone of the denominational system.

It is fair to conclude that early pioneer leaders of the Church of God movement were not necessarily against education as such. They certainly were against schools as they knew them. So much was this the case that the few leaders who had the benefit of some formal education were known to hide the fact in order to retain status with "the brethren." No wonder, then, that some Church of God preachers, once ordained to the ministry, actually burned all of their books (except the Bible) as a witness to their singular reliance on God and his Word.

Such radical actions were a dramatic form of an earlier and related action of Daniel Warner. Sensing his call to the ministry and feeling that he must prepare to be a laborer in the Lord's harvest while it was yet day, he had cut short his studies at Oberlin College. He went home and for a season applied himself to prayer and Bible study, things he judged directly necessary for ministerial preparation.

It certainly was common for the pages of the *Gospel Trumpet* in those first decades after 1880 to carry negative comments about institutionalized education. Typically, the specific issue under attack was either substituting human learning for the grace of God, using schools for sectarian ends, or implying that the primary credential for effective Christian ministry could be issued by a school. Warner, for instance, argued that "as to men prescribing a course of study as a condition of preaching the Gospel, that is the vilest form of popery" (*Gospel Trumpet*, Dec. 1, 1883). Seminaries were branded sectarian training grounds and hot beds of heresy. Colleges were seen as examples of human arrogance.

Again, the target of the criticism was rarely education itself, but wrong motivations for it and uses of it. Education was seen as a potentially good and helpful thing. After all, persons like Warner and Enoch E. Byrum, while writing strong anti-educational articles, at the same time were building significant personal libraries and proving themselves diligent students of the Bible and related subjects. But there was little time to give much attention to such things. More important things were at hand. The gospel workers were hurrying around the country as a "flying ministry," rarely pausing long enough to establish congregations, and certainly not stopping to build things as suspect as colleges.

In the early 1890s, however, at least a hint of changed attitude emerged. A home was organized in Grand Junction, Michigan, for the children of itinerant preachers. Regular classes in music, taught by Andrew L. Byers, and penmanship, taught by Jeremiah Cole, were conducted. Daniel Warner envisioned something more, an "extensive educational project." Persons often had spoken and written to him about the possibility of a course in Bible study that would better equip them to labor in the Lord's vineyard. His heart had become stirred to make an effort in this direction. Even a simple curriculum was projected, with the possibility of three teachers. Suggested courses included Bible history, perhaps archaeology, the critical study of the New Testament, lectures on prophecy, and experimental and spiritual truth. Music and elocution would be added later.

Then came a major turning point for this idea and for the young movement itself. On the day of the first scheduled class in 1895, Warner fell ill. Within days he was dead. Enoch E. Byrum became the new editor of the *Gospel Trumpet* and was quick to make clear his view and intent. He wrote: "Some have asked if we have a theological school here. We answer, no. Neither do we expect to have. We have Bible readings and special faith meetings almost every evening which are wonderfully blessed of God by way of spiritual advancement and real soul food, and holiness is lifted up to the Bible standard" (*Gospel Trumpet*, Dec. 26, 1895).

This hesitancy and almost defensiveness about the most modest of projected educational ventures reflected a widespread attitude in the young church movement. Lawrence Brooks, for instance, started his ministry in Arkansas in 1915. Soon he felt the need for some systematic preparation for his life's calling. The advice he got from older ministers was what he later recalled as the common attitude in those days: "Why fool around in school while souls are going to hell?" So it was in the early years.

This advice to Brooks, however, came in the face of a growing discussion about the appropriateness of formal education for the work of Christian ministry. By at least 1912 the discussion included more than the status quo attitude of Byrum or the negative opinion received by Brother Brooks in Arkansas. The ranks of the young movement were filled with common folk with little or no school experience. But many of that first generation of leaders were educated persons by the standards of the time. On the one hand, both Warner and Byrum had attended college. According to sociologist Val Clear, the first person representing the movement to preach in Anderson, Indiana, was a physician-turned-preacher and, at one time, forty-one of one hundred volunteer workers were school teachers (*Where the Saints Have Trod*, 1977, 20). The literary level of the early church publications suggests a highly literate leadership if not readership. On the other hand, most church people came from a rural background and had little inclination to use an educational approach to general church work. They often ranged from antagonism to apathy in their attitudes toward formal education.

This situation made possible the development of a deep and difficult cleavage. D. O. Teasley argued that spirituality must be central and the apprentice method basic to the training of gospel workers:

> Having recently seen some sad effects of human effort to train
> men and women for the ministry, I feel led to set forth the New
> Testament method of training those whom God has called to

his work…. All theological institutes and missionary training schools are run too much on the theoretical plan, which is detrimental to spirituality and tends to fill the head and empty the heart. In ninety-nine cases out of a hundred, a man goes into a missionary training school or theological institute a thousand times better fitted to win souls than he comes out…. It is the special duty of pastors to encourage, and care for, and instruct young workers. Good workers are the natural fruit of an able pastor and a spiritual church…. Workers are needed, but only those can be used who are able to convince the gainsayers, cast out devils, heal the sick, save souls, and perfect the saints" (*Gospel Trumpet*, April 6, 1905, 1).

H. A. Brooks, in the same publication only seven years later, developed a somewhat different thesis:

To the ignorant and unlearned, the advantages of education are unknown…. Surely there is no evil in knowing how to do and say things well. Yet the unlearned maintain that it tends to pride and worldliness. This is not so; and indeed it is true that there are many more self-conceited people among the uneducated than there are among the learned…. There is talent in the church of God lying dormant in the hearts and minds of men and women, through lack of education. Education would give them tact and diligence to bring forth their talents to the rescue of the perishing world in good, plain, proper language in the form of literature…. Men and women upon whom God lays his hand for the ministry in their youth must be public speakers, singers, readers, and writers all the days of their lives…. They should qualify themselves to meet ably every obligation and to fulfill properly each duty required of them in their calling" (*Gospel Trumpet*, June 20, 1912, 4-5).

Such differing perspectives represented more than a temporary problem, something that would fade quickly once the Church of God movement got itself better established. T. Franklin Miller was the executive officer of the national Board of Christian Education for the period 1945-1966. He reported that during those years there was still this deep cleavage among ministers in the Church of God. Some leaders were committed to evangelism and some to education, with little appreciation shown for each other's views. Miller saw as a central feature of his own work in those years the attempt to bridge this gap. But it persisted in some quarters. Val Clear observed in 1984: "That discussion, that dichotomy, that choice never has been eliminated. It juxtaposes the movement between the false extremes of trusting God or trusting humankind, and much of Church of God institutional history and sociology consists of the ways in which we have dealt with that pseudo-issue" (in *Educating for Service*, 1984, 16).

The Sunday School and Missionary Homes

With the Church of God having an essentially negative and yet increasingly mixed attitude toward formal education in those first decades following 1880, there also was a growing band of enthusiastic gospel workers who were anxious to be effective in their work. They did not see a systematic program of education as necessarily a compromise with sectarianism or a flaunting of human pride in the face of God's grace and gifts for ministry. The need became more apparent and various kinds of educational experimentation emerged.

The Sunday school movement was very popular among churches in the United States during the early years of the Church of God movement. At first, Daniel Warner judged the Sunday school just another sectarian tool bringing more division to the body of Christ. But it was a lay-oriented program often separated from the church bodies in whose buildings the classes met. So, it might be seen more positively. He wrote in an 1885 editorial in the *Gospel Trumpet* that "where there are a sufficient number of saints to hold a service especially for the instruction of the children and youths, there is no reason why such a service should not be held."

Classes of this kind became rather common. Some evangelists experimented further by conducting children's meetings alongside their revivals. Special classes were held occasionally in the Gospel Trumpet Home. In fact, by 1892 there was a Sunday school in the Trumpet Home. The editorship of Enoch E. Byrum, while showing no enthusiasm for training schools, did support Sunday school work. By 1903, George L. Cole was writing a weekly column in the *Gospel Trumpet* entitled "The Sunday School Work." Given a concern about employing "Babylon's" literature, and having judged the International Sunday School materials to have "a taint of sectism and erroneous doctrinal views" (*Gospel Trumpet*, Jan. 1, 1903, 9), by 1910 the Gospel Trumpet Company was publishing its own Sunday school quarterlies. The Sunday school avenue of education obviously had been accepted once it had been adapted to the concerns and perspectives of Church of God people.

Also of increasing prominence in the general society during the early years of the Church of God movement was the growth and industrialization of cities. To these complex and problem-ridden urban settings came pioneer ministers of the Church of God. They were burdened for the lost and the destitute. "Missionary homes" began to appear as bases of operation in various centers as teams of gospel workers conducted revival services, distributed literature, and helped the needy.

Probably the first such home was started in 1895 in Chicago by Gorham Tufts. It operated as a rescue mission, an evangelistic center, and later, under the leadership of E. A. Reardon, a place for a wide range of worship, service, and educational activities. Young people were attracted to this and similar urban homes. They had energy for service to others and they had needs of their own for growth and training. In 1909, F. W. Heinly, then director of the missionary home in New York City, described the purposes of that and the several other such homes within the Church of God movement:

> This home offers an excellent place for the training and instruction of young workers whom God has called. No prescribed course of lessons is given, but . . . a number of established ministers and workers are always here, ready to give the young worker the benefit of their varied experiences in gospel work, expound the Scriptures, and present the best methods for the study of the Bible, how to win souls and conduct meetings in the most effectual way.

Adam W. Miller, dean of Anderson School of Theology from 1953-1962, was once a participant in the "Study by Mail" program of the New York missionary home. Albert F. Gray, later president of Warner Pacific College, helped with the beginning of the Missionary Home in Spokane, Washington, in 1904. Robert H. Reardon, president of Anderson College from 1958 to 1983, was influenced deeply by life with his parents at the missionary home in Chicago.

By 1910 all of these missionary homes had begun to decline in strength and effectiveness. Some eventually were sold as apartment buildings, while others became strong and permanent congregations. Whatever the end of each, all had performed in varying degrees a critical educational function. It was typical in these settings that informal counseling and study sessions became regular classes for enthusiastic young gospel workers. Several of the homes developed the name "Bible school" or "missionary training school," including the Kansas City Bible School and the Spokane Bible School. Most significant for the future was Anderson Bible Training School.

Some general softening of the harsh attitudes toward formal education slowly became evident. The missionary homes were bridge institutions between what was slipping into the movement's past and what was about to come. They served for about a generation as the only existing "higher education system" of the Church of God movement. It was becoming increasingly apparent that the "flying ministry" days were coming to an end. Now there was the need for establishing more settled congregations with traditional pastors. Converts needed stabilizing and nurturing. The deep bias against organization was lessening in the face of obvious need. The Trumpet Home and the publishing company itself had become formally organized, had finally settled permanently in Anderson, Indiana, in 1906, and was a significant if informal training base.

Apparently, all institutionalizing in the church's life did not need to be sectarian after all! Slowly, the door was opening both to the importance of education and even to the potential legitimacy of institutions of education being established to more systematically advance the work of the Lord.

A Crucial Year—1917

Between 1912 and 1917 there appeared a series of little booklets for ministers called *Our Ministerial Letter*. Here was a communication link among leaders in the Church of God who needed more than the news and inspiration found in the *Gospel Trumpet*. They needed vigorous and substantive dialogue on topics central to their leadership responsibilities. They needed instruction.

The *Letter* included issues on "The Care of the Churches," "Financial Support of the Ministry," "Ministerial Relationships," and "Secrets of Success in Pastoral Work." Then came a sensitive, but vital concern. In the April, 1917, issue of the *Letter*, a foreword was written by J. W. Phelps. Very much as Daniel S. Warner had reported in 1895 when he was envisioning some systematic educational effort, Phelps now reported: "Young ministers and young men and women who are called to the ministry have been told again and again that they ought to prepare for their lifework. That the young people have realized the need of the best possible preparation is evidenced by the many earnest inquiries as to what they should study, what course of reading they should pursue. These questions are answered in this issue of *Our Ministerial Letter*." Russell R. Byrum, then pastoring in Boston, authored the main material titled "The Preacher Among His Books."

Then, in the August, 1917, issue there appeared Russell Byrum's "A Course of Study for Ministers." He wrote that "a minister who acts wisely may save an immortal soul for heaven, which is infinite gain; but by mistakes, neglect, or wrong-dealing with souls he may be responsible for their being lost in hell forever, and to miss heaven is an infinite loss." Byrum identified two kinds of qualifications for this heavy responsibility of ministry. The *spiritual* comes first and is God-given. The *intellectual* comes also. It requires human effort and consists of knowledge relevant to ministry. The necessary information is "obtained mostly from books." He concluded, "we have no regular means of systematic training. It is not because we are opposed to preachers gaining knowledge, but the dangers and disadvantages that have sometimes attended training-schools have caused us to hesitate in adopting such means." Having laid the groundwork for justifying a course of study, Byrum outlined a five-year reading plan with an annotated bibliography of readings for each year.

That year was pivotal. In 1917 the General Ministerial Assembly of the Church of God organized formally in Anderson, Indiana. After about four decades of the movement's life, there finally was begun that year the first enduring institution of higher education in the Church of God movement. It would also be located in Anderson, Indiana, and Russell Byrum would be a prominent figure in the early phase of its life. When this first school finally was launched, it would have to face periods of suspicion and strong opposition. Nonetheless, Anderson Bible Training School was launched and did survive as the first of several schools that would emerge later. The following chapters describe in brief the histories of all these institutions, including some that were short-lived and others that evolved in Europe, the Middle East, and Africa.

CHAPTER 3

The Story of
Anderson University

Adam W. Miller, a young convert from Baltimore, and several other aspiring ministers of the Church of God were attending the 1915 missionary convention of the Church of God at the missionary home in New York City. They confronted Joseph T. Wilson, a guest leader and general manager of the Gospel Trumpet Company in Anderson, Indiana. Here was their important question for him: "When is someone going to provide young ministers with training for gospel work?" His answer brought some hope. He said, "The Gospel Trumpet Company is about to begin classes for workers and we would be glad to have you come to Anderson and join us." Such inquiries and the urging of Russell R. Byrum had convinced Wilson that he must act. And Wilson was the kind of man who was willing to act creatively in spite of obstacles.

Those were difficult days financially for the Gospel Trumpet Company. Adding to his challenge was the general sentiment among Church of God people toward institutions of higher education. The sentiment was negative to say the least. But there had been signs of change in the attitudes of some, like the 1912 *Gospel Trumpet* article (June 20, 4-5) by H. A. Brooks titled "Advantages and Value of Education." The educational needs were so real that some persons were beginning to believe that there should be a way to address them despite the lack of financial resources and the jaundiced view of "worldly" schools.

Many more competent leaders were needed for the growing church movement. Evangelistic teams needed singers with trained voices. The publishing company needed good writers, editors, and copy readers. There were young ministers like Adam W. Miller who wanted to learn about the Bible, the world, and their own ministerial callings. There were persons writing to the *Gospel Trumpet* magazine wanting to know if there were a Bible school where they could go to learn about the message of the Church of God movement and how to preach and teach as ministers and gospel workers. It was time for something important to be born.

A Modest Place to Begin

A reorganization of the Gospel Trumpet Company in June, 1917, gave it the legal power to publish religious and moral literature, conduct homes for the aged, and maintain schools. The door was open. Joseph T. Wilson, in a visionary act as general manager, prevailed on the members of the company to name a "managing committee" to begin an educational effort. Comprised of J. T. Wilson, H. A. Sherwood, J. E. Campbell, R. R. Byrum, and F. G. Smith, this committee of vigorous men went to work. They (primarily Byrum) arranged a course of study, selected textbooks, secured teachers, and advertised that a Bible training school was being opened in Anderson. It would operate as an educational department of the company, with Wilson as founding principal.

The opening day for Anderson Bible Training School was October 2, 1917, in the Trumpet workers' home on East Fifth Street in Anderson. This very large block building later would be the "Old Main" of the campus.

Space was available because the company had begun paying wages to workers and some families had moved to private quarters. There were five teachers: Russell R. and Bessie L. Byrum, H. C. Clausen, Mabel Helms, and H. A. Sherwood, with only Clausen and Helms full time.

The initial student body consisted of forty-nine persons who were workers at the company and students at night. Courses included Bible, music, English, homiletics, and public speaking. They were delivered as a series of lectures each Friday evening, October through May, with the overall two-year programs designed by Russell R. Byrum after he had studied the program designs of many schools. As the little catalog printed in 1918 clarified, "no attempt at mere intellectual development is intended." What was intended by Anderson Bible Training School was the preparation of persons to fulfill their divine callings through the life of the church.

There was excitement, challenge, and caution being expressed in the school and across the church. Now there was a place to go! Classes were held in the Trumpet Home, with dorm rooms for students on the floor above. Wilson, acting as principal, continued to carry his regular responsibilities as general manager of the Gospel Trumpet Company. The school was a modest operation. It owned no property of its own and gave no formal recognition for work completed (that would soon change). Its faculty and students spent most of their time working at the publishing company. But it was a definite and welcome beginning, one with an amazing future that no one could foresee.

The first year of operation left some red ink on the books. Some in the company thought that this could not be tolerated. War was raging in Europe and many of the young men left to take up arms. The school's second-year enrollment dropped. But there were those like Joseph T. Wilson and Russell R. Byrum who would not let the effort die. Since it continued to exist into the second year of the planned two-year curriculum, the 1918 General Ministerial Assembly decided to give it considerable attention. What the school might become if it did survive worried some of the ministers.

An increasing number of ministers had come to appreciate the need for such a training school. With very few exceptions, there were no pastors in the Church of God who held college degrees, and there were many negative attitudes about "liberal" colleges and "sterile" seminaries. There was a natural concern that the new school would introduce the standard titles and symbols of self-seeking and worldly sophistication, encouraging in the young a reliance on credentials instead of the gifts of the Spirit. Some of the older pastors felt insecure with the prospect of a new generation of trained leaders quite unlike themselves. So the General Ministerial Assembly adopted the following in 1918 as appropriate guidelines for the future operation of Anderson Bible Training School:

1. We believe that such a school can be conducted to the glory of God and the welfare of the ministry and church if kept within certain bounds.

2. We believe that no effort should be made to create a sentiment to the effect that young ministers must attend this school in order to secure recognition.

3. It is our opinion that in many cases the education of ministers can best be obtained in those sections of the country where their ministerial work is to be done, so that the practical can be more definitely combined with the theoretical. In other words, we do not believe that the Anderson Bible School should supercede or replace other training schools of the church.

4. Students should be left free to choose their own course of study from among such branches as the school provides.

5. No recommendation or diploma should be given any student. Satisfactory gradings in school constitute no proof that an individual is called of God to preach the gospel. Hence, every student must be left on his own

responsibility so that he will not possess in this respect any authority proceeding from this school which will give him an advantage over those ministers who have not attended school. In the Church of God, every minister must stand on his own merits and earn his place of responsibility, whether educated or uneducated.

6. We believe that the training of ministers in this school should include more than their intellectual development along educational lines. The most prominent feature must be their personal development in spirituality, faith, and the gifts of the Spirit of God.

Already this young school had gained the attention of the Church of God at large, something to be typical of its coming relationship with the church.

The first persons to complete a program of study in the school were those completing the two-year program in 1919. They were the first of many thousands to come and were remarkable persons. The group included Anna Koglin, later to be a long-term teacher of German and Greek for the school, J. Frank Shaw, who gave his life as a missionary among the Indians of the American Northwest, and Louise Frederici, who became an assistant to the editor of the *Gospel Trumpet* in Germany.

Joseph T. Wilson had a tendency to begin more things than his management skills or available resources could sustain. By 1923 he found himself forced out of the Gospel Trumpet Company and, heart broken, chose to leave Anderson altogether. But he made one move before leaving that would be crucial for the future stability of the young school. In February, 1919, he had written to John A. Morrison, a young pastor in Colorado, and encouraged him to consider teaching homiletics and helping with the administration of the school as assistant principal. Wilson had never met Morrison, but knew that he had some ministerial and teaching (public school) experience. Wilson was also encouraged by Russell R. Byrum who had appreciated what Morrison had written for the *Gospel Trumpet.*

Morrison reflected years later on "the low estate of education in our movement" that "one such as I would be invited to have a place in the one and only educational institution operated by the church" (*As the River Flows,* 1962, 126). He had never been to high school, although he had attended normal school for several terms to prepare for teaching in Missouri. But he was given a place—and what a place it turned out to be! Linfield Myers, later to become a prominent business leader in Anderson and good friend of the school, said it was Morrison's "earthy quality, together with liberal helpings of his equally earthy humor, that helped him achieve greatness." He concluded, "If the leadership role of the new college had gone to someone of lesser human endowments back in 1919, this whole story might have been completely different" (*As I Recall: The Wilson-Morrison Years,* 1973, 78).

Church controversy soon was in the wind and the young school was in the middle of it. F. G. Smith, now editor of the *Gospel Trumpet* and author of influential writings like the book *Revelation Explained,* was a powerful person in the Church of God movement. In effect, he had become the movement's spokesperson, its chief interpreter, the definer and protector of its treasures of truth. Nevertheless, some persons wished for more democratic procedures in the church and even wanted to entertain points of view other than the so-called "standard" literature of the movement—much of it written by Smith.

Smith was particularly disturbed by the fact that Russell R. Byrum had begun using his Bible classes in the school as places to test various points of view, including alternatives to his own interpretation of the New Testament book of *Revelation.* The school was functioning as a stimulator of new ideas, sometimes even new ways of understanding the Church of God movement itself! The popular Byrum left his editorial work at the company in 1927 to cross the street and become full-time at the school where he was appreciated and very much needed. The curriculum had been extended and the school was growing. Despite the school's obvious limitations and the atmosphere of suspicion created by some, students generally were very enthusiastic and appreciative of their education. In 1924, for instance, Canadian graduate Harry C. Gardner returned home burdened to begin a similar training effort (eventually Gardner College). American graduate Nellie Olson returned as a missionary to Jamaica to do the same (eventually Jamaica School of Theology).

In 1925 the Gospel Trumpet Company struck from its bylaws the portion providing the power to operate schools. The school sought a separate charter from the state of Indiana and the 1925 General Ministerial Assembly elected a fifteen-member board of trustees to govern a now independent institution. Joseph T. Wilson was named board chair. John A. Morrison, who had become principal in 1923 when Wilson left, became the first president of the newly named Anderson Bible School and Seminary. The prohibition against granting degrees had been lifted in 1923 and made retroactive to the first graduates in 1919. Now, in addition to Russell R. Byrum as vice-president and Oscar J. Flynt as treasurer, a major figure was to join president Morrison to complete the school's leadership team.

George Russell Olt, Church of God pastor-educator and dean of Wilmington College in Ohio, came in 1925 as a faculty member and the first dean. Although there were no dollar or prestige incentives that could be offered, Morrison convinced him that God had a big job to be done in Anderson and that he was the only person available to do it. It was Olt who would stand by Morrison's side for decades to come as the academic leader committed to excellence. "It was his dogged determination to bring strength and integrity to the educational program," recalled Robert H. Reardon, "that set the standard for a great deal of what has happened in higher education in the Church of God" (*The Early Morning Light*, 1979, 54). With Morrison and Olt, the school had a sterling pair of leaders with complementary strengths. What was ahead would require all that they had.

Struggle for Survival, Identity, and Accreditation

Both the school in Anderson, Indiana, and the Church of God movement were set to enter a period of severe trial. Each would face fundamental questions about its identity, mission, and proper relation to the other. In addition, the stock market crash of 1929 and all that followed in the nation kept the college's very survival a constant agenda item.

Dean George Russell Olt worked diligently to broaden the scope of the school's program by adding courses and requirements in the liberal arts. This addition had the support of many of the school's graduates and prospective students who otherwise had to seek such "college" work in institutions not related to the church. To so broaden the curriculum, however, was an act of faith since the faculty had limited qualifications, there was no equipment for science courses, the total school budget for 1926-27 was only $32,000, and student tuition was not even charged until 1925. But the addition of the liberal arts was judged by school leaders to be the right direction to go, regardless of the higher cost.

This curriculum addition was affirmed by the 1928 General Ministerial Assembly, but not without opposition. What business, argued some, does the school have going beyond ministerial education? The critics argued that the liberal arts would be an open door for "worldliness." But the move was made and in 1929 the school's name was changed to Anderson College and Theological Seminary. A major statement of expanding mission had been made by the school. Its legitimate arena of academic inquiry and professional preparation was potentially the whole spectrum of human knowledge and endeavor. The windows of learning were to be wide open. The college was going to be a "college" in the fullest sense of the word.

Back in 1919, F. G. Smith had published the book titled *The Last Reformation* which had emphasized that the Church of God movement was a fulfillment of biblical prophecy as understood by a particular interpretation of the biblical books of *Daniel* and *Revelation*. John A.

Morrison and Russell R. Byrum tended to disagree and told Smith so. Thus, a basic question was posed openly: Did the movement's integrity rest in the fellowship of redeemed persons, or must there also be a common commitment to a particular understanding of biblical interpretation which understood the movement as prophetic fulfillment? Tension over this question grew in the church.

In the classes he taught at Anderson College, Russell R. Byrum continued to explore various options of biblical interpretation. He offered possible alternatives to F. G. Smith's approach to interpreting prophetic literature. He relied primarily on the Gospels and Epistles to lay a foundation for understanding Christian holiness and unity. Some showdown was coming and the school would be in the middle of it. It would be the clash between an educational institution prepared to test, learn, and grow and a sponsoring church that was questioning its willingness to be open to a fresh examination of its own historic self-understanding. The crisis points were to come in the Anderson Camp Meetings of 1929 and 1934.

In 1929 there was a direct challenge to the orthodoxy of faculty member Russell R. Byrum on a range of issues. Robert L. Berry, who had replaced Byrum as F. G. Smith's managing editor, brought the charges to the board of trustees of the school. A hearing, almost a heresy trial, was conducted over several days during the Anderson Camp Meeting. Although F. G. Smith was a chief witness against him, Byrum's explanations and attitudes were generally acceptable to most who heard. He was exonerated of "heresy," but cautioned in relation to his future teaching. The trustees quickly drafted a statement of their theological beliefs, proposing that the faculty sign it as a way of avoiding any further and unwarranted accusations. Byrum judged this unwise and saw himself as a potential liability to the school. So he resigned to become a builder of homes in Anderson for the rest of his long life. Even with this sad outcome, the conflict was not over. Educational integrity had withstood a challenge, but the church had lost the skilled services of Byrum. Those sympathetic to Smith's views were frustrated. They were to become more so the following year when the Publication Board refused to re-elect Smith to the editorship.

This frustration would fester and be back for another confrontation. It came in the 1934 Anderson Camp Meeting when John A. Morrison's ratification for another term as college president was under consideration by the ministers. Between 1929 and 1934, opponents of the idea of a church-sponsored liberal arts college and those disturbed by reports of "liberal" teachings at the college joined to attempt to force changes. F. G. Smith, now pastoring in Akron, Ohio, used his major influence as a widely accepted spokesperson for the reformation movement. He wanted control over the college within "last reformation" teachings, and he mistrusted John Morrison.

Beginning with resolutions passed by the Ohio Ministerial Assembly in 1933, several similar resolutions were passed elsewhere in the church. They called for an end of the liberal arts college program and a return to a curriculum of "only such studies as are in keeping with a purely religious training school." Another influential Ohio pastor, C. E. Byers, wrote this to A. T. Rowe at the Gospel Trumpet Company: "The College (liberal arts program) is not the work of the Church. Let the Church train and prepare her youth to preach the gospel. It is not the Church's business to run an institution to prepare folks to go out into the world in a business way." Secular truth, the concern of non-church colleges, is always being debated and changing, so the critics of the Anderson campus argued vigorously. But true Bible unity, based on divinely revealed truth and taught in the movement's standard literature, is the only center to which all Christians can be brought. Secular "truths" and Bible truth, they concluded, should not mix in one institution expecting to be supported by the Church of God. Above all, this college in Anderson must not rule the pulpits; the pulpits of the church must rule the college!

There also were charges of disloyalty to traditional teachings of the movement, with much of the focus on President Morrison whose term of office was coming up for reconsideration. The college responded to the criticism. There were mass mailings, articles in the *Broadcaster* publication of the campus, and numerous personal appearances in church and alumni settings. Morrison was sure of his ground and felt responsibility for thousands of the church's young people. When the showdown arrived in June, 1934, the college trustees re-elected Morrison for another term as president despite the pressure to do otherwise. With a majority vote required for ratification by

President John A. Morrison

the General Ministerial Assembly, Morrison was subsequently ratified by a margin of only 243 to 231! A long meeting followed in an attempt to reconcile as many differences as possible for the sake of church unity. The movement had engaged in a major internal debate and would survive. So would John A. Morrison as president, Russell Olt as dean, and the liberal arts program to which both men were committed. In later years, Morrison and F. G. Smith were to be reconciled, finding joy in their common commitment to Christ and his church despite their differences in viewpoint on some things.

So a training school had begun, had matured into a small liberal arts college, had acquired strong executive and academic leadership, and had survived major opposition from some very influential leaders within the sponsoring church. Now the college had to find ways to build a future, even while suddenly existing in the middle of the terrible economic depression of the 1930s. The first attempt at a major financial campaign had been launched by the college in 1929, but that turned out to be the year of the stock market crash. It was to be more than twenty years before the first new building could be erected.

The 1930s certainly were difficult years. An enrollment as low as ninety-one students was experienced in 1932-33. Faculty salaries were most inadequate. As the economy grew worse, the faculty volunteered to have them lowered even more. Dollars and foodstuffs were collected for the students wherever they became available. An old college truck made trips to neighboring states to gather food from sympathetic farmers—once returning with five hundred quarts of sauerkraut from one church! The one large concrete block building, "Old Main," is all that there was. Dormitories, faculty apartments, classrooms, chapel, dining hall, carpenter shop, and laundry room were all housed under this one roof. Dollars and students were scarce, but not determination.

President Morrison continued trying to convince doubting groups within the church of the wisdom of a church-related liberal arts college and the urgent need to support the one in Anderson in very difficult times. He wrote in the *Gospel Trumpet* (Feb. 12, 1931):

Is anyone educated who has not been taught science, music, history, literature, art, philosophy? Is anyone educated who has not been taught in religion? Can the state teach religion? Would we allow it? The fact is, brethren, if we hope to save our young people from shipwreck of faith during the process of their education, we as a church must make it possible for them to receive that education amid Christian environments.... The state universities have so thoroughly secularized the educational process and divorced it from the religious program that, unless the church colleges are enabled to carry on. . .Christianity in America is doomed to be wiped out.... Anderson College and Theological Seminary. . .is having a terrific struggle to survive the present financial crisis. We must have help from those who believe in a spiritual program.

Even with the difficulties, there were encouraging signs of success, growth, and hope. In 1930, significant persons like Carl Kardatzke, Amy Lopez, Earl Martin, D. S. Warner Monroe, and Esther Kirkpatrick were graduated. In 1932 the first liberal arts graduating class of twenty received Bachelor of Arts degrees. There was a director of intercollegiate athletics by 1934, with a team known as the "Tigers," a fitting symbol for a tenacious young college determined to prevail. By 1937 enrollments were growing again and the Indiana Department of Education gave the college provisional accreditation for the education of public school teachers.

The year 1941, the college's twenty-fifth, was characterized by more than Geraldine Hurst and Jack VanDyke being named best all-around woman and man on campus. President Morrison, despite his own struggle with arthritis, was working toward four central and ambitious goals. Have five hundred students enrolled. Remove the school's indebtedness. Establish a loan fund for ministerial students. Achieve accreditation by the North Central Association. In 1941-1942, the faculty consisted of twenty-one persons, fifteen of whom held at least a master's degree. It was the tragic year of Pearl Harbor and soon many of the male students began to leave school to join the war effort. The college was struggling to mature in a world in turmoil. By 1946 many GI's were home from the war and coming to the college as non-traditional students. Student wives, small children, and temporary trailers became common around campus. With student enrollment growing and Jumpin' Johnny Wilson bringing national attention to the campus basketball team, the drive for full accreditation was really on.

President Morrison and Dean Olt had worked systematically for several years to accomplish vital recognition by the academic world. They had given careful attention to improving business operations and the procedures related to student records. Faculty credentials and library holdings had been strengthened according to accreditation standards. Morrison insisted on a constructive wedding of education and religion. Olt was insistent on maintaining academic excellence. They were a great team.

Then, on March 27, 1946, in Chicago, the North Central Association of Colleges and Schools voted to grant the desired accreditation, the first to any institution in the Church of God movement.

It truly was a day of rejoicing! An Anderson city newspaper the next day carried this as a subtitle to its bold headline about the local college: "Institution takes place among academic leaders in country." It was a matter of community as well as campus pride. This bold subtitle had meaning; practically, however, its realization was hindered by a genuine need for new campus facilities and instructional equipment. President Morrison announced the hope of building student dormitories, a library, a science building, a physical education plant, even launching a school of theology at the graduate level. This was more evidence of what the North Central examiners had said in their accreditation report: "The administration is forward looking."

Building on Strong Foundations

In the decade following accreditation, there were many firsts for Anderson College. There was the first football team, honorary societies, a new student residence hall in 1950, and the giving of distinguished alumni awards. The first two went to industrialist Vern Schield and missionary Daisy Maiden Boone. The faculty had grown by 1950-1951 to forty-five full-time and eleven part-time persons and the student body was nearing one thousand. The curriculum had broadened to three degree programs at the undergraduate level (B.A., B.S., B.Th.) preparing persons for Christian ministry, music, teaching, and pre-professional education in a range of fields. It was a time of steady growth.

This growth included acts of conscience and courage. In the city of Anderson, for instance, the Chamber of Commerce became upset with Dean Russell Olt and professor Candace Stone for their outspoken support of the labor, civil rights, and peace movements. Even so, there were positive breakthroughs in community relations. With the help of Linfield Myers of Anderson Banking Company, the successful financial campaign for the new campus library was made possible largely through the generosity and name of Charles E. Wilson, former Anderson industrial pioneer, president of General Motors, and Secretary of Defense in the cabinet of President Dwight D. Eisenhower. While relationships with the local business community had awkward moments in the college's early decades, improvement had begun and would develop dramatically in the coming decades.

In the 1950s, one could hardly have dreamed that the campus by the 1980s would have built Reardon Auditorium, cultural center of the area, have formed a partnership with Purdue University to serve specialized needs in the local labor force, be providing the two city hospitals with a large percentage of their trained nurses, and have brought to town the annual summer training camp of a National Football League team, the Indianapolis Colts. Slowly, from an isolated and even antagonistic relationship between the Church of God agencies in Anderson (including the college) and the city, change came. As the college developed and demonstrated a servant mission to many needs locally, the city and its people responded with increasing pride and support.

In the Church of God movement at large, there was close relationship, constant interaction, and occasional tension with Anderson College. The tension sometimes grew out of an anti-intellectualism in some quarters of the church, but more often from misinformation or the suspicion and mistrust of "headquarters" and its bureaucracy. Occasionally it came because the campus exercised leadership which was needed but not welcomed by all. An example in 1950 was the launching of the graduate School of Theology.

Although there never had been educational requirements for ministerial ordination in the Church of God movement, the years after World War II saw increasing numbers of young Church of God ministers seeking graduate degrees in seminaries like Oberlin Graduate School of Theology in Ohio. It became the strong conviction of leaders in Anderson like Harold   L. Phillips, Gene W. Newberry, Adam W. Miller, Earl L. Martin, T. Franklin Miller, Robert H. Reardon, John A. Morrison, and Russell Olt that the Church of God should provide such graduate education on the Anderson campus. Morrison, having himself spent time in 1942 at Oberlin as guest of seminarian Robert H. Reardon, recommended the idea to the college board of trustees in 1946. Its desired nature and likely cost were explored by a board committee. When the questions were all addressed and the decision made, plans were developed to actually launch the new graduate school in October, 1950.

Earl L. Martin was the first dean of the new School of Theology. As that first term began, there were thirty-five students and one full-time faculty member, Gene W. Newberry. The three-year Bachelor of Divinity degree was to be offered. All standards and structures were being put in place with the hope of eventual accreditation by the Association of Theological Schools. There was no additional funding from the church for this new venture, so Anderson College underwrote all costs and housed the operation, including the beginnings of a new seminary library located on an upper floor of Old Main. Invaluable assistance came from the Indianapolis-based Lilly Endowment to enable the adding of a new faculty position each year until a full teaching staff was in place. Soon John W. V. Smith and Delena Goodman were on the graduate faculty. Adam W. Miller became dean in 1953. By 1955 there were approximately seventy-five graduate students, twenty-one graduate degrees already granted, and the school's election to the status of Associate Member of the Association of Theological Schools. It was an excellent beginning!

Changing of the Guard

The end of the 1950s was a time of major transition for the institution. The several new buildings, including a library (1957), women's residence hall (1958), School of Theology building (1961), and gymnasium

(1962) gave a very different appearance to the campus. Death claimed leading campus figures Dean Russell Olt (1958), Carl Kardatzke (1959), John Kane (1960), and others. There were financial problems and significant opportunities. President John A. Morrison retired in 1958 after thirty-five years as chief executive officer and, with Dean Olt's death that same year, a new executive team was needed to carry on the long tradition of forward looking and faithful leadership.

The heavy mantle fell on Robert H. Reardon as president and Robert A. Nicholson as dean in 1958. It was the beginning of a new and effective partnership that would last for one-quarter of a century. But it was a beginning marked by rich continuity with the past. Reardon, who had grown up around the campus almost from the school's opening year, and who had returned to the campus in 1947 to be the president's assistant, observed this to the board of trustees as he was retiring in April, 1983: "It has been helpful to have known the college in its infant days of struggle and to have caught during my high school years the dream of its future shared by Dr. Morrison and Dean Olt."

Robert A. Nicholson, who first came from Minnesota as a student in 1940, and in that same decade became a faculty member and chair of the music department, was to have a long and distinguished tenure with the institution. He served as dean of the college for twenty-five years and then as president beginning in 1983. His autobiography, *So I Said Yes!*, was published by Anderson University Press in 2006.

Six major institutional objectives had emerged from the work of the President's Study and Planning Commission that president John A. Morrison had established and Robert H. Reardon had chaired. These objectives, significant directional priorities for the new administration in 1958, were basic concerns: exalt the spiritual and train for responsible Christian citizenship; improve instruction; attract qualified students; raise faculty salaries; build and conserve the physical plant; and broaden the base of financial support for the institution. It was a big challenge indeed, but there were good foundations on which to build—and the builders were skilled, experienced, and dedicated. The objectives were surrounded by core convictions that Robert H. Reardon reaffirmed at his presidential inauguration in 1958 (*Alumni News*, Nov., 1958):

> We believed that the youth of the church and the nation are our greatest wealth, deserving our best since what happens to them will happen to the future; that the heart of a Christian liberal arts college is a qualified and inspired faculty; that there is an essential unity in the truth and no honest Christian student need repudiate his or her faith to maintain integrity; that without the claims and insights of religion, education loses its way...; that learning is neither for wealth nor prestige, but for responsible Christian citizenship; that a church that will take a college and seminary to heart. . .will reap rewards in enrichment of its own life.

The eventful years 1958 to 1983 saw the Reardon-Nicholson administrative team lead, conserve, innovate, and bring increasing maturity to every aspect of campus life. Student enrollment approached the two thousand mark in 1971-1972 and was to remain quite stable despite the volatile forces then affecting the world of American higher education. New campus facilities were provided to accommodate the growth in student population and range of academic and support programs. A men's residence hall and a science building were completed in 1964. In 1967, another residence hall, apartments for married students, and additional athletic facilities were completed. The next year the historic and beloved "Old Main" was demolished so that Decker Hall, a major administrative-academic complex, could be built on the site in 1968-1970. Olt Student Center was doubled in size and a natatorium was erected. A beautiful, modern campus was quickly becoming a reality.

The Vietnam war years brought turmoil to the nation and related tension to the campus. President Reardon, a strong leader determined to retain the distinctiveness and integrity of the campus, both applauded the sensitive consciences of students—he always loved students and was loved by them—and held the line when they wanted to go too far (like wanting to abolish mandatory chapel/convocation attendance). He said in 1972 that he hoped "the turbulent 1960s, with its rebellious, impatient, tuned-in, turned-on, tell-it-like-it-is, revolutionary approach to the world," was over and the college would "recover something of the quiet thoughtfulness and balanced judgment which are marks of civil and refined people" (in John W. V. Smith, *The Quest for Holiness and Unity*, 1980, 389). The campus had not burned as many had, but it had not escaped the strain of those difficult years for the nation. President Reardon's 2004 biography by Barry L. Callen would appropriately be titled *Staying on Course*.

One of the significant and creative programmatic developments during these volatile years was the beginning of the TRI-S (Student Summer Service) program in 1964. With Norman Beard, then Dean of Students, as its skilled administrator, this program began exporting student labor and love all over the world through international learning and service experiences. Another significant development came in 1972 when the Center for Pastoral Studies began under the leadership of Barry L. Callen. It was the special unit of the School of Theology to coordinate the professional development of ministerial students on campus and to be the agency for accrediting, recording, and sometimes sponsoring programs of continuing education for active ministers (more than one thousand ministers soon became involved nationwide). A third such development was the creation in 1973 of the Center for Public Service under the leadership of Larry Osnes. It supported selected students from many major fields of study who desired assistance in preparing to serve the public effectively through utilizing their own careers as service opportunities.

Academic majors continued to expand and gain national recognition. New accreditations were granted by the National Council for the Accreditation of Teacher Education in 1963, the Association of Theological Schools in 1965 (related to the School of Theology), the National League of Nursing in 1975, the National Association of Schools of Music in 1974, and the Council on Social Work Accreditation in 1979. The Master of Religious Education degree was added in the School of Theology in 1967, and other specialized masters programs began there in 1973.

The campus administration was active and innovative throughout these years. Many highly gifted and credentialed persons were brought into the life of the institution and given the encouragement to grow and be creative. President Reardon identified a central reason for this growth: "Young Christians and their parents want a school that has standards of behavior, that has a framework of faith, a religious root system, but where there is a strong academic program, a strong sense of freedom to think, to explore within a sense of community where people come to know one another and participate in one another's lives" (in *Vital Christianity*, Sept. 11, 1983, 11).

Relationships between the campus and the Church of God remained vital. Thousands of young persons had come to the campus from local congregations and then taken their places of leadership and service across the nation and the world. Significant financial support came to the campus annually from the church's World Service budget. Many students who had gone abroad first on a TRI-S project began moving into the ranks of the full-time missionaries sent by the church. Graduates of the School of Theology were filling more and more church leadership positions.

By 1971, some issues in the School of Theology had to be faced. The enrollment was low, the faculty aging, and the church, maintaining no educational requirements for ordination, apparently was satisfied to allow the campus to carry the full financial responsibility for this, the one seminary of the church. It was time to explore program and even affiliation options. The board of trustees authorized: (1) new degree programs (Master of Ministry and Master of Arts in Religion) which required less completion time and gave more specialization potential than the standard Master of Divinity degree; (2) the beginning of the Center for Pastoral Studies which would allow new stress on the internship and continuing education aspects of ministerial education; and (3) affiliation with the evolving Foundation for Religious Studies in nearby Indianapolis which would enable student program enrichment opportunities in the several seminaries involved.

The church's 1972 General Assembly, pleased with some of these developments, nonetheless had some objections, particularly to the affiliation arrangement which was seen by many ministers as an inappropriate way to educate future Church of God ministers. When the debate had subsided, resolutions passed by majority vote called for: (1) an end to this affiliation; (2) the development of a plan for the continuation of a Church of God seminary responsible more directly to the General Assembly; and (3) the launching of a multi-year study by the Commission on Christian Higher Education on theological and ministerial education in the Church of God. For the first time, the School of Theology, born and nurtured by the Anderson campus, was being examined closely, disciplined, and even adopted by the church at large. This process had its pain, pitfalls, and real potential.

The 1973 General Assembly heard its study committee announce that a free-standing seminary separated from Anderson College, a model advocated by some, was not desirable functionally or feasible economically. Instead, the committee recommended and the Assembly agreed that the School of Theology should receive separate and increased World Service support, its Church of God students should receive new scholarship funding from the church, and its dean, still to be elected by the campus trustees, should be ratified by the Assembly as was the campus president. Barry L. Callen was so ratified as the seminary's new dean in 1974, succeeding the retiring Gene W. Newberry. Student enrollment grew dramatically from 68 in 1974 to 188 by 1977. In 1975, the Adam W. Miller Chapel and library addition were added to the School of Theology building. Exciting days had arrived!

Another tension-filled but eventually constructive period for the campus was 1980-1981 when an "open letter" sent to ministers by a pastor charged the college with yielding to liberalism and "humanism" in certain of its teachings and practices. The 1981 General Assembly received a major report from the campus board of trustees in which charges were addressed and stances taken. This well-prepared report cleared the air and left no doubt that the college was committed both to the church and to the integrity of an open educational process. Some changes were made on campus. A new faculty application form was developed that made more explicit the school's expectations of belief and ethical practice. The board of trustees created a new Committee on Educational Policy and Personnel designed in part to review and approve recommendations by the president to grant tenure to faculty members.

The times of tension between church and campus often were reflections of struggles within the larger Christian church, and certainly between differing groups within the Church of God. Such struggles easily focused on the Anderson campus because of its visibility, central geographic location, strategic influence, and many contact points with the life of the church. The college had played a pivotal role in the general development of the Church of God movement and even of several of the church's other institutions of higher education. In 1981, for instance, the college granted honorary doctoral degrees to four of its own graduates of earlier years, persons who had gone on to make major leadership contributions to sister Church of God colleges. They were: Milo L. Chapman (B.Th., 1939) from Warner Pacific College; Walter M. Doty (B.A., 1939) from Mid-America Bible College; Leslie W. Ratzlaff (B.A., 1940, B.Th., 1941) from Warner Southern College; and J. Horace Germany (B.Th., 1944) from Bay Ridge Christian College.

The School of Theology on the Anderson campus was a gathering point for graduates from all the Church of God schools as these persons continued their ministerial educations at the graduate level. For example, in 1983 first-time seminarians joining the School of Theology student body included twenty-five graduates of Anderson College, one from Azusa Pacific

College, one from Bay Ridge Christian College, twenty-three from Gardner Bible College, five from Mid-America Bible College, three from Warner Pacific College, and six from Warner Southern College.

Organizing for the Future

The year 1983 would mark another new beginning. Robert H. Reardon retired from the presidency after twenty-five years and his dean of all those years, Robert A. Nicholson, was elected by the board of trustees to become the third president of the institution. Nicholson had deep roots in higher education, the Church of God, and the history of the college. In his inaugural address on October, 1983, he expressed his profound debt for leaders of the past and his intent not necessarily always "to stand where they stood," but rather "to stand on their shoulders, to seize the strength of their steadfastness, to peer further out into the unknown...." This he would do with exceptional success.

Excellent foundations had been laid; now it was time to organize for the demanding times that lay ahead. It would not be easy in the face of declining numbers of eighteen-years-olds in the country, reductions of student financial aid from the government, and aggressive recruitment by public institutions of higher education with low tuition charges. It would take new efforts and resources to retain the distinctiveness of the institution. Sharply rising costs had to be faced, while remaining affordable for those students, particularly from the Church of God, who would want this special alternative in higher education. The local Anderson newspaper may have been premature in announcing in 1946, at the time of initial accreditation, that the "institution takes place among academic leaders in country." The 1990s, however, could bring substance to such a bold assertion if the campus could find ways to meet these challenges. It would.

Robert A. Nicholson made good use of his year as president-elect. When he assumed the presidency in the summer of 1983, he had put in place a formal mission statement, accompanied by eight institutional goals for the years 1983-1987. The goals addressed campus distinctives, student enrollment aspirations, personnel development needs, a major growth goal for the endowment of the institution, and so on. It was time for purposeful and disciplined action. The new president reorganized the administration and, with the help of Barry L. Callen, who moved from the deanship of the School of Theology to that of the college, he reorganized the college into three schools. The intent was to accomplish a level of academic and personnel administration better suited to the college's expanding future. New commitment was made to the cruciality of the liberal arts program after the completion of an intense review of its philosophy and curricular structure.

Working closely with the chair of the board of trustees, Ronald J. Fowler, the president proposed a reorganization of the manner in which the board did much of its work. The board adopted the new plan in the belief that it would increase its direct involvement in informed campus governance. The institution joined the Coalition for Christian Colleges and Universities and soon was recognized as one of its more prominent members nationally. Attempts were made to devise an effective campus planning process. A systematic way of setting annual priorities was sought for an increasingly complex institution, using the best wisdom and the wisest allocation of available resources. After some frustration and excellent consultant assistance, a strategic planning process was put in place in 1987.

In 1985, President Nicholson launched a five-year "Campaign for Anderson College" which sought $25 million for the heart of the institution. With chief financial and development officer Ronald J. Moore assuming leadership, and Bill and Gloria Gaither co-chairing a national campaign cabinet, significant funding was sought for endowment of student financial aid, faculty development, key academic programs, and a major expansion of library space, including a computer-automated modernization of its services. The stress on endowment was seen as essential if the future was to be marked by stability and excellence. By the end of 1987, with two of the campaign's five years completed, approximately $12 million already had been committed, with groundbreaking for the library project anticipated in the summer of 1988.

The campus continued its tradition of innovation as it sought to fulfill its stated mission of being "an institution of Christian higher education at its best." The Krannert Fine Arts Center had been erected in 1979 to house the music and art programs and provide general classroom space. In 1984 Reardon Auditorium was opened as a worship, cultural, and entertainment center for the campus and city (local citizens and businesses shared in the cost by providing 1.7 of the 5.5 million dollars in a time of high local unemployment!). The campus and its fine facilities had become host to activities as diverse as a symphony orchestra, special olympics, and the training camp of a National Football League team (Indianapolis Colts). The undergraduate college was increasing in its attractiveness to young persons with church backgrounds other than the Church of God. The graduate School of Theology continued to serve graduates from all colleges related to the Church of God, and from many others as well.

The School of Theology, under the leadership of Jerry C. Grubbs, developed its Florida extension program on the Warner Southern College campus, while the Center for Pastoral Studies, directed by James W. Bradley, continued to broaden its services to ministers nationwide. After several years of offering the associate degree in Nursing, the first Bachelor of Science in Nursing degrees were granted. The campus entered a unique and widely heralded relationship with Purdue University, enabling Purdue to offer associate degrees in technical fields to non-traditional students in the Anderson area. The first of these Purdue degrees were granted in 1987 as part of Anderson's commencement ceremony, a signal event in a partnership of public and private institutions formed to serve most efficiently a real public need. Also in 1987 Anderson initiated its own adult education program for a range of local persons not served by Purdue's technology-oriented programs. Michael E. Collette was key to guiding the development of these new efforts.

Even though the 1980s were difficult years in higher education, including significant problems experienced by all of the other Church of God colleges, Anderson remained relatively stable in enrollment, innovative in programming, and well managed financially. It began to serve some new constituencies without violating its distinctive mission. It sought to strengthen faculty salaries and obtain expensive instructional equipment without raising student costs beyond affordability. It was seeking to retain that precious quality of community, that atmosphere of personal caring, sharing, and learning in the midst of both the diversity of ideas and vocational goals, all with the unifying factor of Christian faith.

Then in May, 1987, the board of trustees determined that it was appropriate and timely to change the institutional name to Anderson University. This would reflect more accurately an institution that had come to comprise a strong liberal arts college with some sixty majors, a graduate School of Theology with a range of masters degree programs, a new division of adult continuing education, and the possibility of new masters and even doctoral programs not related to ministerial education. In President Nicholson's May 15, 1987, recommendation to the trustees on behalf of the name change, he stressed that "acknowledging God as the source of truth and wisdom, we seek unification in a Christian faith perspective. . .*university*, unity in the midst of diversity, and not *multi-versity* as is often seen today in higher education." This name change, effective September, 1987, was a result of an institutional maturing with deep roots in its own history and longstanding commitments; it also was an act of openness to the widening doors of the future and a sign of resolve that those doors would be entered with creativity and courage.

The University Today

The year 1992 was something of a new beginning on the Anderson campus. It was time to mark seventy-five years as a school, with the year-

Anderson University Presidents: James L. Edwards, John A. Morrison,
Robert H. Reardon, and Robert A. Nicholson

long celebration using the theme "Kindle the Flame." The Gospel Trumpet
Company of the Church of God movement had birthed the campus in
1917 and shared with the new school its own leaders. In 1990, Robert A.
Nicholson retired as president after an unprecedented career of forty-five
years on campus beyond his student days. From the publishing company

across the street, now called Warner Press, came the new executive officer for the university, James L. Edwards, to be only the fourth president of Anderson University. Typical of the history of this campus, the resulting transition was smooth, there was a great outpouring of love for the retiring leader, and the new president represented considerable continuity with the past, even while charting new paths into the future.

Major elements of the diamond jubilee celebration in 1992-1993 were: (1) the launching of a $75 million capital funds campaign (that would be exceeded); (2) beginning of the Master of Business of Administration degree program, the first new graduate program outside the School of Theology; and (3) the publishing of a range of key historical materials related to the campus. In 1991, Barry L. Callen, faculty member and former dean of the undergraduate College and graduate School of Theology, compiled and published *Faith, Learning, and Life*, views from the president's office of Anderson University. Presidents John A. Morrison, Robert H. Reardon, and Robert A. Nicholson had spoken and written often with a wisdom that was captured for future generations. Then in 1992 the university published its own official history, *Guide of Soul and Mind*, also authored by Dr. Callen. This same author would write the biographies of Daniel S. Warner in 1995 (primary pioneer of the Church of God movement) and President Robert H. Reardon in 2004 (*It's God's Church* and *Staying on Course* respectively). In addition, under Callen's editorship of Anderson University Press, founded in 2000, came the 2006 publishing of the memoirs of President Robert A. Nicholson, titled *So I Said Yes!*, and this 2007 history of higher education in the Church of God movement.

Anderson University currently maintains seventeen academic departments, a full liberal arts program, three colleges, four professional schools with undergraduate and graduate degree offerings at the master's and doctoral levels, and a school of adult education. There also is the Purdue Statewide Technology Program offering two associate degree programs functioning in cooperation with Anderson University. The university sponsors sixteen intercollegiate athletic teams (eight men's and eight women's), competing as the "Ravens" in the NCAA Division III. Celebrated and longstanding campus programs include TRI-S, the Center for Public Service, the Center for Christian Leadership, Covenant Productions, the University and Church of God Archives, the Wilson Galleries, and the Gustav Jeeninga Museum of Bible and Near Eastern Studies.

Signs of dramatic campus development in recent years have included construction of the Kardatzke Wellness Center, the Fair Commons student residence hall, York Seminary Village, and the addition of Hardacre Hall now housing the highly successful Falls School of Business. Participation in the new Flagship Enterprise Center, a local not-for-profit business incubator, involves a new Anderson University education center that serves the I-69 business corridor and northern Indianapolis, and is the home of the university's cooperative associate degree programs with Purdue University. Over the last decade, the university has experienced a substantial strengthening of its financial condition. Assets over this period of time have increased 81%, from $60.8 to $110.3 million, and net assets have increased by 238% from $18.5 to $62.5 million. Gifts for 2006 were at the second highest level recorded, and over the past ten years have totaled an average of nearly $10 million annually. The endowment investments of the university have increased from $3.3 to nearly $21 million, or a 528% increase. Financial progress has been funded through careful planning of balanced budgets, retaining of annual operating surpluses for each of the last ten years, and the procurement of gifts through the generosity of many persons and organizations.

Unique to the Anderson campus are: (1) the School of Theology, the seminary of the Church of God movement: (2) the WQME campus radio station; (3) the treasured collection of some 2,000 hymnals representing the entire American Christian tradition; (4) the Sallman paintings, including the famous "The Head of Christ"; and (5) the Mack M. and Irene Smith Caldwell peacemaking endowment fund of over $700,000 that supports campus programs designed to enhance conflict resolution in our troubled world. The university takes pride in its thousands of highly successful graduates, like 1978 graduate John Pistole, now deputy director of the Federal Bureau of Investigation who was the 2006 commencement speaker. Also in 2006, the campus purchased 37.7 acres of adjacent prime property from Church of God Ministries, thus continuing its historic relationship with its sponsoring church and positioning itself for additional growth in the near future.

Anderson University has been listening to dreams, encouraging discovery, and offering direction to new generations for almost a century. In its classrooms and laboratories, at chapel in worship, over lunch and during late-night discussions in the residence halls, students have shared dreams and discovered life direction. The university has remained determined to continue ensuring the kind of environment that invites debate, teaches discernment, and supports growth—both academic and spiritual. To enable the possibility of this determination in challenging new times, the university launched another major capital funds campaign in October, 2006, this time with the goal of raising $110 million by May, 2010. It is an aggressive plan to enhance several facets of the campus, particularly the school's permanent endowment and select new facilities. Campaign leadership is being provided by Tom L. Ward and James B. Winner, co-chairs of the National Campaign Cabinet, and Bill and Gloria Gaither, co-chairs of the National Campaign Advisory Commission. Staff leadership is being provided by Robert L. Coffman, vice president for advancement.

At this campaign's launching in October, 2006, President James L. Edwards made the dramatic announcement that, of the $110,000 million goal, over $61 million already had been secured! The university's expanding future appears to be a soon-coming reality. It will include a new University Center for student life, a Center for Communication and Performing Arts, a state-of-the-art Recital Hall for gifted student musicians, and the York Seminary Village for housing many future leaders of the church. All of this is urgently needed since estimates are that, by 2008, the student population of the university will be more than 3,000. This estimate is based in part on the strength and range of academic programs and their level of accreditations. In part, it is based on the excellent and growing reputation of the university. Beyond the regional accreditation of the entire campus by the Higher Learning Commission of the North Central Association, the additional seven professional accreditations are a key reason for the deserved national reputation for quality education. These specialized accreditations presently are held in the fields of athletic training, business, graduate ministerial education, music, nursing, social work, and teacher education.

The prestigious *U. S. News and World Report* has ranked Anderson University among "top-tier" master's degree-granting universities in the Midwest. *Business Reform* magazine has recognized Anderson University's Falls School of Business as its "Dean's Choice" among business schools with a biblical foundation. The *Princeton Review* has cited the university as a "Best Midwestern College," and the Templeton Foundation has commended the campus for its work in building character and preparing graduates to make a positive difference in today's society. The state of Indiana has chosen Anderson University as the site for the Center for Character Development. The Center for Christian Leadership of the School of Theology hosted its twenty-fifth annual Newell Lectures in Biblical Studies in 2006. This history of world-class scholarship began with Dr. Bruce Metzger of Princeton Theological Seminary in 1982, with the most recent lectures in 2006 delivered by Dr. Morna Hooker of the University of Cambridge in England.

With all of the accolades received and scholarships featured, the university remains committed to its core values and mission, largely unchanged since its founding in 1917. According to the 2006 financial campaign book *Dreams, Discovery, Direction*, "Anderson University was and is a community of believers that expects and celebrates academic rigor and Christian discovery. As we help students develop their God-given talents, so do we encourage them to use those talents in answering God's call on their lives." The university already has some twenty-five thousand living alumni. There soon will be many more.

The Campus at a Glance

Institutional Names:

1917-1925	Anderson Bible Training School
1925-1929	Anderson Bible School and Seminary
1929-1964	Anderson College and Theological Seminary
1964-1987	Anderson College
1987-	Anderson University

Accreditations:

1946-	North Central Association of Colleges and Schools
1963-	National Council for the Accreditation of Teacher Education
1965-	Association of Theological Schools
1974-	National Association of Schools of Music
1975-	National League of Nursing
1979-	Council on Social Education
1988-	Commission on Accreditation of Athletic Training Education
1994-	Association of Collegiate Business Schools and Programs

Chief Executive Officers:

1917-1923	Joseph T. Wilson (principal)
1923-1925	John A. Morrison (principal)
1925-1958	John A. Morrison (president)
1958-1983	Robert H. Reardon
1983-1990	Robert A. Nicholson
1990-	James L. Edwards

Chief Academic Officers (College):

1917-1925	(Chief Executive Officers)
1925-1958	George Russell Olt
1958-1983	Robert A. Nicholson
1983-1988	Barry L. Callen
1988-1996	A. Patrick Allen
1996-	Carl H. Caldwell

Chief Academic Officers (School of Theology):

1950-1953	Earl L. Martin
1953-1962	Adam W. Miller
1962-1974	Gene W. Newberry
1974-1983	Barry L. Callen
1983-1988	Jerry C. Grubbs
1988-1989	Barry L. Callen (acting)
1989-1985	James Earl Massey
1995-	David L. Sebastian

Mission Statement

The mission of Anderson University is to educate persons for a life of faith and service in the church and society…. This university is committed to being a teaching-learning community of the highest order, engaged in the pursuit of truth from a Christian faith perspective.

Campus Alumni Publication

Signatures

Contact Information

Anderson University	Phone:	765-641-4080 or
1100 East Fifth Street		800-428-6414
Anderson, Indiana 46012	Email:	info@anderson.edu
	Web Site:	www.anderson.edu

President James L. Edwards

CHAPTER 4

The Stories of Arlington College and Azusa Pacific University

T he story of Arlington College is a combination of its own history and the history before and after its time of what now is Azusa Pacific University. The earlier portion of the combined story began at the close of the nineteenth century when the Church of God movement was very young and still not favorable toward institutions of Christian higher education. A school emerged beyond the movement's borders that, much later, would be an important educational partner for the life of the Church of God movement, especially in California.

"God First" Since 1899

A training school for Christian workers was established in 1899 in Whittier, California, by leaders of the local community of Friends

(Quakers). This modest educational beginning was the forerunner of today's Azusa Pacific University. The school's founders insisted on a strict evangelical confession of faith, including "the verbal inspiration of the Holy Scriptures," "the entire sanctification of believers," and "the speedy evangelization of the world." Mary A. Hill from Mount Pleasant, Ohio, served as the first president (principal). Most of the early teachers were local pastors who received no salary for their part-time services. The curriculum stressed biblical study, but included subjects judged to be important practical skills for Christian ministry and missionary service—music, physical culture, Spanish, and nursing.

The 1900-1901 catalog directed that "we would see this school a healthy hotbed of germinating missionaries." Mary Hill answered her own call to missionary service in 1901, initiating a series of new presidents and locations for the little school in the following years. Its leaders all stood firmly against "modernism" and "liberalism," remaining orthodox in theology and missionary in focus. The international flavor of the student body was seen in the 1928 enrollment that included students from Canada, China, England, Germany, Japan, Mexico, Norway, the Philippines, Romania, and Wales. Eleven students from as many nations formed a Gospel band and called it "The League of Nations."

Meanwhile, officials of the school remained active in national Friends circles. The school struggled through the economic depression of the 1930s and occasional controversy among differing leaders of California Friends. By 1940, reports school historian Sheldon Jackson, "the Training School began a period of consistent growth to the stature of a superb Christian evangelical college that represented many evangelical denominations, yet was not controlled by any one" (*Azusa Pacific University: 1899-1999*, 1999, 28).

A key turning point in school history came in 1939 with the naming of a new president. Cornelius P. Haggard had been a student at the Training School (1930-1933) and then a part-time teacher and pastor. He was a visionary man with a charismatic personality. It had been forty years since this small Bible school had been founded on the Pacific Coast at the end of the nineteenth century. Now, despite all the limitations faced by such pioneering schools, there was beginning under President Haggard what would be a thirty-six year administration (1939-1975). During this long tenure, President Haggard led the school from a fledgling training school to an accredited Bible and liberal arts college.

The school's name was changed to Pacific Bible College while it was located in Huntington Park, California. Under whatever name and in whatever location, however, the intent always was to maintain a Bible school with three years of intensive Bible study for all students, while raising academic standards and curricular breadth so that credits would be accepted by colleges granting the standard B. A. degree. President Haggard, a positive and practical man, was determined to stay close to the spiritual aspirations of the school's founders without getting embroiled in fruitless theological debates that broke out among constituents on occasion. He also was determined to build a strong and respected institution of higher education.

When World War II ended in 1945, school growth became rapid and the Huntington Park location was entirely inadequate. A move was made to Azusa twenty-six miles away. The beautiful Maybelle Scott Rancho School for Girls had ceased operation and was purchased. It was a twelve-acre site allowing much room for future expansion. A new era had begun for Pacific Bible College. By 1947 there was a new School of Music and the offering of the Bachelor of Theology and Religious Education degrees. The 1949 catalog announced accreditation by the Accrediting Association of Bible Institutes and Bible Colleges, and approval by the California State Department of Education for the educating of veterans (thirty-nine veterans had come to Pacific Bible College in 1946 alone). There was exhilaration characteristic of a school clearly on the move.

Malcolm R. Robertson joined the faculty in 1949 and soon would be Dean of Education and then Vice-President. He became President Haggard's right-hand man. Under this skilled and visionary leadership team, in 1957 the school's name was changed to Azusa College and attempts were made to one day achieve accreditation by the regional body, the Western Association of Schools and Colleges. The intent was to broaden the liberal arts curriculum while retaining the school's evangelical testimony, moral standards, and spiritual life. Buildings were constructed, faculty and library improved, and, in 1964, full regional accreditation as a liberal arts college was achieved.

With all of this change and growth, four concerns of the school's founders in 1899 remained central for Azusa College. The school was to be consistently "evangelical." It would always cherish the spiritual motto "God First." The school would give practical training for Christian service and be interdenominational. It is in the context of these four concerns of the Azusa founders that the Church of God movement entered the scene. Azusa's historian, Sheldon Jackson, summarizes:

> Although the institution maintained a doctrinal position of Wesleyan convictions, it represented several supporting denominations. In 1965, this interdenominational structure provided a favorable arrangement for the merger of Azusa College and Los Angeles Pacific College—the Free Methodist Church joined as another sponsoring denomination of [the newly named] Azusa Pacific College. Then in 1968, the Church of God, Anderson, Indiana, joined as a sponsoring denomination to effect the merger of Arlington College with Azusa Pacific College. In 1998, five religious organizations were officially affiliated with the university [Azusa Pacific]: Brethren in Christ, Church of God, the Free Methodist Church, the Missionary Church, and the Salvation Army (*Azusa Pacific University: 1899-1999*, 1999, 243).

The Beginning of Arlington College

The early 1950s in the Church of God movement in Southern California were years marked by an evangelistic zeal and missionary spirit. The church was truly alive. It was a time of learning, growing, and serving. Realizing that training was needed to maximize the service gifts given by God, a lay academy was organized. In the Whittier, California, congregation of the Church of God, with area pastors Carl Swart as dean and Clifford Tierney as registrar, the Southern California School of the Bible began operating on thirteen successive Tuesday evenings between February and May, 1953. Every church school teacher in the congregations of the Los Angeles area was urged to attend, with the promise that the school would "strive for academic proficiency, but the spiritual emphasis and personal evangelism will remain pre-eminent.... At no time will the academic life supercede the spiritual life of the student." About two hundred persons participated enthusiastically.

Between September and December of 1953 another such educational effort operated on thirteen successive Monday and Tuesday evenings in the East Los Angeles Church. This time it was called California Christian College with David Martin, layperson in the Pomona Church of God, acting as president and C. Herbert Joiner, Jr., pastor of the Whittier Church of God, acting as dean. This "college" program continued the previous lay-leadership training, but operated on two levels by adding some actual college-level education.

The result of such training efforts was enough excitement and momentum that a young Church of God evangelist and graduate of Anderson College, Maurice Berquist, was called from his seminary training in Louisville, Kentucky, to become the executive secretary of the Association of the Church of God of Southern California. He arrived in 1954, bringing his new bride and much youthful enthusiasm of his own. Berquist later called what he found a "fantastic program" involving nearly three hundred committed Christians seeking to grow through these educational efforts.

Soon he was pastoring the Arlington Church of God congregation and stimulating missionary interest in every way possible. He published the *World Evangelism* newsletter, spoke on a daily radio broadcast in Los Angeles, and consulted with others in drawing plans for a new school. As his biography reports, he was "in his element"—preaching, writing, and creatively putting together "a new thing" (Berny Berquist and Maxine McCall, *Posthumorously, Berk*, 2000, 82-83).

In the spring of 1954, the educational effort began another term, this time maturing into a daytime program in more of a campus setting. Camp Anza, an old Army camp near Riverside, had been purchased by the area churches and turned into a campground. It now became the site of classes that stressed evangelism and missionary preparation. Several students came from across the United States and Canada to be part of what now was being called World Evangelism Institute. David Martin and Herbert Joiner continued as president and dean.

The first issue of the little publication *World Evangelist* sought to spread across the continent the news of this most recent development. Letters praising the intent and early success of this enhanced educational program came back quickly. In the publication's second issue, a few of these letters were reproduced, including those from ministers O. L. Johnson in Warsaw, Indiana, Kenneth G. Prunty in Smith Center, Kansas, and Gordon A. Schieck in Camrose, Alberta, Canada.

Missionary zeal was very much alive in Southern California. An educational program had begun as a way to bring substance to this zeal. Word of early success was getting out by the summer of 1954. The ministers of the Association of the Church of God of Southern California met in the Whittier church and voted overwhelmingly to expand the training program into a full-time college. Enthusiasm ran high for this expansion of the World Evangelism Institute, even though finances were limited and few of the pastors had any experience in operating a college. These negative issues notwithstanding, God seemed to be in this effort.

When the Study Commission on Christian Higher Education of the Church of God met in Anderson, Indiana, in June, 1954, the Association of the Church of God of Southern California was represented by C. Herbert Joiner, Jr., Maurice Berquist, Herschell Rice, Albert Kempin, Mark Denton, and John Neal. The proposed new college in California was discussed at length. Questions were raised by representatives of existing colleges of the Church of God about whether the movement had the strength to support another college. There was careful consideration of the difficulties inherent in such a proposed venture. Finally, given the Commission's proposed criteria for starting a new college in the church, and its assumption that these criteria could not be met in time to launch a new college by the fall of 1954, the Commission recommended delay, further study, and another report of findings and developments.

Church historian John W. V. Smith, in his *The Quest for Holiness and Unity* (1980, 340), recalled that in the 1940s and 1950s there were several "regional enthusiasms" calling for new colleges. The national Commission on Christian Higher Education of the Church of God, formed in part to help control the development of excessive competition with established schools, related to circumstances likely related to the possible emergence of a new college, now being called Arlington College. "With little assistance and considerable discouragement from the powerless commission," wrote Smith, "this school began nevertheless." This fact reflects something of the glory and agony of the Church of God movement in general.

Creativity and local initiative is frequent and clearly prized in the movement—expressing the valuing of freedom in the Spirit. Effectiveness and accountability as a united church are also envisioned and prized—expressing the value of disciplined coordination of ministry efforts for maximum impact. Both of these values are widely and simultaneously cherished. The problem is that sometimes freedom of initiative and disciplined coordination clash, and middle ground is not easily found. Too often, a serious search for the middle ground waits until a given situation has reached crisis proportions. Such is life in a free-church tradition like the Church of God movement.

Arlington College, choosing not to delay despite the Commission's judgment, opened its doors in the fall of 1954 with about fifteen students. Included was young Gerald J. Marvel from Oklahoma who had been encouraged to come by Maurice Berquist. A central aim of the new school was "the inculcation of vital missionary vision and passion for worldwide service." Standard Bible courses were offered. It was suggested that students could supplement their work with liberal arts courses through the nearby University of California at Riverside or at Riverside College.

Why had this educational effort emerged? Partly it was because of the encouraging response to the World Evangelism Institute. No doubt it was helped by the growing influx of people into the Southern California area and because of a regional concern strongly held by the local congregations. It was a long way to Portland, Oregon, or Anderson, Indiana, where the established colleges of the church were located. Air travel was not yet common. The established colleges had not developed regional outposts to serve regional needs. Accordingly, it was judged that area needs justified an area response. California had an extensive and, for students, very inexpensive network of institutions of higher education that could supplement what seemed beyond Arlington's own resources.

So Arlington College had begun. The new college was near industry, which brought hope for student employment, and new housing developments where the practical opportunities for meeting spiritual needs were many. Gerald Marvel recalled that the college really began as a child, cared for tenderly by local Church of God congregations. Meals and bedding were brought in for students. The campus, operating on the Arlington campground property, provided the atmosphere of a small family that was pioneering for God.

In those first years, faculty and students felt a sense of urgency and were dedicated to a compelling mission. President Joiner provided the heart of the venture. He modeled a rich blend of evangelistic fervor and scholarly integrity. With him was dean Fred Shackleton who had come from Pacific Bible College, the Church of God school in Portland, Oregon, arriving at Arlington in its first year of existence. He believed deeply in the mission of the new college and gave freely of himself. By 1958 there were fifty-seven students (twenty-one from California, nine from Ohio, five each from Kansas and Oklahoma, two each from Colorado, Indiana, Michigan and New York, one each from six other states, and three from outside the United States). The *Aletheia*, the college's new yearbook publication, began capturing the school's history.

The story of how the nine students migrated all the way from Ohio is revealing. This group came from the Newton Falls congregation pastored by Lillie S. McCutcheon. It began when young Jack Winland wanted to go into the ministry, did not have his high school diploma, and heard about Arlington College through the ministry of Maurice Berquist. Arlington accepted Winland despite his educational deficiency. His experience at Arlington was good, and, in the summer of 1958, he and the gospel team of John Adams and Doug King visited the Newton Falls youth group. By August several other young people were on their way to California, including Norman and Marge Patton who had just been married and drove across the country even though Norman was only seventeen years old! In another year, still others followed from Newton Falls. Although the beginnings were humble, one day Norman Patton would be the chief executive officer of the Missionary Board of the Church of God. Arlington College played a role in this significant ministry.

These first years for the school were characterized by explorations designed to find a permanent location and a respectable accreditation status for the college. During 1954, Arlington College attempted a bold step forward by laying plans for buying a new site in Riverside. Potentially it would include a merger possibility with Pacific Bible College in Oregon. But neither ever materialized. PBC decided not to proceed and Arlington was not able on its own to capitalize on the opportunity.

In 1956 Maurice Berquist left the area for a pastorate in Florida. He later recalled that, after the collapse of the merger talks with Pacific Bible College, circumstances pressed Arlington not to attempt building a four-year college and shouldering alone all the accreditation requirements. Dewayne B. Bell recalled that by 1958 the regional accrediting association had led Arlington to believe that its best hope was an affiliation with an accredited institution. At the same time, some questions were being raised within certain quarters of the Church of God movement about the need and viability of another college. So the future seemed clear. Arlington would need to seek some cooperative arrangement in the Los Angeles area. Meanwhile, it decided to seek recognition and support as a national agency of the Church of God. This status would offer a regular flow of funding from the national budget of the church.

On December 6, 1957, President Herbert Joiner officially informed the Executive Council of the Church of God that, by direction of the Arlington College board of trustees and with the support of the Association of the Church of God of Southern California, "Arlington College hereby requests. . . admission into the family of agencies which receive regular support through World Service funds." Joiner said that since 1954 the college had done "everything possible to achieve and maintain harmony and unity with all the Church's general agencies." During that time, the churches of Southern California had both carried the financial load imposed by Arlington's educational program and maintained their previous level of World Service support.

On February 19, 1958, the Executive Council reviewed this request, assured Arlington College of its interest and concern, and forwarded the matter to the Study Commission on Higher Education. Its decision in 1959 featured expressed appreciation for the cooperative attitude of Arlington and a recounting of the established requirements necessary for any ministry desiring to be a national agency. They included that "any institution should be expected to demonstrate wide acceptance and approval by the church and some history of success in achieving stability and purposes consonant with the policies and program of the other general agencies of the Church of God before being invited to participate in the distribution of World Service funds." It was determined that Arlington College had not yet qualified for funding participation in light of such criteria. More time would have to pass and more progress made.

The Long Beach Plan

The necessary progress in institutional development being required of Arlington College was sought through an informal cooperative arrangement with a state institution in Southern California. President C. Herbert Joiner, Jr., explained the plan to the Commission on Christian Higher Education of the Church of God in its January, 1960, meeting. Long Beach State College had a dean with Church of God background who promised cooperation with Arlington College. Wilford Denton pastored the College Park Church of God congregation located just blocks away from that state campus. Arlington College, therefore, decided to buy five acres of prime property, part of an old ranch on the hill just behind the state campus. In the summer of 1960, Denton opened his church for college use while a new building was constructed (mostly with donated labor).

Moving the campus brought its difficulties. Gerald J. Marvel, who graduated in 1960, did not feel good about abandoning "our family" out in Arlington for this very different setting. President Joiner, now seriously ill, initially supported the move. By the time the actual move came, however, he had difficulty handling a decision of this magnitude, became fearful, and withdrew his support. The executive committee of the college's board of trustees tried to reverse the board's decision to move. When this attempt failed, the executive committee resigned and a leave of absence was granted to the president. The college did move, but, according to Everett Richey, "the community spirit that had founded the college was now fractured. It was never restored." The illness, absence, and later death of Joiner was a great loss to the college. He was a man of vision who was an effective scholar, fund-raiser, and encourager of students. The beloved Earl L. Martin from Anderson College in Indiana brought temporary leadership during 1960-61. George H. Ramsey assumed the presidency in 1961, but in 1963 he left the area for a faculty position at Anderson College.

Hope for the future of the college was judged to lay in developing a relationship with the nearby state institution of higher education. It was the Long Beach plan. In brief, the plan was that an Arlington student would take a program of liberal arts courses at the state school and a program of religious studies at Arlington, often simultaneously. It was thought to be an academically strong plan and a good stewardship of resources. Back in the 1920s, when Anderson College first introduced its own liberal arts program, some Church of God ministers were critical of the move, charging that it was bad stewardship for a church school with limited resources. They had proposed the alternative of students going elsewhere to take whatever liberal arts courses they wished, while the church's school stayed focused on its particular mission and expertise, religious education. Anderson College chose to do both and eventually prospered. Now Arlington chose to pursue the path proposed by the critics in the 1920s—not for any lack of valuing the liberal arts, but out of sheer financial necessity.

The Long Beach plan hoped that student costs, in significant part, would be underwritten by California subsidies of higher education through its state institution affiliated with Arlington College. After one year of residence in California, a student qualified for very low resident tuition rates at the state college. So, the intention was that students would come from across the country to a promising and affordable educational environment. The liberal arts program was strong on the Long Beach State College campus and, according to President George H. Ramsey, the secular dangers were recognized and could be handled successfully. It was thought that any negative influences coming from the state curriculum could be counteracted by the

Arlington faculty. It was made clear that the college would continue to operate as a Church of God institution. It was announced that Arlington College could successfully fulfill the purposes and aims of a Christian liberal arts college, but would be spared the prohibitive cost of actually executing a liberal arts program on its own campus. It was an innovative and idealistic plan.

Arlington's relationship with Long Beach State College was very informal. Arlington students took accredited liberal arts courses at the state college and had their records transferred to Arlington to supplement the religious studies, thus comprising the four-year Arlington program. It was hoped that soon the religion portion of this cooperative program would be accredited so that the full four-year program would be covered by accreditation. President Ramsey referred to this arrangement as "a breakthrough, a revolutionary idea." But it was not an idea fully understood or appreciated by many in the church. A "secular" education in a state school was questioned. The recruitment of students remained a struggle. Some students did not have the qualifications for admission to Long Beach State College, and most found it very difficult to pay the out-of-state costs for the first year. By 1968 there were fewer Arlington students than ten years before. According to the annual publication, *Aletheia*, the 1968 total was only thirty-seven, twenty-seven of whom were from California. Something had to change.

One attempt at fundamental change had occurred in 1966 when serious discussions were held with Warner Pacific College about the potential of a merger of the colleges on the site of a gift of land in San Jose, California. Excitement ran high. Warner's board authorized the relocation of its college. But then came a period of questions and indecision, with much unrest related to the feasibility of the move. It finally ended with Warner's board of trustees deciding that achieving a sound fiscal operation on the Portland campus was the college's first obligation. President Louis F. Gough presented his resignation because he judged that his leadership had been eroded seriously. Another possibility for Arlington College had finally died in discussion. So Arlington continued to hope that the Long Beach plan would catch hold and prove fruitful, despite the considerable obstacles.

In the period just prior to 1968, the stance of the Western Association (official area accreditation body) changed in regard to cooperative endeavors, such as the one between Arlington College and Long Beach State College. Earlier, a program with limited objectives, such as Arlington's religion program, could be accredited in a special category if it were part of a recognized cooperative endeavor and the objectives were being achieved. But by 1968 this special category of accreditation had been dropped, forcing an institution to mount the full four-year program on its own. Arlington just did not have the resources necessary for such a broadened venture. All doors seemed to be closed since the cooperative plan was no longer viable and a small, unaccredited college was not adequate for the needs and desires of most of the church's youth. Soon to come was another merger possibility, the one possibility that would materialize and determine the shape of the future.

Merging with Azusa Pacific College

In 1967, an historic connection between Azusa Pacific and Arlington Colleges began. Cornelius P. Haggard, president of Azusa Pacific College, was resource leader at a retreat of Church of God ministers in Southern California. He shared with Arlington's president, Dewayne B. Bell, board chair, Charles Benson, and board member, Wlford Denton, about how God had blessed a merger in 1965 of Azusa College and the nearby Free Methodist school, Los Angeles Pacific College. He reported his own tie with the Church of God through the long-term use in his classes of Russell R. Byrum's *Christian Theology* volume. After the Arlington leaders told Haggard of Arlington's four discouraging years of seeking accreditation, Haggard issued an invitation for Arlington to consider a merger with Azusa similar to that successful one in 1965. The invitation seemed timely, even providential.

At first the Arlington board of trustees and area Church of God ministers were hesitant about this merger proposal. For instance, all Church of God faculty members would have to sign a statement of faith, a practice traditionally considered "denominational" in the Church of God movement. Some wondered about the unknowns of educating Church of God leadership in an interdenominational setting, despite the irony of members of a movement committed to Christian unity entertaining such a sectarian concern. But, whatever the cautions, the options were few, and this particular possibility seemed to present some promising features. For instance, Azusa represented a compatible theological tradition, Wesleyan in nature.

The merger idea was shared with the Commission on Christian Higher Education of the Church of God, which responded with the following in its January, 1968, meeting: "The Commission concurred with President Bell that there appears to be compatible educational concerns and impressive theological affinities with Azusa Pacific…. This Commission commends President Bell for the creativity and courage of his Board in appraising the options and recommends this one as worthy of consideration."

Finally, in 1968, the Arlington board of trustees voted unanimously to proceed with this merger. On March 4, 1968, this action was ratified by vote of the Association of the Church of God of Southern California. The Church of God movement would join six other church bodies in supporting Azusa Pacific College. Student enrollment at Azusa had grown dramatically from 223 in 1963 to 1,007 in 1968—with much more growth still to come. Arlington would be part of a vigorous and rapidly expanding Christian campus, one providing full accreditation to all its students.

The Long Beach campus of Arlington College was sold by the area Church of God association, with a good profit realized. Some of the proceeds were designated to fund a course in Church of God history and doctrine and scholarships for Church of God students at Azusa Pacific. Several hundred volumes, including the back issues of the *Gospel Trumpet*, went to the Azusa library, with many of the others going to two of the young

Church of God schools that were just building their libraries, Warner Southern College and Gulf-Coast Bible College. There was some transfer of remaining funds, about fifty thousand dollars, and the establishment at Azusa of an "Arlington Room" as a perpetual memorial.

Several Arlington students went on to leadership in the Church of God movement. For example, Norman S. Patton became a prominent pastor and missionary leader. Willard K. Reed became a professor of philosophy at Anderson University. David C. Shultz was an Arlington student who went on to Azusa to complete his degree and become pastor of several of the larger congregations in the Church of God and editor in chief of Warner Press. Sharon Clark Pearson would later teach Bible at Azusa and then become a professor of Bible at Anderson University School of Theology.

Church of God leaders at Arlington College who transferred to Azusa went on to play significant roles in the newly merged campus. President Bell became Assistant to the President and Director of College Relations at Azusa. Frederick G. Shackleton, dean at Arlington, became Coordinator of Graduate Studies. Arlington faculty members Everett Richey and Frederick Shackleton joined the Azusa faculty, as did Fredrick Shively who, while pastoring, had taught at Arlington in 1966-1967 and then taught the Church of God history/theology course at Azusa from 1968 to 1973. Several Arlington board members became part of the Azusa governing board, including Charles Wyant for many years and Greg Dixon currently. All things considered, a significant Church of God presence went to Azusa Pacific as a result of the merger. Arlington finally had found its permanent location, its means of achieving accreditation, and a way of providing long-term service to the church.

After years of experience with the results of this merger, reflections and analyses vary, of course. Dewayne Bell expressed satisfaction at his central role in achieving the merger. "Arlington added to the weight of the Church of God in the Southwest," he said, "and at least some of that valuable reality has been perpetuated through Azusa." Arlington never could have provided such service to the Church of God on its own and under the circumstances that existed at the time of the merger. Charles Benson, board chair of Arlington at the time of the merger with Azusa and then an Azusa board member, has affirmed both that the merger was "a great move forward" and that, even so, the Arlington years were "the peak years of excitement" for the churches in Southern California, unmatched before or since.

With the retirement of President Haggard in 1975, a transitional presidential team was named. One of the three members was Dewayne Bell, former president of Arlington College who had served Azusa as Assistant to the President for planning and development since the 1968 merger. In 1976, Paul E. Sago, a Church of God minister and former vice-president for financial affairs of Anderson College, became president of Azusa Pacific College. He pledged "to take up where Dr. Haggard left off." Under his strong leadership for the next thirteen years, Azusa Pacific grew in strength and influence in the higher educational community. It officially became Azusa Pacific University in 1981 and has continued to be related, both structurally and programmatically, to the Church of God in Southern California. President Sago left in 1989 to accept another presidency.

A typical analysis of the Arlington experience is that of Maurice Berquist. A necessary thing (the merger) had become a good thing. While Azusa "salvaged much of what we had hoped to do through Arlington," Berquist observed with some sadness that Arlington on its own might have been such a school if a few circumstances had been different. It had been a worthy venture, but suffered the untimely loss of C. Herbert Joiner, Jr. Finally, the dollars, students, and church support just were not adequate.

Milo L. Chapman, longtime leader of Warner Pacific College and faculty member at Arlington College from 1964 to 1967, expressed some disappointment, feeling that Church of God efforts on the West Coast would have been served better if the earlier merger talks with Pacific Bible College had proven successful. There is good reason for a church body to maintain its own higher education, he felt. The Church of God has enjoyed only modest control or visibility at Azusa, with a continuing confusion in the minds of many about whether it is "our school." But George Ramsey judged the merger with Azusa a "very fine liaison with kindred denominations."

Frederick Shackleton, longtime dean of Arlington and then chair of Azusa's Department of Religion and Philosophy, not sure that control should be the issue, stated that this multi-denominational model of Christian higher education is actually a fine expression of what the Church of God movement has always said it believed. Azusa's Church of God president, Paul E. Sago, once said that, "if control is an issue to be discussed, it should be pointed out that no church controls Azusa Pacific." In this interdenominational setting, with Wesleyan theological commitments, a painting of Daniel S. Warner, primary pioneer of the Church of God movement, hangs proudly today in "Founder's Hall," part of the Haggard School of Theology of Azusa Pacific University.

The University Today

Arlington College had become part of what now is Azusa Pacific University in 1968. For Arlington, in one sense, that merged identity represents a dream that died of practical necessity. In another sense, the dream now goes on in a larger way than originally thought possible.

In 1991, Haggard School of Theology of Azusa Pacific University established the annual Malcolm R. Robertson Lectureship for Holy Living. The intent was to honor a long-time academic leader of the campus and demonstrate commitment to the vitality of the historic Wesleyan message in response to the complex spiritual and social issues facing Christians today. Recent lecturers have included three scholars from the Church of God movement, Cheryl J. Sanders, Susie C. Stanley, and Barry L. Callen. The twenty-first century opened with the launching of a three-year Wesleyan-Holiness Study Project designed to revitalize this theological tradition among today's churches. It is a tradition central to the histories of both Arlington

College and Azusa Pacific. Barry L. Callen and several leaders of the Church of God in Southern California participated actively in meetings of this project that convened on the Azusa campus.

President Paul E. Sago

Following the death of President Cornelius P. Haggard in 1975, Church of God minister-educator Paul E. Sago served as president of Azusa Pacific until 1989. By 2007, the university was meeting the academic needs of more than 8,000 students with about fifty areas of undergraduate study, twenty master's degree programs, six doctoral degree programs, and numerous educational sites in the southern California area. The campus maintains an affiliate relationship with Church of God Ministries in Anderson, Indiana, and has Church of God membership on its board of trustees.

The Campus at a Glance

Institutional Names:

1954-1968	Arlington College
1968-1981	Azusa Pacific College (merger)
1981-	Azusa Pacific University (merger)

Accreditations:

1954-1968	Not accredited (Arlington College)
1968-	Joint with Azusa Pacific University, which is regionally and professionally accredited.

Chief Executive Officers:

1954-1955	Maurice Berquist
1955-1960	C. Herbert Joiner, Jr.
1960-1961	Earl L. Martin (acting)
1961-1963	George H. Ramsey
1963-1968	Dewayne B. Bell
1968-	Joint with Azusa Pacific University (including Paul E. Sago, 1976-1989)

Chief Academic Officers:

1954-1956	Albert J. Kempin
1956-1968	Frederick G. Shackleton
1968-	Joint with Azusa Pacific University

Mission Statement

Azusa Pacific University is an evangelical Christian community of disciples and scholars who seek to advance the work of God in the world through academic excellence in liberal arts and professional programs of higher education that encourage students to develop a Christian perspective of truth and life.

Contact Information

Azusa Pacific University
901 E. Alosta Avenue
P.O. Box 7000
Azusa, California 91702

Web Site: www.apu.edu
Phone: 800-825-5278 or
          626-815-6006

CHAPTER 5

The Story of Bay Ridge Christian College

Daniel S. Warner (1842-1895) demonstrated in his ministry one reason why the Church of God movement has had unusual success in carrying on a productive ministry to African Americans in the United States. In 1890 he engaged in an evangelistic tour in Mississippi and became the victim of an angry white mob. The anger came, in part, because Warner showed no discrimination toward African Americans in his public meetings or his visitation of the sick. While recuperating from personal injuries in a cabin outside Union, Mississippi, he wrote the words to the hymn "Who Will Suffer With the Saviour?"

J. Horace Germany was born in 1914 about six miles west of Union, Mississippi. Together with seven siblings, his childhood was on a farm, the same land where slaves once had tilled the soil and picked cotton. One day the practical skills he learned early in life would be very important to his Christian ministry. So would his faith that would sustain him through very hard times ahead. Being true to the implications of the Christian gospel will bring opposition from the world. Several decades after Warner's difficult experience, and also near Union, Mississippi, a small school would be launched. It would be for the benefit of disadvantaged African-Americans. The founder was J. Horace Germany, a white minister ordained by the reform movement pioneered by Daniel S. Warner. The persecution would again be very real. The school would be part of the larger story of the significant presence of African Americans in the Church of God movement, and their many contributions to it. This story has been told by James Earl Massey (*African Americans and the Church of God*, 2005).

Early Pioneering Efforts

Mack Caldwell became an early pioneer in attempting some training effort for African-American leaders in the Church of God movement. He moved to Augusta, Georgia, in 1925 to direct a small educational effort known as Southern Bible Institute. There was an adequate facility there that housed an annual camp meeting for the area African-American church. Caldwell directed the institute as a branch of Anderson College, receiving some funding from the College and drawing heavily on the teaching outlines of Anderson's professor Russell R. Byrum. This institute was a sacrificial effort to assist with the needs of the "colored" people. It existed for two years, served about fifteen students, and then closed because of lack of adequate finances. But it had been a beginning.

In 1937, along the very rural road in Mississippi which ran close by where Daniel Warner had been nurtured back to health after the mob violence nearly fifty years earlier, a young, white farm boy dedicated his life to whatever God had for him. J. Horace Germany did not know then that his later ministry would focus on the particular needs of African-Americans. Like Warner before him, it also would nearly cost him his life at the hands of an angry Mississippi mob.

Horace Germany's commitment to Christian ministry led him to Indiana and Anderson College in 1937. It was there, in a sociology class taught by Leona Nelson, that he did research and wrote a paper on "The

Negro Educational Problem in the South." He came to feel very uncomfortable because of the magnitude of the problem. He noted that there was not one college graduate in the 228 little African-American congregations then associated with the Church of God movement in the South. There was ignorance of the problem among white leaders, and there existed the status quo of segregated ministerial assemblies. He felt "thoroughly condemned" about how little the church was doing to help.

President J. Horace Germany

African Americans were not permitted to go to non-black schools in the South in those years. A few did come North, like Isom R. Crockett and a few others at Anderson College, but only a few, and often they did not return home after their educations were complete. Germany concluded that what was needed was a new school in the South designed for the particular needs of young African-American church leaders. He now was a young Christian man with a sensitive social conscience and a cause to bring focus to his own life and ministry.

In 1944, having completed the Bachelor of Theology degree at Anderson College, Germany returned to pastor his home church near Union, Mississippi. He built a new building out of blocks made by hand, modeled after the Old Main building at Anderson College. In 1948 he returned north to Muncie, Indiana, to pastor a congregation near Ball State University. There he started one of the first university student fellowships in the Church of God movement. He continued to build acquaintances with African-American students at his alma mater, nearby Anderson College, learning that he could have "good fellowship" with men like Isom Crockett and Emery Williams, despite the racial and cultural differences. An early step by Germany, however, proved awkward. He reports in his autobiography that it happened during the International Convention of the Church of God convened in Anderson, Indiana, in June, 1952.

> I shared with black and white ministers alike my dream of going back south to build a Bible college for black ministers. But I made a grievous social error while talking with a group of black ministers from Louisiana and Mississippi. "If you boys will join hands with me," I said, "we will roll up our sleeves and work together and get something going for the Lord." I thought I had made a perfectly innocent statement. However, George Burns. . .took exception to my use of the term "boys." He confided to me later that. . .he told several of his black brothers, "If that long, tall, Mississippi white man thinks he's going anywhere with us, he's sadly mistaken, standing up there calling us 'boys.' Ha!" (*At Any Cost*, 2000, 77).

Later, once back in Mississippi, Germany continued sharing among his African-American friends his idea of an integrated, Church of God sponsored school in the South, but he met skepticism. They had not often worked quite that way with white persons before. It was an idea not commonly accepted in the South, even among Church of God leaders, although there were colleges for African Americans with vocational orientation such as Germany envisioned. But Germany persisted. He began attending the New Orleans Institute and became a friend of the host pastor, George W. Burns, and many other African-American ministers who heard and appreciated his vision and courage.

This New Orleans Institute had been operating since the mid-1940s as an annual two-week training experience for African-American pastors. The idea had been conceived by A. T. Rowe of the Gospel Trumpet Company located in Anderson, Indiana. It had been operated for several years with financial support from the company and the Women of the Church of God. Organizational direction had come from T. Franklin Miller of the national Board of Christian Education, and instructional support had been provided by many persons in the Anderson church agencies and elsewhere.

Included among the supporters from the South was Charles W. Cheeks from Laurel, Mississippi, who had become burdened for the fair treatment and education of African Americans when he visited Mack Caldwell's Southern Bible Institute in the 1920s. Another was James Stewart, a native of Mississippi, a white Church of God minister, and also a graduate of Anderson College in Indiana. However, Horace Germany learned quickly that the forces of white supremacy in the South were not ready for a program that included whites and blacks, with blacks being treated as equal partners. When the United States Supreme Court ruled in May, 1954, that school segregation was now to be illegal, strong white elements in the South galvanized into overt resistance to such a federal mandate.

In 1956, Mississippi established the State Sovereignty Commission to be the watchdog for creeping integration in the state. From then on, the emerging educational dream of Horace Germany was under critical surveillance, both locally and statewide. He determined to stay the course, knowing that the church's African-American leaders would come to believe in him and his righteous cause only if they saw him and even his family "suffering their pain without running for cover" (*At Any Cost*, 2000, 106).

Dairy Cattle and Ministerial Education

The dream of J. Horace Germany was similar to that of Berea College in Kentucky. He needed to get a dairy program going that could provide for his family and also support a Bible college. "Then," reports Germany, "once we had the school up and running, we could have students come to our seminary and work in the dairy and on the farm, and thus pay for their room, board, books, and tuition. I calculated that each cow could produce enough milk to pay the expenses of one student" (*At Any Cost*, 84). The problem was that he did not have any cows.

While still pastoring in Muncie, Indiana, Germany began building a dairy cattle herd in Mississippi. Various persons from Anderson College started a project among themselves and helped buy one of the first cows. By 1952, Germany had moved back to Mississippi to work toward the fulfillment of his dream. With the help of a $10,000 loan from the Board of Church Extension and Home Missions of the Church of God, he bought sixty acres of ground south of Union, near Decatur, built a barn, and began a small dairy operation that he hoped would allow black students without money to earn their education and develop work skills necessary for a tent-making ministry in the South (model of the Apostle Paul).

Germany spread word of his dream in places like the New Orleans Institute. His intention was to start a college for the church by offering classes scheduled around the working demands of the farm. He believed that long-term leadership development was vital for the African-American churches of the South. These leaders must be trained to be self-sufficient and responsible, breaking the welfare cycle by allowing them to work for their education. It must not be a school *for* blacks (another white handout), but a venture *with* African Americans (there has always been a majority of African-American persons on the governing board of the school that evolved). While later history would raise questions about whether this method of approaching the problem was viable and adequate, certainly the cause was right, Germany saw no other way to go, and his commitment to it was complete.

The Board of Church Extension and Home Missions, located in Anderson, Indiana, had interest in opening a work among African Americans in the South. In 1952, Isom and Ola Crockett were added to the staff of the Board for work in Mississippi. The Crocketts, James Stewart, Harold Chesterman, and Horace Germany formed a ministry team for the state. But Germany's particular dream was a school. In March, 1953, the first session of a planning committee for a training school met in the very modest home of Horace and Janetta Germany near Decatur, Mississippi. It considered how a board of trustees should be formed. Isom Crockett acted as group secretary. Additional acreage was secured across the highway from the original land for a "manual training school."

Germany traveled back to Indiana to share his dream with the general church offices. He reports: "When I visited the Anderson graduate School of Theology and told the students what my dream was, they thought it was a great idea. Some of them volunteered to come and help with the training or write up materials we would need to get our curriculum under way. Some of the Anderson faculty volunteered to help us write our first catalog—and we just about had our first school started" (*At Any Cost*, 93-94). A tentative organizational plan for guiding the school project was agreed to by the Board of Church Extension and Home Missions, involving a committee on planning and operation. The committee consisted of Germany, four members from each of the white and black state church constituencies, and two officers of the Board. William E. Reed of the Board made numerous trips to Mississippi in the years that were to follow. Isom Crockett recalls that the new school was patterned somewhat after Piney Woods Country Life School near Jackson, Mississippi. Germany had studied the goals and operation of the School of the Ozarks in Missouri and Berea College in Kentucky. Students could work at a trade to help pay their bills.

Financial problems soon plagued the project. Interest payments became delinquent on the loans made by the Board. In 1956, ten acres of the total land involved was deeded to the Board as a way of beginning to address the delinquency. At about the same time, local opposition began to build against the idea of a college for blacks. The Germany family decided that the local resistance and the limited acreage for cattle were obstacles too great for the success of the school. In 1957 they bought 140 acres from a relative. This was six miles west of Union, near where Horace Germany had pastored for seven years. By 1959 another 120 acres were purchased and an excellent site for the school had begun to be developed. In March, 1960, the original 60 acres, which had become deeded to the Board of Church Extension, were sold so that the Board's investment could be recovered. Later, the additional acreage across the highway also was sold by the Board.

These years of relationship between the Board and the school project directed by Germany had been frustrating and tension filled for both parties. The finances had been a major problem. A pronounced philosophical difference existed regarding the type of training needed. Germany was committed to a college approach, and the Board questioned the necessity or wisdom of this approach, not having the resources to support such a program. Finally, Germany felt abandoned by the Board and the Board felt, because of Germany's decision to leave the farm that the Board had financed, that Germany had separated himself from the administrative guidance of the Board. The Board felt this estrangement even further when a separate corporation was set up to operate the school. Germany continued to believe that the Board lacked real commitment to the project and had backed off in the face of pressure from southern white ministers. But the Board insisted that to call the venture a college was misleading to prospective students and was promising more than could be delivered. It suggested rather that the focus should be on the original concept of a "manual training school."

Bay Ridge Christian College was formally organized in 1959 in a meeting to which all Church of God state chairpersons in the South, black and white, were invited. Forty-six persons were present. They elected J. Horace Germany (white) president and George W. Burns (African-American) vice-president. The first students were enrolled in January, 1960, with Fred Dixon (an African-American school teacher from Georgia) elected as acting dean and James Stewart (white) as secretary-treasurer. Persons like professors Val Clear and Louis F. Gough from Anderson College served voluntarily on an advisory committee and assisted in the development of the first curriculum design and catalog.

The Commission on Christian Higher Education of the Church of God was approached by the new college for guidance and recognition, but the

Commission saw the project as more of a home mission venture than a college—Germany thought of it as a trade school and Bible college. Since the Board of Church Extension and Home Missions did not support the college emphasis, and then had become separated formally from the project, the school had to seek such guidance from interested persons until a formal organization could be established. For a time it was a fragile institutional reality, with no parent body and virtually no resources. A parent body soon was formed in New Orleans during an Institute meeting. It was to be known as the Southern Association of the Church of God. But before it was a meaningful reality, a near tragedy occurred that could have ended the entire venture.

A Mob and a Move

On June 13, 1960, the Secretary of State of Mississippi informed Bay Ridge Christian College that its application for a charter of incorporation had been denied by the governor. Racial tension was high. In Little Rock, Arkansas, national attention was drawn to the refusal by state officials to allow Blacks to enroll at Central High School. Germany was branded a "Yankee" probably sent in by the federal government to force a confrontation over integration in Mississippi. Governor Ross Barnett sent sheriffs and warnings to Bay Ridge. This integrated activity (a white president and six black students) was to stop or there would be severe consequences. And there were. On August 21, 1960, in Union, Mississippi, a mob of about thirty white men beat Germany and left him for dead! With Germany at the time had been Herman Fontenot, George Burns, and two students. They were driven away by members of the mob, fortunate to have survived.

With the help of a sympathetic doctor and a Catholic hospital in Meridian, Mississippi, Horace Germany survived this brutal attack. The local KKK then tried to bankrupt the school before Germany was out of the hospital, but a white feedstore man in Union, Mississippi, Ray Richardson, bought the school's outstanding bank notes and saved its property at the risk of his own life. Since the students were threatened with hanging if they remained at the school, they went to George Burns' church in New Orleans to finish the school term. There they were taught by James Stewart and Isom Crockett, while president Germany recovered and then traveled to generate fresh support for the school.

Some embarrassment was felt in Union. On August 23, these words appeared in the *Delta Democrat Times* of Greenville, Mississippi:

> What is wrong with a town or a county in which wanton brutality is tolerated, ignored, or gleefully applauded? What is wrong with a people when they consider it a crime to build a college dedicated to training men, no matter what color, to be preachers of God's word? What is wrong with the moral climate in which this kind of barbarism can be safely perpetrated?

The college's board met in Houston, Texas, where the racial climate was much better. Richardson received payment for the $19,000 of notes he had secured, and he personally provided the trucks to move the school's cattle to Texas. Fearing likely reprisals, ministers of the area did not involve themselves openly by offering any assistance. Others, however, did help, including the Emerald Avenue Church of God in Chicago, pastored by Marcus Morgan.

Although the separation between the school and the Board of Church Extension and Home Missions had occurred prior to these violent events, it was perceived by many, particularly in the black church community, that the Board had forsaken Germany at the time of his greatest need. There were confrontational meetings in which the Board had to explain and defend its position. The move from Mississippi made permanent the school's separation from the Board.

Preston Ervin was pastoring in Kendleton, Texas, a small place not far from Houston, with virtually all of its residents being African American.

There was interest among town leaders in a college being built there. Three Texas residents formed a new board of trustees and soon this the new Texas location would be the future home of the school. Germany began his personal promotion of the school across the church. It now had its own charter from Texas, was governed by its own board of trustees, and had the Southern Association of the Church of God as its parent body. Isom and Ola Crockett remained in Mississippi and continued to serve the Church of God faithfully, sometimes at the risk of their own lives and property. Harold Chesterman and his wife moved to Florida.

So the school, to be known as Bay Ridge Christian College, began its life over in a rural setting in Texas. About 230 acres of land were purchased near Kendleton, located forty miles southwest of Houston. The property was adequate and would grow in value. Facilities were built on the new property so that the cattle could be moved from Mississippi, with the Germany family living in a borrowed mobile home. Vocational training was developed, including a dairy herd and print, auto, carpentry, and machine shops. It was a self-help program. In 1967 the farmland and livestock enterprises generated $44,000 of the college's $110,000 budget, and furnished milk and meat for staff and student needs.

Classes were scheduled as faculty and students could be available. But the operation remained small and struggling. President Germany traveled extensively, telling the school's story and seeking funds and students. John A. Buehler, former faculty member at Anderson College in Indiana, came to teach science and religious education. Horace Germany handled the theological instruction and his wife Janetta Germany taught the English classes. Others soon joined on a part-time basis with little or no pay, including pastor Al Donaldson.

In addition to teachers, the little school was blessed with some generous friends, like Louisiana cotton farmer H. H. Humphries and Iowa businessman Everett Lawson. It also suffered from a hurricane in 1961 and then two different tornados—and always from a lack of funding. But it survived and managed to serve more extensively than its meager resources would have suggested was possible.

Search for National Recognition

In 1965 the college, represented by the Southern Association of the Church of God, contacted the Commission on Christian Higher Education of the Church of God. It wanted a closer association with the commission. But members of the commission were not well informed about the personnel, programs, management, facilities, and other resources of Bay Ridge. In January, 1967, therefore, following a request from Bay Ridge for formal membership in the commission, the commission proposed to send a team to gather information and perspective as a way of helping to determine an appropriate response to the request.

The team of James Earl Massey, Robert A. Nicholson, and Hollie W. Sharpe conducted a campus visit at Bay Ridge on May 19-21, 1968. It then formalized a set of observations and recommendations for Bay Ridge. They included the need for clarifying educational objectives, giving much higher priority to the educational program (over the "farm program"), and facing the dilemma of the church being asked to support two colleges so close together (Gulf Coast Bible College was located in nearby Houston, Texas).

President Germany responded to these observations and recommendations in a document dated May 16, 1969. He defended the necessity of the trade school department and stated an aspiration for academic progress. Some attention was being given to the admittedly inadequate library. The board of trustees of Bay Ridge had determined that the college would "work toward becoming an accredited Bible College and an accredited trade school." Germany argued that the fact that Bay Ridge and GBC were only forty miles apart was not relevant to the potential of the church supporting both. In fact, "BRCC has no overlapping in service or reason for existence with the GBC program.... BRCC has a specific purpose not touched by GBC."

Disagreeing with the team's assertion that BRCC "is by and large a vocational college," Germany insisted that "our major emphases are in the fields of religion and communications, equipping the students for the gospel ministry with enough vocational training to aid them in carrying out this ministry." He asserted that the Church of God was failing in its responsibility to serve the real and very practical needs of southern African Americans. His question was: "Could our general agencies, then, not join in promoting a program which is already in existence [BRCC]?"

This criticism of the church's institutions, and the related call for church-wide recognition and support of Bay Ridge, were to receive considerable attention in the next few years. Through the Southern Association of the Church of God, Bay Ridge formally requested "general agency" status and thus an annual share in the national World Service budget. The 1975 General Assembly of the Church of God referred this request to the Commission on Christian Higher Education. At the Assembly's direction, the Commission considered the request in the broader context of determining the best way to train African-American leaders for service to the church in the South. More study of Bay Ridge was done by the Commission, several black consultants were brought in from across the country, and some thirty black congregations in the South were visited as one way of assessing the nature and extent of the need.

The result was that in June, 1977, the Commission reported to the General Assembly its judgment that "the need is urgent, complex in nature, and national in scope, necessitating an approach other than the recommendation of general agency status for Bay Ridge Christian College." Instead of highlighting Bay Ridge as the primary answer, a Black Ministerial Education Fund was established. It was raised each year until being discontinued in 1981. The money was divided among the academic development needs of Bay Ridge, scholarships for eligible black ministerial students to attend their choice of Church of God colleges, and an in-service training program designed by the Center for Pastoral Studies of Anderson

School of Theology primarily for black church leaders with limited education. When the fund ended, the commission was given the continuing assignment of identifying and addressing "the gaps and shortcomings" of several national programs of ministerial education for African Americans, and donors to Bay Ridge were given the privilege of credit for gifts to Bay Ridge channeled through World Service.

Bay Ridge was again urged by the Commission to explore with nearby Gulf Coast Bible College "the possibilities of joint programming and other mutual uses of the available human and material resources." After a few modest attempts at such exploration, this effort was dropped. The personalities and differing philosophies and objectives of these schools, as well as the forty miles, kept them quite far apart. In 1985, Gulf Coast moved to Oklahoma City and that move ended the possibility of any cooperative effort.

Another crisis time for Bay Ridge came in the early 1980s. President Germany was talking of retirement. A search was conducted for a successor, with some persons hoping that a black leader would emerge and accept the presidency. But that hope was not realized. Black persons with the necessary qualifications either were not considered for some reason or seemed not to share the vision of Bay Ridge as the way to meet the needs of the next generations of young African Americans. So Charles G. Denniston, a young, white construction supervisor who had been with Bay Ridge since 1970 and had earned a degree from it, became president in 1982. He felt unprepared for the task and was aware of the criticism, even cynicism about Bay Ridge in some quarters. But he was committed to the task and determined to serve in a sacrificial manner. At the conclusion of his five-year term in 1987, Denniston expressed willingness to step aside if appropriate black leadership became available. And, in fact, that is what the future held.

In 1987, the board of trustees of Bay Ridge Christian College and the Southern Association of the Church of God announced the election of Robert C. Williams as the new president of the college, succeeding Charles G. Denniston, who was to remain as faculty member and director of development. This move to an African-American chief executive officer with significant academic credentials (M. Ed. and Ed. D. from the University of Southern Mississippi) and educational experience was intended to be an aggressive step toward making longstanding hopes more viable in the future.

President Williams announced soon after his election a new "commitment to excellence." He declared that "we can build an institution of Christian higher education. . .looked upon as one of the finest Black colleges in the nation." To do this, he envisioned a new drive toward accreditation and the establishment of a more secure financial base, to be accomplished in part by one thousand congregations giving regularly to the college through their local budgets. It was a bold hope in the face of significant odds; but, to this school, significant odds were nothing new. What was new was the fresh enthusiasm and leadership that was determined to find a way to move hope in the direction of reality.

A 1987 brochure of the college reported that, among more than 13 million black citizens in eleven Southern states, the Church of God movement had 187 churches, 58 of which were without pastors. There were 7 million young persons in the region in need of Christian training. This was a large part of the need that Bay Ridge heard calling it forward. So President Williams brought experienced educator Walter Doty as the new dean. Soon the academic programs had undergone extensive review, a significantly revised catalog was published, and applicant status was achieved with the American Association of Bible Colleges. A more sturdy foundation was beginning to be built for the future.

Yesterday and Tomorrow

Bay Ridge Christian College always has been small, has struggled for operating resources, and has depended heavily on the vision and personal sacrifice of relatively few persons. Nonetheless, past and present school leaders like J. Horace Germany and Robert C. Williams would point proudly to many churches in the South and elsewhere, both rural and urban, now being pastored by Bay Ridge graduates. They would recount with satisfaction the names of faculty members who have served without salary and a series of former Bay Ridge students who have gone on to Anderson School of Theology and other graduate schools and have been successful. The Bay Ridge history was told in a 1998 doctoral dissertation by Tracey Walker (University of Houston) titled "An Ethnohistorical Study of a Small Historically Black Ministerial College."

Although the numbers of such persons are small, college leaders would suggest that, when compared with the success levels of other church colleges in preparing and placing black church leadership, the success of Bay Ridge has been remarkable. Understandable pride is taken when names like the following are recalled, all Bay Ridge Christian College graduates: Percy Lewis, Benjamin Leon, Andrew David Johnson, Iris Pearson-Mayshack, Reginald Alford, Richard Prim, and Robert C. Williams. In the summer of 1986, pastor George W. Burns, himself key to the history of Bay Ridge Christian College for many years, reported to the readers of *The Shining Light* that, by that time, two of the school's graduates had earned doctoral degrees and twelve masters degrees. Further, he said, "more of the black pastors serving Church of God congregations today are graduates of Bay Ridge Christian College than from any of our other Church of God colleges" (July/Aug., 1986, 11).

Margaret Ann Dunn completed a masters thesis in 1989 (Ball State University) that described the Christian education programs in black congregations in select southern states. Most of them were being served by graduates of Bay Ridge Christian College. At the time, Dunn was an Assistant Professor of Christian Education at the college. A major purpose of the study was to determine specific ways that the college could better serve the needs of the churches. In contrast to the early focus of college mission, many of the pastors surveyed were not serving in rural, but in urban or suburban congregations. In line with the school's history, the majority of these pastors were bi-vocational. One recommendation from Dunn's study was that college professors should keep in mind that "most students will be ministering in small churches in a variety of locations, and most students will have a job in addition to pastoring the church" (85).

The presidential years of Verda E. Beach were ones during which there was a significant upgrading of campus facilities. The sewer system was brought up to state standards and an attractive facelift was given to the kitchen and cafeteria. Various classes and conferences were held off campus during this process. On campus, the chapel, auditorium, and Germany Ministry Center were made available for conferences. Bay Ridge also provided, through the Ministry Leadership Development Institute, workshops for ministers and laypersons designed to enhance the effectiveness of their ministry assignments. President Beach established on the Bay Ridge campus the first public library in Kendleton, Texas.

Coming to the presidency of Bay Ridge Christian College in May, 2005, was Stanford Simmons. He was an experienced educator who felt himself ready and anxious to lead in the development of bi-vocational programs guided by strong Christian values. The chair of the board of trustees was James Phillips, a professor of pediatrics at Baylor College of Medicine in nearby Houston, Texas. These men brought an academic sophistication not known before by the school. The mission remained the integration of respectable academic standards with an applied education and Christian worldview that can enable effective ministry to the church and world (story in *One Voice*, Feb./Mar., 2006).

Pastor Ronald J. Fowler of Akron, Ohio, wrote the following as an endorsement of the 2005 social history written by James Earl Massey and titled *African Americans and the Church of God*: "Now the work and sacrifice of those in the past will neither be forgotten nor their lives unappreciated by those who carry on the good work our pioneering giants began." One such giant was J. Horace Germany. His legacy is the continuing educational ministry of Bay Ridge Christian College. His alma mater, Anderson

University, awarded him the Distinguished Alumni Award in 1970 and an honorary Doctor of Letters degree in 1981 for "his accomplishments in education and as a bridge-builder during the years of severe racial unrest in the South."

In 2005, the History Channel aired a documentary called "Mississippi State Secrets." It depicted the struggles for civil rights in the state and featured the life of J. Horace Germany as he had sought to launch Bay Ridge Christian College. Germany had been persecuted, almost murdered, trying as a Church of God pastor-educator to train young African Americans for leadership in the churches of the South. This legacy of vision and courage persists in the present life of this pioneering school.

At Bay Ridge today, one finds a two-year residential Christian college designed to meet the needs of a culturally diverse student body. Students can complete general education requirements while earning ministerial and entrepreneurship certificates. They then can transfer to one of the four-year campuses of the Church of God to pursue the bachelor's degree. Affiliated with Church of God Ministries, Anderson, Indiana, and endorsed by the National Association of the Church of God, Bay Ridge is carrying on a specialized tradition of education and ministry. It is doing so, however, with troubling operational restrictions. On one occasion, all students had to leave campus because of the need to update the sewage system to meet new county requirements. Classes ended early in the spring of 2006 because of storm damage. In the fall of 2006, all students (about twenty-five) again were removed from the campus because of a failed safety inspection resulting from new federal and state requirements for residential dorms.

The current story, however, is more than the facing of big challenges. There is a significant board of trustees in place, including James Phillips, board chair. Its members are committed to the school's future and bring with them a wide range of outstanding competencies, including architecture, medicine, strategic planning, etc. This is unprecedented in the school's history. The current school president and dean, Stanford and

Beverly Simmons respectively, are experienced and credentialed educators.

A particular educational vision is inspiring the school's future. While major universities and colleges bemoan the failure of their institutions to serve ethnically-diverse students, national, state and local political leaders, social activists, and clerics are seeking new and creative ways to increase academic achievement for all students. Bay Ridge Christian College is primed to help previously underserved populations experience educational and economic success by engaging them in transformational teaching and learning. Because many of today's students leave high school without acquiring the necessary skills to be successful in college or to compete for meaningful employment, Bay Ridge is planning an "ability-based" curriculum in a two-year, residential, Christian junior college.

The Campus at a Glance

Institutional Names:

1959-   Bay Ridge Christian College

Accreditations:

Not accredited.

Chief Executive Officers:

1959-1982   J. Horace Germany
1982-1987   Charles G. Denniston
1987-1991   Robert C. Williams
1991-1993   Wilfred Jordan
1993-1995   Percy Lewis
1995-1996   Charles G. Denniston
1996-2005   Verda E. Beach
2005-   Stanford Simmons

Chief Academic Officers:

1959-1960	Isom R. Crockett
1960-1970	John A. Buehler
1970-1971	J. Horace Germany (while president)
1971-1974	Raymond E. Hastings
1974-1975	Sawak Sarju
1975-1976	J. Horace Germany (while president)
1976-1977	Charles G. Denniston
1977-1987	Elbert Williams
1987-1991	Walter M. Doty
1991-1993	Dean Stork
1993-1996	Sadie Fletcher
1996-1998	Margaret A. Dunn
1999-2000	Kimberly Thomas
2001-2005	Tracey Walker Moore
2005-	Beverly Simmons

Mission and Vision Statements

To challenge, educate, equip, and empower students in a Christ-centered environment to be effective servant-leaders in their chosen careers, churches and communities, while modeling exemplary excellence in character, values, and integrity.

Bay Ridge Christian College will strive to be a leader among institutions of higher education with an emphasis on providing a Christian environment conducive to transformational teaching, learning, and leading by responding to the needs of diverse, post-modern students, seeking to understand their purpose and destiny. We are committed to academic integrity and excellence and sound operational procedures and fiscal management.

Campus Alumni Publication

A newsletter found on the campus website.

Contact Information

Bay Ridge Christian College   Phone: 979-532-3982
P.O. Box 726   Email: info@bayridgecc.com
Kendleton, Texas 77451   Web Site: www.bayridgecc.com

President
Stanford Simmons

CHAPTER 6

The Story of
Gardner College

The Church of God movement spread in the final years of the nineteenth century primarily through the influence of its periodical, the *Gospel Trumpet.* By the 1880s this paper was greatly appreciated in eastern Canada and soon would move westward with its influence. Wherever this paper was read, the number of believers associating themselves with the movement increased.

Several Canadians joined the "Trumpet Family" when the publishing work was located in Moundsville, West Virginia (1898-1906). They helped with the editing and printing work. William Ebel, a worker in Moundsville, moved to Winnipeg, Manitoba, in 1905 and gathered a group of German-speaking Church of God "saints." The next year William H. Smith, an African-American minister from Colorado, arrived in Edmonton, Alberta, preaching and distributing literature of the Gospel Trumpet Company. In 1907 Gottlieb Butgereit, a North Dakota minister fluent in English and German, also came to Alberta, beginning a new work in Irvine.

Through such people and publications, the work of the Church of God movement took root in western Canada. The story is well told by

Walter Froese in *Sounding Forth the Gospel on the Prairies* (1982). Some program for educating Canadians for the ministerial work in Canada would not be far behind. The influence of Anderson Bible Training School in the United States would be one key factor.

Time for a Bible School in Western Canada

By the 1920s the leaders of the Church of God movement in western Canada felt the need for a training institute for preparation of future ministers. Various Christian institutions were being founded in the area, including the 1922 beginning of Prairie Bible Institute in Three Hills, Alberta. Denominational motivations for these new schools related closely to preparation of leaders for the particular culture of the prairie.

Anderson Bible Training School had served well the Church of God in Canada, but it was thought that it would be more advantageous to have a western Canadian school rather than one in a "foreign" country (the "lower 48"). The Ministerial Assembly of the Church of God in Canada discussed the matter in 1927, set up a planning committee the next year, and then in 1929 heard a favorable report from the committee. However, because of a crop failure and difficult economic and church conditions in general, specific action to launch a school was postponed for a few years.

The hope for a school had been nurtured by key individuals who had attended the young school in Anderson, Indiana, founded in 1917. One was Victor Lindgren from the vicinity of Camrose, Alberta, who went to Anderson in 1919. Edgar Busch from Saskatoon began his studies in Anderson the same year as Lindgren, with two others from Rocky Rapids going in the fall of 1920. Of particular significance for the future was Harry C. Gardner, who graduated in 1924 from Anderson Bible Training School in Anderson, Indiana.

Gardner returned to his native Canada and soon became the respected pastor of the Church of God congregation in Edmonton, Alberta. He carried home with him a concern that went beyond his new pastoral responsibilities. He had a burden for establishing in the Canadian setting a Christian training program something like what he had experienced in Anderson, Indiana. The college that finally would evolve from this burden, although never large, would prove to be pivotal in the development of much of the general work of the Church of God in western Canada in the decades to follow.

President Harry C. Gardner

Fulfilling such a dream, however, would have to occur in the midst of the prevailing realities of the Church of God on the western Canadian prairies. Those realities included relative newness as a church movement, pronounced ethnic and language diversities among the people, and the lack of organizational development within the church. It also was a time of widespread financial hardship that soon would grow even worse. The need for Christian education was far more evident than were the ways and means of meeting it.

For several years the possibility of a new school was discussed among the area ministers, with action always being postponed until circumstances became more favorable. The concern persisted because trained leadership was lacking and many of the church's young people were being lost from the life of the Church of God movement. It was difficult and expensive for most Canadian young people to go as far away as Anderson in the mid-western United States for the necessary education. Some had been choosing to attend an interdenominational Bible school near Edmonton. These persons, however, often were drawn away from the Church of God movement by the new relationships made and opportunities encountered.

Finally, in a minister's meeting in Lashburn, Saskatchewan, in 1932, Harry C. Gardner shared persuasively his vision and burden for starting a

Bible school in Edmonton. His sharing inspired agreement that this proposed school project had potential and deserved encouragement and support. The ministers passed a brief resolution authorizing the establishment of a training school. Initial implementation was left to Gardner's best judgment and efforts. It was a time of severe depression economically and determined hope spiritually. Considerable dedication and sacrifice would be required. There were only a few well-established congregations of the Church of God in western Canada, although there were many more saints living in isolated communities and reading the English *Gospel Trumpet* or the German *Evangeliums Posaune*. Probably there were some six hundred Church of God persons in all, about half German speaking, a few Ukrainian and Russian, and the rest English.

One Church of God woman, Sarah Monroe, responded to the difficulties of the times by moving with her husband to Edmonton to start the Mission of the Open Door ministry as a way of helping some of the economically hardest hit people in the heart of the city. The hungry, mostly unemployed men, were fed with donated food supplies. A meal was served at the mission each evening after a gospel service conducted by Harry C. Gardner and others whom he supervised. In this mission, on January 3, 1933, with eleven students enrolled in classes, the school long hoped for actually began. Students lived with local Church of God families. "Mother" Monroe, Harry Gardner, and Walker Wright, also a graduate of Anderson Bible Training School, were the teaching staff. Gardner directed the small enterprise, a long dream beginning to materialize, if only in a modest way.

Those first students soon were expressing deep gratitude for the supportive atmosphere and the learning opportunity. They wanted their lives to count for God and the work of God's kingdom. A good report of that first term reached the Ministers and Workers Assembly at the Church of God camp meeting in Ferintosh in July, 1933. Apparently, such an educational effort was viable, despite all the problems. Persons were chosen to promote the school and guide its development. The school already had moved from a prayerful dream to a functioning reality. Gardner had put out the challenge for support in these words: "Let us pray and work for a bigger and better School next winter. Do not forget the Bible School in your future plans. If you cannot come, perhaps you can raise a few extra chickens, feed a calf or a pig, grow some extra vegetables, sow a few acres of wheat, or do something to help the School next winter" (*Canadian Messenger*, April 1933, 3).

The next winter term (January-March, 1934) found the school operating with thirteen students in the basement of the Edmonton church. Another thirty-three students were in a German school in Medicine Hat under the direction of Jacob Wiens, bilingual pastor of the German congregation there. By that summer, the new school, now known as Alberta Bible Institute, solved the problems of two locations and poor facilities by merging the operations into one at Ferintosh where Victor and Elsie Lindgren were host pastors and the large camp meeting tabernacle was located. These two language groups in the church worked together smoothly as this joint venture of faith proceeded. Instruction was to be in English, but a German language class was provided whenever it was needed.

A New School Home in Camrose, Alberta

In 1935 an old hospital building became available in Camrose, Alberta. The decision was made for the Institute to move one more time, this time to a location which was to be the long-term home of the Canadian school. Jacob Wiens moved to Camrose as vice-principal. He and the principal, Harry Gardner, determined that together they would build the school.

Although 1936-1938 were severe years of economic depression, Alberta Bible Institute flourished, reaching an enrollment of sixty students and sponsoring the "ABI Gospel Hour" radio program. Camrose, in the province of Alberta, was becoming the focal point of the work of the Church of God in western Canada. The Ferintosh tabernacle was dismantled and moved the thirty miles to Camrose. Publication of the

Western Canadian Contact was also now based in Camrose. When the first issue appeared under the new name *The Gospel Contact* in October, 1942, ABI was its featured subject. By then, it was clear that the school had become an important part of the life of the approximately thirty-five Church of God congregations in western Canada. Over half of these were in the province of Alberta.

Real trouble, however, soon came over the horizon. There was war in Europe. Some Church of God young men became active in the Canadian military. Feelings in the country intensified against German people. In spite of efforts to avoid it, some strain developed in German-English relationships within the Church of God in Canada. After the war, a large number of refugees from Europe came to Canada, including many displaced Germans. Among them in 1949 was Gustav Sonnenberg, a widely-known Church of God leader in Europe. Coming with him were his family and many others who had known and respected him in their former homeland. He became pastor in Wetaskiwin, drew many of the newcomers, and traveled widely as a successful evangelist. He then moved to Edmonton to pastor a German congregation that became the largest Church of God congregation in Canada.

In the midst of this social tension and change after World War II, Alberta Bible Institute continued to develop and play a vital role in the western Canadian church, including being a means of positive communication and fellowship between the English and German church leaders. The Legislative Assembly of the Province of Alberta granted to ABI an act of incorporation in 1947, with the church's General Ministerial Assembly now empowered to elect the school's nine-member board of trustees. The stated purpose of ABI was "the providing of intellectual and spiritual training for prospective ministers, missionaries, and gospel workers, and of promoting the true principles and teachings of the Bible as taught and exemplified by Jesus Christ."

A high school was established in 1949 by the Ministerial Assembly. Connected with Alberta Bible Institute, it was under the leadership of

Wilhelm and Irene Ewert and in part had developed out of a concern about the educational level of many ministers who had not completed high school. Even though this new educational project was accredited by the Department of Education of the province, which certainly increased the public stature of ABI itself at the time, library and laboratory resources and enrollment levels were not adequate to justify continuance. By 1957 the high school was discontinued, as the radio program had been in 1956.

By 1950, President Harry C. Gardner of ABI was facing a series of problems, including some criticism of his own leadership of the school. He decided to contact a young American minister, Kenneth Jones, to see if he would consider coming to Canada as the first formal dean of the school. Jones, a graduate of Anderson College and Oberlin Seminary, was then in Princeton, New Jersey, doing further graduate work. He had felt a divine call to a teaching ministry and so decided to accept the ABI opportunity and challenge. When he arrived, Jones found ABI going through difficult times. Gardner soon left the school, partly in response to criticism of his own leadership and partly for reasons that, according to Jones, kept his own service limited to only one year.

The lack of educational resources and low student enrollment were not the only problems. Some continuing tension was rooted in a conflict commonly experienced by a dedicated immigrant community seeking to retain the integrity of its own traditions. Rev. Sonnenberg, for instance, was very concerned that the introduction of the English language into the German church in Canada would bring cultural decay and religious compromise, particularly to a new generation of German young people. Only the German language was judged appropriate for public preaching and praying. The German Christians formed their own church organization, held occasional Bible classes in Sonnenberg's congregation beginning in 1956, and actually formalized their own Bible school in 1964.

These concerns and developments inevitably came to involve Alberta Bible Institute. Sometimes the results tended to be divisive, even though efforts were made at understanding and reconciliation. Kenneth Jones returned to the United States to pastor, Harry Gardner ended his long tenure of leadership, and Gordon Schieck attempted to bring some new stability to the institution and help it be a positive force in the life of the church. But student enrollments, always small, declined during the 1950s. Church support was not adequate and, at times, not even enthusiastic. Gordon Schieck, wanting missions experience and hoping to bring that thrust back to enrich the ministry of the school, left for India in 1955.

Thomas M. Hall served as president from 1955 to 1957. Then, in an especially difficult period for the school, Gardner was called upon to return to the presidency of ABI. He served again from 1957 until his sudden death in 1961. His years of service had been many and had included challenges and frustrations as well as the joys of leadership training for the church. It had been "his school" for many years. Now his death demanded the entering of a new era.

Whatever the persistent problems, there continued to be quality persons of real dedication associated with the school, persons who had vision and stimulated program development despite the problems. Harry Dodge became dean in 1953. Soon the four-year Bachelor of Theology degree program was initiated. Russell Olt, dean of Anderson College, visited during 1953-1954 to assist in establishing the necessary new courses. Douglas E. Welch, later a long-term missionary in East Africa and then professor of Christian mission at Anderson School of Theology, was one of the first students to enter this expanded program.

Richard N. Yamabe, a graduate of the University of British Columbia and Anderson School of Theology, continued the upgrading of the program through his teaching and academic administration over a period of almost twenty years. This tradition was carried on by others, particularly Siegfried Belter, educated at ABI and the University of Alberta and an excellent bridge person to the German church. Belter was a strong academic man who worked tirelessly to strengthen the educational life of the school. At Belter's untimely death in 1984, John Alan Howard, who was educated at Anderson College, its School of Theology, and the University of Winnipeg, came to carry on this tradition as dean. Over these years the college worked as it could at strengthening academic programs despite severe economic restrictions. It kept in touch with the larger community of higher education through its affiliation with the Association of Canadian Bible Colleges and its involvement in the Commission on Christian Higher Education of the Church of God.

Years of Discouragement and Determination

The 1960s continued to be difficult years for Alberta Bible Institute. The school made a series of efforts to develop options and set new and clearer directions. It requested assistance from the Commission on Christian Higher Education of the Church of God. After the Commission's Milo L. Chapman and Robert A. Nicholson had visited the Canadian campus, the Commission recommended that the Church of God in western Canada outline its objectives so that ABI could then align its efforts with them. Common vision and clearer communication were essential.

In 1968 an important relationship began between ABI and the neighboring Camrose Lutheran College. Consideration was even given to an amalgamation of ABI, Mountain View Bible College (Missionary Church), Hillcrest Christian College (Evangelical Church), and Aldersgate College (Free Methodist Church). In 1971 an extensive study was undertaken with the leadership of former ABI student and skilled researcher John Wesley Hughes. Hughes and Gordon Schieck made visits to Canadian congregations and colleges. Concurrence was given to the earlier Commission recommendation. The result was a call for the school to remain in Camrose and develop one-year and two-year programs that could be the foundation for continuing studies at Anderson College and Warner Pacific College or elsewhere. A multi-institutional strategy appeared wise.

Beginning in 1972, some new optimism began to build. An aggressive development program for the school had been launched. David W. Davis, having graduated from Anderson School of Theology and pastored in Canada, became president of ABI in 1974. Ralph Farmer was now in place as director of development. A prime piece of land in Camrose, not far from the old school facility, became available. It was seen by some as an excellent opportunity for the school to relocate and expand. Planning began toward the possibility of new construction so that the school, the western Canadian camp meeting, and offices for the national work of the Church of God in Canada could be housed in a conveniently designed and common complex. This would symbolize and help to bring to increasing reality the essential interdependence of these several church organizations—and ABI would be appropriately and closely related to all of the work. But what might have been a giant step forward instead brought turmoil and eventually the resignations of both David Davis and Ralph Farmer.

Another possible site near Edmonton had become an alternate possibility. It was both attractive and expensive. To some, including Farmer, it seemed almost too good to be true, well worth the risks and major costs involved. To others, including President David W. Davis, it appeared to be an unwise idea that tantalized some egos but would turn out to be a practical disaster. Sides developed and positions hardened. The resignations followed. Both sites were eliminated, one by the city of Camrose for safety reasons (old coal mines under the property) and the other by lack of the funds necessary for ABI to act in time to secure it. Gordon A. Schieck again was asked to fill the sudden leadership vacuum and try to carry on the school in the old location and facilities, and in the midst of many deeply strained relationships. There now were very few students and even some talk that it might be necessary to close the school altogether. But that was not allowed to happen.

The pattern for ABI over many years had been one of determination mixed with discouragement. Then in 1977 another era of renewed hope began. Robert J. Hazen from Lansing, Michigan, accepted the school's presidency. He had been a member of its governing board, knew its problems, but was nonetheless optimistic about the potential that could be its future. Some new plans were drawn for long-term development. President Hazen knew that his task was to try to salvage the situation.

At least a few things gave him the necessary hope to proceed. There was some strong lay leadership in the church and on the ABI governing board. Alberta was a rapidly developing province with a strong economic base. The students who did come to the school tended to be persons with talent, drive, and a willingness to adapt and work hard (they often came from immigrant families). Finally, in President Hazen's view, the school was needed if the Church of God in western Canada was to have identity and cohesion. Otherwise, the church probably would deteriorate into a scattered collection of essentially community churches.

The years following 1977 were guided by a series of goals that were achieved in varying degrees. President Hazen identified these goal areas as follows:

1. To bring to the Church of God movement at large the unique benefits of "the German theological mind." The coming to the faculty of Anderson School of Theology in 1980 of Dr. Walter Froese from the faculty of ABI is an example.

2. To help the Canadian church capitalize on opportunities not available to the church in the United States or not addressed by the American church. The relatively neutral posture of the Canadian government on the international scene opens some unique mission opportunities.

3. To be a unifying force in the Canadian church. The very large distances within the country, as well as Anglo-German and other divisions, have created a real need for such a force. There have been attempts and progress toward ending the polarizations among the college, the Canadian Board of Missions, and the local churches.

4. To establish a sense of continuity and longevity in the school by ending the frequent administrative and faculty changes which had been endured in previous years. The leaving of Dr. Froese and the death of Dean Belter have worked against this goal, but Hazen's own long-term commitment and that of the new dean, John Howard, are positive events.

5. To bring improvement in the aged and inadequate facilities of the college. In fact, two new student dorms and a music hall have been added, and now the offices of the Executive Council of the General Assembly of the Church of God are on the edge of the Gardner campus. This brings increased unification of the school and the ministry agencies of the church in the region.

6. To enhance a significant relationship with the nearby Camrose Lutheran College which had been evolving over the years. This is being accomplished so that Gardner students have convenient access to a range of liberal arts courses. CLC has managed to gain degree-granting status through the Private College Accreditation Board of the Province of Alberta. Gardner is able to grant theological degrees without such accreditation. It relies, then, on the availability of the wider range of CLC courses, a practical way to approach the hope of a quality program with limited financial resources.

In 1981 the name of the Canadian school was changed to Gardner Bible College in honor of its founding president. Then, in June, 1983, the General Assembly of the Church of God, meeting in Anderson, Indiana, joined with Gardner Bible College in celebrating its fiftieth year of service to the Church of God. The college was recognized as the second oldest institution of higher education in the Church of God in North America (only Anderson University is older) and one that had played a significant role in the life of the church. Gordon A. Schieck earlier had reported through the pages of *Vital Christianity* (July 2, 1978) some of the accomplishments of the college over the years. An alumni association had been formed in 1949. By 1978 there were over seven hundred on the mailing list. Some of these had gone on to excel in additional academic studies at Anderson and Warner Pacific Colleges and elsewhere. Most were active in Christian service as educators, pastors, and leading laypersons.

Thirty-two of the Church of God ministers in Canada at the time were Gardner alumni, while others were serving as missionaries in other countries. A wonderful example of missionary service was Irene Engst who served in Kenya from 1947 to 1974. These numbers have continued to grow. Between 1972 and 1986 there were a total of 163 graduates of Gardner Bible College. Thirty-four of these persons completed the four-year Bachelor of Theology degree. A significant percent of these graduates are in full-time Christian ministry or are pursuing further studies toward that goal.

The additional name change in 1993 to Gardner College, removing the word "Bible," did not alter the primary purpose of the school, which at the time was said to include "the promotion of the principles and teachings of the Bible as taught and exemplified by Jesus Christ." By the 1980s, four published sources had sought to record portions of the long history of Gardner College (Alberta Bible Institute). They were:

1. Walter Froese, *Sounding Forth the Gospel on the Prairies* (Gospel Contact Press, 1982).
2. H. C. Heffren, *Voices of the Pioneers* (n.d., about 1969).
3. Daniel Nelms, "A Comparative History of Three Selected Bible Colleges in Alberta," a Ph.D. dissertation, Walden University, 1982.
4. Gordon A. Schieck, "A Brief History of ABI," in *Vital Christianity* (July 2, 1978).

Looking Backward and Forward

Gardner College (Alberta Bible Institute) has never been large in numbers of students, but it has survived and persisted in its prime purposes since 1933. It has been a pivotal force in the development of much of the general work of the Church of God in western Canada and, through many of its graduates, it has provided significant leadership for the church in Canada and worldwide. The college's challenge is substantial as it seeks with limited funding to serve a relatively small and geographically scattered church constituency. That challenge has been faced for decades with persistence and high aspiration.

The constitution and bylaws of Gardner College calls for two key leadership positions, Chief Operating Officer and Dean of the Faculty. It allows that they may be held by the same person given the size and resources of the school. In fact, John A. Howard held both positions for some years before his retirement in 2006. He had begun serving the school as professor of Christian education and campus chaplain, and then he accepted the role of academic dean in 1984. During his teaching and administrative years, stretching beyond two decades, he oversaw the construction of new facilities and expansion of the academic program to include early childhood development and child youth care work.

Consideration of possible change in the relationship of Gardner College and the Church of God movement in western Canada has been a prominent agenda item since at least 1995. A proud tradition has been facing major challenges. It may be that, in order to compete for the church's students, an answer must be found for the school's limited facilities and financial resources. Many leaders in the Church of God in western Canada have suggested that the school needs to reinvent itself, re-emerging in some new form. The school is being forced to rethink its options.

The Church of God in western Canada has called in recent years for a reassessment and strengthening of the relationship between itself and

Gardner College. In 2000, an outside consultant group argued against a more direct structural relationship between college and church. In fact, it suggested that the school be a stand-alone entity. That idea was soon rejected by the school's board of trustees in favor of the college seeking an affiliated agency status with Church of God Ministries, Anderson, Indiana. The board's stated intention was "to continue offering ministerial education in accordance with the Anderson School of Theology, such that ministry preparation for the Church of God remains a highest priority for the College." The Executive Council of the Church in western Canada developed a transitional plan for structural changes, stating in December, 2000:

> The Church of God in Western Canada is a work in progress. It always has been. At this point in time, we are embarking on a journey for which we don't have all of the answers. But it is our desire to begin the journey of restructuring and revisioning in the hope that the Church of God in Western Canada could celebrate its diversity of character and live out the unity of mission and service shared…. Perhaps in this process, we will truly know what it means to be "a movement."

The Viability Committee appointed by the Canadian church's Executive Council had observed in 1995 that Gardner College has always operated "with several clear disadvantages: never enough dollars, inadequate facilities, limited staffing, too narrow a focus of purpose." Even so, the school's track record was a proud one. In 1995, congregations of the Church of God in Canada being served by Gardner College alumni (pastor or pastor's wife) were: 4 out of 7 in British Columbia; 14 out of 19 in Alberta; 3 out of 6 in Saskatchewan; 2 out of 2 in Manitoba; and 9 out of 17 in Ontario. Many other alumni were serving outside Canada in various ministerial roles and in other church fellowships.

In the college's publication *Gardner Matters* (spring 2006), the retiring president, John A. Howard, reported with pride that 42 of the 79 ministers in Canada had been Gardner students. For Howard, recent relations between the General Assembly of the Church of God in Canada and the college had left the college more unsure of where it fits into the grand scheme of the church's ministry. Howard had served the college since 1983 and seen many changes, challenges, and successes. He was retiring, hopeful that the future would be bright for Gardner College, whatever new model of curriculum and relationships might emerge. Howard was replaced in 2007 by the new chief executive officer, Donnalyn Froese, who had served as chair of the board of trustees since 2001.

Currently, Gardner College offers the opportunity to secure a liberal arts degree through cooperative programs with Warner Pacific College, Warner Southern College, and Azusa Pacific University. A student may attend Gardner for two years and then transfer to one of these schools in order to complete the program. Also, a student may reside at Gardner and complete liberal arts study with the Augustana Campus of the University of Alberta. Four full-time and eight adjunct faculty members are currently employed by Gardner and assigned among three departments, Early Childhood, Child and Youth Care, and Bible and Theology.

With Donnalyn Froese assuming the college presidency in 2007, various new initiatives were in the wind. A new Bachelor of Ministry degree program was under consideration. A new four-floor building was projected, with the main floor housing a day care facility. An increased interest in distance education had been noted. Hope abounded that a new day was dawning for the college.

The Campus at a Glance

Institutional Names:

1933-1980	Alberta Bible Institute
1980-1993	Gardner Bible College
1993-	Gardner College

Accreditations:

Membership in the Association of Canadian Bible Colleges. Through affiliation with Camrose Lutheran College and Warner Pacific College. The Early Childhood program is licensed by the Private Institutions Branch, Advanced Education of the Province of Alberta.

Chief Executive Officers:

1933-1953	Harry C. Gardner
1953-1955	Gordon A. Schieck
1955-1957	Thomas M. Hall
1957-1961	Harry C. Gardner
1961-1964	J. Milton Chugg
1964-1966	Albert F. Irving
1966-1967	Hugh C. Wolkow
1967-1974	Gordon A. Schieck
1974-1975	David W. Davis
1975-1977	Gordon A. Schieck
1977-1989	Robert J. Hazen
1989-1997	M. Bruce Kelly
1997-2006	John Alan Howard
2006-2007	John Bruneau (interim)
2007-	Donnalyn Froese

Chief Academic Officers:

1933-1950	Harry C. Gardner (while president)
1950-1951	Kenneth E. Jones
1951-1953	Gordon A. Schieck
1953-1957	Harry L. Dodge
1957-1962	Richard N. Yamabe
1962-1968	Jarvis C. Wiuff
1968-1974	Richard N. Yamabe

1974-1975   David W. Davis (while president)
1975-1984   Siegfried Belter
1984-2006   John Alan Howard
2006-   John Bruneau

Mission Statement

The mission of Gardner College is to develop followers of Christ by providing a faith learning community.

Campus Alumni Publication

Gardner Matters

Contact Information

Gardner College   Phone: 780-672-0171
4707 56th Street   Web Site: www.gardnercollege.org
Camrose, Alberta
Canada T4V 2C4

President Donnalyn Froese

GARDNER
COLLEGE
entre For Christia Stud

CHAPTER 7

The Story of the Caribbean Colleges

Jamaica School of Theology and West Indies Theological College

T he Caribbean region between the Americas includes many islands and independent nations. Those that are English-speaking were former British colonies that now have gained their independence. Jamaica, for example, became a sovereign republic in 1962. Unfortunately, a rather narrow insular mentality has characterized many relationships among these island nations. This has complicated the higher education work of the Church of God movement in the region that has hoped to serve the various nations equally.

The missionary work of the Church of God movement in this region has tended to develop with an insular mentality, true to the general circumstance prevailing. Each nation has its own leaders, leadership structure, and program priorities. Efforts at leadership training, often related to institutions and academic leaders of the church in the United States, have not managed to survive the disadvantages of such a lack of integrated effort toward a common goal. A series of missionaries from the United States has sought over the decades to be a force for unification, evangelism, and leadership development. More recently, there has evolved the Caribbean Atlantic Assembly, an expression of the church in the region seeking a more structured means to make unified ministry a growing reality.

Two institutions of higher education have emerged in the life of the Church of God movement in the Caribbean region. The first was in Jamaica and has not functioned beyond the high school level since 1970. The second is in Trinidad and Tobago and is struggling to survive and find its way toward a more viable and productive future.

Jamaica School of Theology

The work of the Church of God movement in Jamaica began in 1907 with the pioneering ministries of George and Nellie Olson, former workers in the Gospel Trumpet Home in Anderson, Indiana. During the early years of the Jamaican work, the church had no system of theological training for ministers and other leaders except what missionary Nellie Olson managed to provide in the Kingston Sunday school. Soon she became burdened for a Bible school and was encouraged in her hope when J. W. Phelps, secretary-treasurer of the Missionary Board in the United States, visited Jamaica in 1921. A furlough followed which allowed Mrs. Olson to complete a two-year ministerial course in the new Anderson Bible Training School (now Anderson University). When she returned to Jamaica in 1924, she was both better prepared herself and more determined than ever to start a similar school for others.

The Jamaica Bible Institute was opened in January, 1926, in Kingston. Classes for the original five students were held in the facilities of the High Holborn Street congregation pastored by George Olson. Nellie Olson served as principal and the only teacher. A four-year theological course was outlined for the purpose of preparing young men and women for

Christian service. Obviously, the personally experienced model of Anderson Bible Training School was prominent in the principal's mind and heart. The new institute was operated under the auspices of the Missionary Board in the United States, but there was a local guidance committee that included Jamaicans. It was hoped that the institute would serve the needs of persons from Jamaica, Barbados, Trinidad, and elsewhere in the Caribbean. Ambitious plans were laid in faith, despite the scarcity of resources. Soon, small cash gifts began arriving from concerned persons in Cuba, Panama, and the United States.

In the second year of operation, Alva Ramsey was engaged to assist in the teaching. Arithmetic, Latin, and Spanish were taught to assist students with the Junior Cambridge examination, with geometry and algebra to follow for those preparing for the Senior Cambridge exam. This circumstance enabled the development of a level of student academic achievement recognized and valued by the Jamaican and neighboring societies of the time. Also during this second year of operation, Edith Young was sent to Jamaica by the Missionary Board in Anderson, Indiana. She spent her entire missionary career teaching in the Kingston school, not retiring until 1964.

Jamaica Bible Institute was gaining in strength and general recognition by 1929. Eleven acres of land were purchased. They faced both Ardenne Road and Hope Road in a suburban section of Kingston and were set aside for the use of the Institute. In 1930 the first three students completed the four-year course and were graduated. Nine more were to be so honored by 1942. Although the numbers were small, the accomplishment was meaningful to the life of a relatively small church community. The Institute's life was primarily the vision, faith, and perseverance over the years of one woman, Nellie Olson, the Institute's founder and first principal.

During this initial phase of the history of Jamaica Bible Institute, a major opportunity developed. There was in the region a great demand for schools that would enable persons to gain a secondary education that permitted passage of the Cambridge exams. Passing this standardized exam, based in England, opened doors for employment in many fields. Since the Institute provided this educational service, one clearly in demand, that aspect of the school's operation grew more quickly than the portion related specifically to leadership training for the church. So, partly to enhance the primary reason for the Institute's existence, in 1938 the two departments were separated into two institutions, Jamaica Bible Institute facing Hope Road and Ardenne High School facing Ardenne Road. Mary Olson, daughter of George and Nellie, was principal of Ardenne High School by 1940, and in 1946 Charles and Florence Struthers were sent by the Missionary Board in the United States to devote their time to the Institute.

By the late 1940s the Institute was offering three courses of study: a short-term Christian Education program; a two-year gospel workers program; and, for an additional two years, the full ministerial training program. Students who needed financial assistance for room and board worked in maintaining the property or in the agricultural and industrial projects of the Institute. Over these years, many students came from and then went back into the life of the church better prepared to serve effectively. Administrative leadership was through missionaries appointed by the Missionary Board in the United States. Both missionaries, including Raymond and Elna Mae Hastings, Leslie and Nina Ratzlaff, and Edith Young, and local Jamaican leaders taught and otherwise contributed to the significant work of the Institute.

The Jamaican society was developing rapidly and eager for progress on all fronts. Educational standards and expectations were rising. Now the question was: How can Jamaica Bible Institute graduate more highly qualified students? W. W. King wrote from Anderson, Indiana, in 1959 that "plans are now being worked out to upgrade the school as the growing need for leaders demands." Part of that plan turned out to involve Kenneth E. Jones, a young American minister-educator who spent 1960 as mission secretary in Jamaica. He traveled and preached in the churches and served on the governing boards of the Institute and high school. He came to understand the challenge and began to develop a strategy for further development of the educational work in Jamaica.

After two years of pastoring back in the United States, Kenneth E. Jones was asked by the Missionary Board to return to Jamaica to reorganize the Jamaica Bible Institute and be its principal. He and his family arrived in 1962 with a strengthened curricular design and a desire to help work out some of the organizational problems hindering the possible expansion of the Institute's work. In a series of meetings, the basic concepts were conveyed and accepted by the Institute's governing board. But then Mrs. Jones fell ill and the family was forced to return to the United States, delaying the opening of a new school term. New leadership was needed urgently. Fortunately, a gifted young pastor in the United States was willing to assume this responsibility.

James Earl Massey of Detroit, Michigan, had preached periodically in Jamaica since 1958. He had become a close friend of Samuel G. Hines, a Jamaican graduate of the Institute and pastor in Kingston. When invited by the Missionary Board to provide leadership to Jamaica Bible Institute, it was made possible when Massey arranged to also work with the congregations of Hines in Kingston, who in turn would preach in Massey's Detroit congregation and continue his education in the United States. Massey was appointed to become the new principal for a three-year term. He needed to get the Institute open again. He and his wife Gwendolyn Massey arrived in January, 1964. According to Kenneth Jones, Massey "went to fit into the new organization and carry out my plan."

Under Massey's leadership, the Institute did indeed experience a new day and a new enthusiasm. There was stress on achieving a serious educational environment. The academic program was lifted to the level where students could be tutored to take the external examinations for the Diploma in Theology or the Bachelor of Divinity degree from London University. The curriculum was operated at a university level, with passage of the Senior Cambridge exam expected for admission. The Institute had moved more seriously into efforts at "higher" education.

This was a new day that justified a new and more appropriate name for the school. Accordingly, the more prestigious name Jamaica School of Theology became official in April, 1964. There was new excitement and momentum. The student body of thirteen was large by local standards, and several faculty members were now Jamaicans. Indeed, as a result of the intensified curriculum, there were students who passed the difficult external examinations. Persons with London degrees were considered genuinely educated and could enroll for other degree programs in almost any college or university in Great Britain or the United States. Some did just that, becoming gifted leaders in their own right, the pride of Principal Massey. In the background, but supporting much of the academic thrust throughout this time, was the school's vocational department. Led by Ralph Little, a small furniture factory and its "Master Craft" products provided the needed employment for many of the students.

It was the conviction of James Earl Massey that the cost of quality theological education was far more than the Jamaican church could afford alone or that the American church should be expected to bear. So he encouraged leaders "to be forward-looking and see the importance of an ecumenical venture in this regard." An opportunity and a major decision soon arose in this regard. George and Nellie Olson, first missionaries to Jamaica, had been progressive and ecumenically-minded Christians. For instance, under George's influence many years before Massey's arrival, the Church of God movement in Jamaica had become a charter member of the Jamaica Council of Churches. Nellie Olson had always welcomed to the Institute students from many denominational backgrounds. Now, in 1964, Jamaica School of Theology was reaching for quality programming with a small student body and inadequate resources. Several other theological schools in the country were facing the same dilemma and looking to each other for an answer.

An ecumenical plan developed that called for the formation of the United Theological College of the West Indies. Merging were the resources of three local colleges (Anglican, Baptist, and Methodist) into one institution. It began to operate in Kingston in close relationship with the University of the West Indies, offering a Licentiate in Theology comparable to the Diploma in Theology from London University. The Church of God movement in Jamaica was invited to be involved in this joint venture, with the understanding that a proportional number of Church of God students could attend. Classes and requirements would be the same for all cooperating schools, except where distinctive denominational doctrines required special classes and qualified instructors.

This plan, in the mind of Principal Massey of Jamaica School of Theology, offered a way to further strengthen instruction and achieve accreditation for Jamaica School of Theology. He had become a personal friend of Dr. Wilfred Scopes, an Englishman who served as president of the United Theological College. Massey delivered the valedictory address to UTC in June, 1966. But the majority of Church of God leaders in Jamaica were hesitant. They were concerned about the possible loss of their own identity and influence in such an ecumenical setting, particularly because of the Church of England presence in the United Theological College (some preachers in the Church of God movement thought of its hierarchy as a major obstacle to true Christian unity). They questioned the wisdom of Church of God ministerial students training under largely non-Church of God instructors. Although a movement calling for increased Christian unity, the Church of God in Jamaica had clear "sectarian" concerns about the kind of unity being proposed in a United Theological College.

So, in December, 1964, the offer to join in the ecumenical venture in higher education was declined by the Church of God in Jamaica. A disappointed James Massey knew then that it would not be wise for him to remain and work in Jamaica beyond his three-year term. Here is his later recollection of this difficult time for him personally, as reported in this 2002 autobiography: "I was gravely disappointed.... I entered into a period of depression that lasted about three months.... I felt dark and dead within.... It was like the horror of seeing no future for what you are doing" (*Aspects of My Pilgrimage*, 233). In fact, only four years of life were now left for Jamaica School of Theology. Insight is available in the 1958 masters thesis by Raymond Hastings titled "The Church of God in Jamaica: A Critical Study of Its Structure and Work" (Anderson School of Theology).

James Massey's term of service in Jamaica ended in 1966. He and Gwendolyn returned to waiting pastoral responsibilities in Detroit, Michigan, and later to major roles on the Anderson University campus. Although Massey stated to the Missionary Board in the United States that "the school will have become sufficiently established during our stay that its future could well be handled by other leaders," without his strong leadership and the necessary resources of the ecumenical venture, the fortunes of Jamaica School of Theology deteriorated. Missionary George Buck continued to make efforts to implement aspects of the cooperative educational plan envisioned by Massey. Even so, the Missionary Board became discouraged by the few students and the failure of the school to develop cooperative relationships, even with West Indies Bible Institute, a Church of God school which had been in existence in Trinidad since 1950. Consequently, without an adequate base of operation or a supporting cooperative relationship to broaden the base, Jamaica School of Theology closed its doors in 1970.

Since that fateful year when their school ended, the Jamaican church has sorrowed over the loss. The Missionary Board has sent scholarship assistance to help support select persons seeking their educations elsewhere. Local churches have relied on the leadership of ministers from the United States and Jamaicans with limited theological education, education gained earlier from Jamaica Theological Seminary in Kingston, a proud and productive venture that is no more.

West Indies Theological College

Parallel to Jamaica School of Theology, with its institutional roots going back to 1926, is another school that evolved in the southern Caribbean. The first reference to a pattern of theological education in this area was in 1922. Representatives from the Church of God movement in Barbados, British Guiana, and Trinidad and Tobago had begun meeting for a one-week period each year. A fixed part of each day was devoted to educating for church leadership. There was serious reading and even written examinations. The need for learning was obvious, and this modest effort was at least a beginning.

During the lifetime of Jamaica School of Theology in the northern Caribbean, there was both the need and desire to begin a more formal, residential, educational work in the southern Caribbean. But the islands of this area were relatively small, scattered, and independent, presenting practical problems not experienced by the single, large island nation of Jamaica. Travel among the islands was inconvenient, costly, and complicated by immigration procedures and employment restriction on non-citizens. Nonetheless, the need for some means of educating church leaders for the region was obvious, and the will of the churches and missionaries to do something became clear. The motivation was strengthened further in the 1940s by the rising demand for self-government and the corresponding need for the training of indigenous leadership.

In 1948 a plan for the possible beginning of an educational program was proposed to the Missionary Board of the Church of God movement in Anderson, Indiana. Knowing the financial limitations of the Board, and concerned about the self-respect of those to be educated, Clair and Retha Shultz and Ralph N. and Ruth M. Coolidge, American missionary couples who had arrived in 1945-1946 in Trinidad and Tobago, proposed a practical self-help program. The board approved, emphasizing that the project had to be self-supporting. Soon a total of $700 was raised by a challenge presented at the Church of God state youth camp in Pennsylvania. Tools were purchased and a shop was set up in a garage behind the mission residence at 15 Carlos Street in Port of Spain, Trinidad. With an offering from the church in Trinidad and Tobago for some working capital, the operation of the vocational department of the new West Indies Bible Institute began.

The first classes met in 1950 in the Sunday school rooms of the church at 40 Carlos Street in Port of Spain. There were nineteen part-time and seven full-time students, the latter including three from Trinidad and Tobago, two from Barbados, and one each from British Guiana and Grenada. The faculty were the Coolidges and Shultzes and two members of the Port of Spain congregation, Carlton Cumberbatch who taught English and Leopold Lynch, a local medical doctor, who taught hygiene. Ralph Coolidge was the principal. Cumberbatch was in secular education at the time, but would become vital to the future of Christian higher education in the southern Caribbean. He would resign his government teaching service in 1954 to devote the rest of his life to the educational effort of the church.

Clair Shultz later recalled that the subjects to be taught at the church would be "about the same as those in the Theological Department of Anderson College or Pacific Bible College and would cover a period of four years." It was the substance of a two-year program spread over four years to accommodate the necessary work schedule of students. Typically, students would attend classes several hours each day and work the rest of the day making coat hangers, ladders, ironing boards, and souvenirs for tourists. It was a workable arrangement in that setting.

Facilities soon were inadequate for the shop. Space for the materials and tools became a problem and the noise of the shop's operation disturbed the quiet residential neighborhood. Something had to change. Then Wilbur Schield, friend of the Schultzes and businessman from Iowa, visited during one of his business trips to South America. Challenged by the need and opportunity, he and his brother Vern Schield gave $15,000 to help purchase a new site, five acres in the Santa Cruz valley some miles away over a nearby mountain. A small factory was built in the new location, more tools were provided, and the assignment of a third missionary couple was made possible. The Oakley Millers came in 1952, she to teach and he, a woodworker, to staff the shop.

The first students of West Indies Bible Institute graduated in 1954. An all-purpose building and a small dormitory had been built by then. The shop was very active, and school morale was high. Students were now coming from St. Kitts, Antigua, St. Vincent, and even Dutch-speaking Curacao and Spanish-speaking Panama and Costa Rica. Graduates began assuming leadership roles in the churches. Theodosia Cumberbatch, previously a young evangelist, became the pastor in San Fernando, Trinidad, and later would serve as president of the Institute. Carlton Cumberbatch became a full-time teacher in 1954, leaving his government teaching role, and later would also serve as the president of the Institute. Clifford Payne became pastor in Port of Spain, Trinidad, and Earl Proctor in Tobago, with others going to Barbados, Grenada, and Guiana. Sam Dhanraj became of professional counselor.

Over the years, the shop operation was both a blessing and a burden. It was promoted heavily in the churches, sometimes being referred to as "the sleeping giant" because it was seen as having great potential for generating funds for the school and the local churches. It appeared essential for the viability of the academic program since most students had no other way to pay for their educations. But conflict arose. In Jamaica, the rapid growth of the secondary education department had threatened to overwhelm the theological education mission of Jamaica School of Theology. In Trinidad, it was the vocational department. On the one hand, it became the view of the missionaries that the shop was too much of a competitor for the primary time and energy of students. On the other hand, many local church members felt that the shop's potential was being limited to the provision of student needs when it should be further expanded to assist the churches as well.

Donald D. and Betty Jo Johnson arrived as missionaries in 1956 to join the staff of the Institute. As dean and then acting president, Donald

Johnson helped bring into being an administrative reorganization that established a board of trustees representative of the Missionary Board and the churches in Barbados, Grenada, Guiana, and Trinidad and Tobago. The intent was to enable the local churches to assume more responsibility, partly through granting to the board of trustees the right to ratify officers of the Institute appointed by the Missionary Board. Carlton Cumberbatch, a local graduate of the Institute and one its faculty members, was appointed and ratified as the third president of WIBI, effective in June, 1959.

A key year was 1967. President Carlton Cumberbatch graduated from Anderson College, the Oakley Millers ended their missionary service (the last missionaries assigned to the work of the Institute), and WIBI graduate Clifford Payne was appointed dean, making the entire staff of the school West Indian. Since then, the Missionary Board in the United States (now Global Missions of Church of God Ministries) has continued to invest substantial dollars in support of the operation of the Institute rather than sending American personnel. A new phase of the school was the opening of a nursery school in 1969.

Clifford Payne was followed as dean in 1975 by another West Indian, Frank Drakes. By that silver anniversary year of WIBI's existence, forty-nine of its graduates had served as pastors, eleven as teachers in public or private schools, five as nurses, four as social workers, nine as Christian education workers, two as church leaders in ecumenical work, two as nursery and child care workers, three in secretarial work, and one in radio broadcasting. Over the years, several graduates have gone to England, Canada, and the United States as students in accredited colleges and universities and earned undergraduate and graduate degrees (including from Anderson University in several cases). Clinton Providence of St. Vincent and others graduated and served the church widely.

In the 1970s, the academic programs of WIBI included a two-year course of general preparation for the General Certificate of Education examinations. Also, built on that course with two additional years, the school offered a Ministerial Diploma course and a Christian Education Diploma course. An expansion in 1975 introduced a series of third and fourth year courses designed to assist selected students with the advanced-level General Certificate of Education examinations. Then in 1978 the Institute's name was changed to West Indies Theological College.

Over these years, the dilemma of the shop continued and worsened. Finally, the shop's operation failed altogether. There were business management problems, worker inefficiencies, and the increasing disrepair of equipment. The college, determined to keep this mainstay of student finances going, converted the shop into a commercial enterprise. But the dream of profits from this move never materialized. The new company, Masterbilt Products Limited, replaced the college's vocational department, began operating in 1972 after a delay, stopped functioning in 1974, and was liquidated in 1977—all without managing to contribute any revenue to the college's operations. This was indeed a depressing sequence of events.

Two major issues over the decades of the life of West Indies Theological (Institute) College have had a negative impact on its development, and are yet crucial to its future. One is its geographic isolation from most of the Church of God constituency in the Caribbean, and the other is its lack of formal accreditation as an institution of higher education. In the late 1950s, an experimental Caribbean ten-nation federation was launched and then failed. This was another evidence of the insular mentality and nationalism that have hindered regional progress in many ways. Jamaica, with its large Church of God population, went its own way. Any hope of a merger of the Church of God schools in Jamaica and Trinidad ended. Although each school was weak, there was no apparent way to cooperate for the good of both. Isolation prevailed.

But geography and politics were not the only isolating factors. Church identity inclined both schools against formal involvement in any significant ecumenical arrangement. The Jamaican school rejected such a possibility in the 1960s and soon closed. Although WITC developed an informal relationship in 1985 with the nearby Caribbean Nazarene Theological College, nothing more seemed feasible or desirable to either of the church constituencies involved. WITC has remained largely a very small school of the south Caribbean only, and of the Church of God movement only.

This isolation has been countered in part by the active involvement of WITC in the development of an interdenominational Caribbean association for theological education beginning in 1971. There also have been a few well-known educators from the American church who have taught for brief periods at the college, including Earl L. Martin in 1958 and John W. V. and Margaret Smith in 1984 (both from Anderson University and after John's retirement from his teaching position at Anderson School of Theology). Also in 1984, an agreement was reached with Warner Southern College in Florida that promised some practical help to the college and some of its students. Little, however, has come of this.

With such isolation and very limited financial resources, WITC has been poorly equipped to face the other challenge, that of needed accreditation. In its early years, the school recruited many of the most gifted Church of God youth of the area. Despite its lack of institutional standing in the world of higher education, several of its graduates were able to excel because of their own ability and motivation. Over the years, however, educational aspirations and standards have risen sharply in the Caribbean. For the more gifted persons, education in the local university or abroad has become more feasible and popular, affecting adversely both the size and quality of WITC's student body and the focus of its educational programs. More of the students now attracted want preparation for the certificate exams on their way to "standard" higher education, rather than only theological training for service specifically within the Church of God of the south Caribbean. In recent years, the annual student body has ranged from only eight to twenty-five persons.

Presumably, formal accreditation would help this circumstance, and such an accrediting body has arisen. It is the Caribbean Evangelical

Theological Association (CETA) that works jointly with the American Association of Bible Colleges. Carlton Cumberbatch of WITC was involved with the early development of the Caribbean Association of Bible Colleges that later evolved into CETA. The church's WITC campus has had an active relationship with this association since 1971, but has not been able to qualify fully for its accreditation. Without such formal recognition from the wider educational community, and without a substantive ecumenical relationship or a major new source of support from within the Church of God movement in 1985, it became questionable whether the college had a future. To date, for instance, nothing has ever replaced the supportive role played by the shop operation in the earlier years, except for some direct support from the churches in the region and substantial dollar support from the Missionary Board in the United States.

In 1986, Barry L. Callen, then Vice-President for Academic Affairs of Anderson University, visited the college in Trinidad to research its history and counsel with president Carlton Cumberbatch as he contemplated retirement after many years with the school. Out of the resulting conversations came a call for a formal consultation of Caribbean leaders of the Church of God, the WITC board of trustees, a representative from the Missionary Board, and Dr. Callen as special resource person. An era seemed to be ending for the college and a new future had to be found.

The consultation convened on the campus in Trinidad in June, 1986. Ten countries were represented, including Jamaica where the other Caribbean school had once functioned. In 1985 the organization of the governance of WITC had been changed to extend the right of board membership to all of the countries associated with the Caribbean/Atlantic Assembly of the Church of God. This consultation began to demonstrate the widening circle of interest in and potential commitment to WITC. Nine consensus statements were developed and agreed to by all participants as crucial guidelines for the future. They were:

1. It is affirmed by the Consultation members that the Church of God in the Caribbean needs a Church of God institution which seeks to prepare Christian leaders for service to the life of the Church of God in the Caribbean and to enable that church to fulfill its world mission.

2. Given the level of educational expectations in the Caribbean and the desire of the Consultation members to see provision for development of the best possible leadership for the church, every effort should be made to gain accreditation for this Church of God institution.

3. For this institution to be viable, the assemblies of the Church of God associated with the Caribbean/Atlantic Assembly must take increased responsibility for the necessary support of this institution and its students.

4. Since the leadership needs of the Church of God in the Caribbean are various, including traditional college education, extension education, and the continuing education of ministers, this Church of God institution should be creative and flexible in its programming.

5. This Church of God institution, to become a reality, must be built within the limits of available resources and should take advantage of a foundation already laid. West Indies Theological College has laid such a foundation. It is the theological training institution currently recognized by the Caribbean/Atlantic Assembly of the Church of God and affirmed by members of this Consultation as the proper place to begin.

6. The instructors at the West Indies Theological College should include representation from the entire Caribbean to the greatest extent possible. Their compensation should be at a level appropriate to their experience, their credentials, and the local cost of living.

7. The generation of adequate support for the operation of West Indies Theological College will require the development of some enterprise/plan which can produce income for the college in addition to church contributions.

8. Review should be made of the current nomination process for membership on the board of trustees of West Indies Theological College to ensure that the process is structured to bring to the board the strongest potential membership. This review should include a reconsideration of the number, and the length of terms of service, of members of this board.

9. The members of this Consultation have been informed about and heartily endorse the recent decision of the board of trustees to seek funding for the construction of an administration and academic building for West Indies Theological College.

As the participants left this consultation for their several home countries, the college still was small and struggling. But there was renewed hope that the college had a future. Some sense of direction had been achieved and a group commitment had been made. Within weeks, the faculty of WITC proposed plans to offer the fourth year segment of the curriculum, thus hoping to implement the full four-year Bachelor of Theology program and working toward accreditation at that level. By 1988 there was government approval of plans for a new administration and academic building. Fundraising for it had begun among the Caribbean churches. These were steps of faith.

Edward Cumberbatch, who had come to Trinidad from Barbados in 1905, had been converted under the preaching of missionary George Pye and then ordained in 1913. He was the first West Indian ordained minister of the Church of God in Trinidad and, in fact, in the entire southern Caribbean area. His son, Carlton, educated at WITC and then Anderson University and its School of Theology, was the West Indian president of

WITC from 1959 to 1988. He retired from his long tenure in that responsibility, being replaced for a decade by his wife Theodosia Cumberbatch, former dean who herself was replaced in 1998 by WITC graduate Clinton Providence. This marked the end of an era; by faith it would be the beginning of another.

The College Today

As West Indies Theological College prepared to move into the twenty-first century, it continued to survive the many obstacles it always has faced. In 2003 it opened new academic programs, including both bachelor and associate degree programs in psychology/counseling and social work. Having learned about the requirements and processes of accreditation through relationship with the Caribbean Evangelical Theological Association, WITC completed a self-study and has been granted provisional accreditation by the National Institute of Higher Education, a body set up by the government of Trinidad and Tobago. This advance in program and recognition has attracted some interest from the general public, requiring that classes be scheduled both morning and evening hours.

An encouraging ecumenical development saw the Mennonite Church in Trinidad and Tobago adopt West Indies Theological College as an agency for educating its local leaders. Mennonite students have been on the WITC campus since 1994. Five of them have graduated with the Bachelor of Theology degree. One of them, Linda Gunpath, now serves the school as dean. Observed the now-retired Carlton Cumberbatch to Barry Callen in 2006: "For several years the church failed to attract [to WITC] the more capable young people to theological study; now, however, that keen minds are enrolling here in the new courses, even from outside of the Church of God fellowship, this level of encounter in common courses may well lead young people to see the idea of being a student at WITC in a new light."

A board of trustees of fourteen members guides the school. The members come from eleven different islands of the Caribbean, with one from the United States. The current catalog lists sixteen faculty members, not all full-time. Prominent graduates of the school include Carlton Cumberbatch (1944), Clifford Payne (1955), Eustace Rawlings (1970), Clinton Providence (1972), and Linda Gunpath (1999).

The Campus at a Glance

Institutional Names:

1950-1978	West Indies Bible Institute
1978-	West Indies Theological College

Accreditations:

National Institute of Higher Education, Trinidad and Tobago

Chief Executive Officers:

1950-1956	Ralph N. Coolidge (principal)
1956-1957	Clair Shultz (president)
1957-1959	Donald D. Johnson (president)
1959-1988	Carlton Cumberbatch (president)
1988-1998	Theodosia Cumberbatch (president)
1999-2000	Donald Blankenship
2000-	Clinton Providence

Chief Academic Officers:

1950-1959	(no one so designated)
1959-1961	Donald D. Johnson
1961-1964	Walter Lehmann
1964-1967	(no one so designated)
1967-1974	Clifford Payne

1974-1988	Frank Drakes
1988-1998	Theodosia Cumberbatch
1998-2002	Clinton Providence
2002-2005	Frank Drakes
2005-	Linda Gunpath

Mission Statement

West Indies Theological College is committed to being an instrument of education and training through which the Church of God contributes to the guidance and preparation of Christian leaders to serve the church and the community in the Caribbean and beyond. It seeks to be a provider of the highest quality education and training for its constituents and to enable graduates to serve with a keen sense of purpose, responsibility, diligence, and distinction.

Contact Information

Located on LaPastora Road, Santa Cruz, Trinidad and Tobago.
Mailing address: P. O. Box 572, Port of Spain, Trinidad and Tobago
Phone: 868-676-7020
Email: witcol@tstt.net.tt

CHAPTER 8

The Story of Mid-America Christian University

MID-AMERICA
CHRISTIAN UNIVERSITY

I n one way, the origin of Mid-America Christian University stretches as far back as the early 1930s. In that Depression period, Warner Memorial University was forced to close its doors in Eastland, Texas. President Joseph T. Wilson and others had sensed a need for educated church leadership in the Southwest and had begun to build an educational dream for making that possible. Wilson also had begun Anderson Bible Training School twelve years earlier in 1917. The school in Anderson already had matured considerably, although there was debate in the church about the wisdom of its moving into the liberal arts curricular arena. Financial circumstances in Texas caused by the Great Depression, however, did not permit the Texas dream to survive for long.

Within a year of the 1933 closing of Warner Memorial University, Gordon Bible School was begun in Nebraska, primarily the dream of R. A. Germany. As the school in Nebraska was nearing its end in the early 1950s, a third dream emerged in the region, this one launched in Houston, Texas. South Texas Bible Institute would have the longevity denied to Warner Memorial University and Midwest (Gordon) Bible School. Credit for this third visionary launching of a school lies mainly with the strong-willed and spiritually disciplined Max R. Gaulke. His biography by Arlo F. Newell is titled *A Servant in God's Kingdom* (Warner Press, 1995).

A Determined New Beginning

The hope that had birthed Warner Memorial University and Midwest (Gordon) Bible College persisted despite the weaknesses and demise of these educational efforts. There was a continuing sense of need for a Church of God college somewhere in the southwestern part of the United States. Following the failure of Warner Memorial University in the early 1930s, Joseph T. Wilson became pastor of the First Church of God in Houston, Texas. He led the congregation in purchasing property on West Eleventh Street in the Heights area. In 1935 he shared with this church his vision that one day there would be a college on those grounds. After founding Anderson Bible Training School and Warner Memorial University, Wilson's educational vision was relentless! This current dream would be realized through Max R. Gaulke, a later pastor of that congregation. When Wilson died in 1954, the new school in Houston renamed its young library in his honor.

By 1950 this hope for a new institution of higher learning had begun to gather some potential concreteness. Concern was expressed in the Midwest Assembly of ministers, and soon the ministerial assemblies of the Church of God in Colorado, Kansas, Nebraska, Oklahoma, and Texas had each appointed representatives. Together they formed a board of directors working on behalf of a proposed new college. This group of church leaders included Elmer Case, an alumnus of Midwest (Gordon) Bible College. Of the seventeen group members, most were ordained ministers and graduates of Anderson College. Under the leadership of Max R. Gaulke, a 1934 Anderson College graduate and pastor in Houston, Texas, since 1947, the group met in Oklahoma City in 1951 to discuss prayerfully the need and possibilities. They were both optimistic and cautious. Arlo F. Newell observes: "Whether by sociological evolution, as outlined by Val Clear in his book *Where the Saints Have Trod*, or by spiritual maturation in Christian faith, the church was losing some of her fear of education" (*A Servant in God's Kingdom*, 1995, 25-26).

At this point, it was the opinion of the working board of directors, being chaired by Max R. Gaulke, that a new college, tentatively referred to as Central Bible College, should be founded in either Wichita, Tulsa, or Oklahoma City. The felt need was a large city setting that could provide adequate student employment. Studies of the potential of these locations began. Meanwhile, Gaulke explored with Frellsen Smith, Church of God layperson and college professor, the possibility of locating the school in Ruston, Louisiana, in relation to Louisiana Tech University.

Smith pursued this idea with the university president and State Board of Education, thinking that students of a new church college could take general classes at Tech for academic credit, enabling the college to concentrate on studies in Bible, theology, and church ministries. Gaulke, however, came to feel that there would be better student employment in a major city setting, so the idea of Ruston, Louisiana, was dropped. One oil man offered a large gift if Oklahoma City were chosen as the site. But there developed no sense of rightness, no clear view of practical possibility in this or any of the other options considered.

Gaulke, himself a well educated and sometimes driven leader, began to despair of this process of searching for the right location. Someone had to take action, even if it were only the first step and not eventually the long-term solution. He took matters into his own hands, sure that God was leading. As he later wrote, "I was finally pressed by a sense of duty to do something concrete as a start." He initiated plans to open an "institute" in Houston, Texas, "as a beginner effort." The multi-state board was agreeable to this temporary development, while it continued to plan for the founding of a college more centrally located than was Houston. In reality, no other college ever would be founded in the region, except for Bay Ridge Christian College that would have a different vision and constituency. The new South Texas Bible Institute in Houston became the modest base on which the future would be built.

The Sunday school of First Church of God in Houston, Texas, grew to about 500 persons during Max R. Gaulke's pastoral years there. He continued his own education. Having received the Bachelor of Arts degree from Anderson College and the Bachelor of Divinity degree in 1948 from Chicago Theological Seminary, he earned a master's degree in 1950 from the University of Houston. Then in the spring of 1953, with the First Church of God in Houston planning to host the new Institute envisioned by its pastor, Max Gaulke approached the Texas Ministerial Assembly meeting in San Antonio to seek its support of the educational effort.

Some of the ministers were hesitant, fearing another failure like the earlier Warner Memorial University in Eastland, Texas. They certainly did not want Texas to be known as the graveyard of Church of God colleges. But Gaulke assured them that the new Institute in Houston would be a small and viable operation, with himself as president and his local congregation being primarily responsible. The ministers were willing for the experiment to proceed on this basis. Thus, the modest beginning of South Texas Bible Institute was in September, 1953.

Esther Acheson had arrived at the Houston congregation in January, 1952, to be the secretary and Christian Education director. Soon she became aware that Pastor Gaulke had become "obsessed with the idea of starting a Bible college" (Newell, *A Servant in God's Kingdom*, 111). Her schedule was already full and it never occurred to her that soon she would also be asked to assume administrative duties for a new school. One day, however, the pastor entered the office and announced that he would be the president and she the registrar. Although a little shocked, she agreed. Soon a neighboring pastor had much the same experience. Gerald Erickson, an Anderson College graduate like Gaulke and now pastoring the Northside Church of God in Houston, was soon convinced to come full-time as dean of the Institute.

President Max R. Gaulke

Max Gaulke had a vision and could be persuasive. He had served in the North Dakota National Guard and once received an appointment to the West Point Military Academy. He now worked very hard, being the full-time pastor, the Institute's president, and the school's professor of homiletics. Observes his biographer, Max Gaulke "was possessed by an insatiable desire to prepare ministers to serve the church" (Newell, *A Servant in God's Kingdom*, 130). His students, like George Golden, were affectionately referred to by Gaulke as his "preacher boys."

A governing board was constituted, including members chosen by the local church and others selected by the State Ministerial Association of the Church of God in Texas. Gaulke judged that the Institute was on a sound foundation with the Texas State Assembly as its "general legislative body," and with its willingness to be "amenable to the jurisdiction of the General Ministerial Assembly of the Church of God." Erickson, Max and Isabelle Gaulke, and secretary Esther Acheson worked hard to get organized for the Institute's opening.

A recruitment flier was passed out during the 1953 International Convention of the Church of God in Anderson, Indiana. The intent, according to Gaulke, was to see "what the Lord would give us by way of students." A small notice appeared in the *Gospel Trumpet* (April 25, 1953), announcing that in September the South Texas Bible Institute would open in the facilities of First Church of God, Houston. It would offer "a three-year curriculum in accordance with Bible School accreditation standards." A letter of explanation was read to the General Assembly in June, 1953. The way was prepared for a modest beginning.

When the Institute opened its doors in September, 1953, it owned no property and had a modest budget of $10,000, with only the dean on salary. Twenty-six students had arrived from eight states (Arkansas, Colorado, Kansas, Louisiana, Nebraska, Oklahoma, South Dakota, and Texas). The promised availability of room, board, and work in the city, as well as the low tuition rate of thirty five dollars per semester had proven attractive. The small staff and "pioneer class," as they were called, were dedicated to an educational and evangelistic mission. President Gaulke announced that the Institute "was born to such an urgency." Lost men and women would hear the good news "through the activities of trained, spiritual, and zealous followers of Christ."

South Texas Bible Institute intended to give "intense training" in the Scriptures, personal and mass evangelism, Christian education, and missions. It was hoped that eventually such training would develop to the point of being on "a college academic level." In the meantime, and clearly emphasizing more than academics, chapel attendance was required of all students, the president functioned as a strong spiritual leader, and strict "holiness" standards of student conduct were maintained. President Gaulke announced a few years later, "we have taken a firm stand against worldliness in all forms" (*Tidings*, summer, 1972). The anti-worldliness was detailed this way in the school's 1963 Student Handbook: "The use of tobacco, alcoholic beverages, gambling cards, profane and obscene language is prohibited. It is expected that all refrain from worldly amusements, attendance at dances, theaters, and other habits that defile the body and mind and bring reproach upon the cause of Christ (1 John 2:15-17)."

The 1955-1956 catalog carried the name Gulf Coast Bible College and featured a cover photo of the First Church of God of Houston, said to be "the temporary home of GBC." Eight faculty members were listed, including President Max Gaulke, Isabelle Gaulke, and Walter M. Doty who was now present and functioning as the school's dean. In April, 1956, the GBC Chorale conducted a spring musical tour in Texas, Oklahoma, Kansas, and Colorado, with Samuel Germany as director. Student enrollments grew steadily, from 26 in 1953 to 118 in 1963 and then to a dramatic 364 in 1977.

The Long Path to National Recognition

President Max R. Gaulke had a national vision in mind from the very beginning of South Texas Bible Institute. He quickly reached out, bringing key figures to share with the students. Charles E. Brown, former editor in chief of the Gospel Trumpet Company, and William E. Reed, Secretary of Evangelism for the Church of God, arrived within the first two years to give sets of lectures. In 1954, the school's publication called the *Tidings* emerged as a means of effective communication nationally. The annual Minister's Refresher Institute began in 1963, a long-term program designed to bring to the Texas campus significant national church leaders and pastors in search of growth and renewal. While the First Church of God in Houston was sharing its pastor, staff, and facilities to enable the school's initial operation, the vision was always far from local. To be accepted more broadly, however, there were significant challenges to be faced.

From the Institute's beginning, there was a degree of tension between it and the national structure of the Church of God movement. On the positive side, and according to the first issue of the *Tidings* (January, 1954): "It wasn't until the brethren in Anderson were notified of our intentions and asked for their criticisms and suggestions that the initial step was taken to organize the school. A letter from the Acting Secretary of the Commission on Higher Education of the Church of God informed us it was all right to go ahead with our plans." But there was another side, one more hesitant. The general church had just come through some years characterized by strong "anti-Anderson" feelings on the part of many ministers. There had been "watchmen on the wall" who had sat in judgment of certain "headquarters" persons and program trends.

President Gaulke did not always see eye-to-eye with some of his own staff or with some general church trends. The presumed "liberal" tendencies of a "liberal arts" curriculum were often highlighted critically. South Texas Bible Institute would take the higher road of strict holiness standards of conduct and serious Bible study for all students, regardless of academic major. All resources would be spent on curricula designed to be immediately relevant to the needs of the church's life.

Numerous prominent church persons caught this focused church vision articulated by President Gaulke and began long tenures of close association with the school. Arah Phillips was an influential trustee who was financially generous at pivotal points in the school's early history. Lillie S. McCutcheon served as a trustee from 1969 to 1988 and gladly directed her church-side prominence toward the school's good. Max and Isabelle Gaulke said at McCutcheon's retirement: "You have been the pattern for countless others who have felt the call to preach and teach the gospel of our Lord Jesus Christ by convictions to hold, courage to speak, and character to live the truth." These are the commitments for which the college stood—a call from God, preaching, teaching, and living the gospel of Christ. This was seen in a major book, *Dynamics of the Faith: Evangelical Christian Foundations,* published by the college in 1972.

Dean Gerald Erickson and others at the school opposed vigorously the idea proposed by some who became related to the Institute. It was that there should be a break with "the Anderson body"—Gaulke and Erickson were loyal Anderson College alumni and hoped to be national team players in the church's life. While the idea of total independence was never given serious consideration, a degree of tension persisted. It was partly a preoccupation with a perceived regional need; but it went deeper than that. Gaulke was critical of what he judged the failure of the other colleges to train preachers true to the Church of God movement. The general church, on the other hand, worried about the financial burden and competition that would result from the existence of another educational institution. Would another school just make the existing ones less viable?

The Institute's leaders contacted the Commission on Christian Higher Education of the Church of God to seek dialogue regarding direction and procedures for the new program. President Gaulke, Dean Erickson, and trustees Lloyd Butler and Loren Rohr went to Anderson, Indiana, in June, 1954, to meet with the Commission. After Gaulke reviewed for the Commission the background of the Institute's beginning and his own view of the need for such a school, the trustees stated their desire that the venture be critiqued carefully. Does a Bible institute have a legitimate place in the life of the Church of God movement? They said that they did not wish to support a reactionary or divisive move within the church, one that could not function in harmony with the Commission and the General Ministerial Assembly.

There followed some vigorous discussion pro and con about educational philosophy, religious fundamentalism, and the value of formal accreditation for a viable program of ministerial education. While the Commission had no legal jurisdiction, it tried to offer counsel and caution consistent with the ongoing educational efforts of the church. Ironically, in this same June meeting, the Commission also handled issues related to the World Evangelism Institute in Southern California (later Arlington College). It counseled that this new training program be "consistent with the generally accepted philosophy of missionary education in the Church of God." The simultaneous evolution of new schools in Texas and California were promising developments in some eyes and unwise regional moves in others.

The life of the new Institute in Texas slowly gained strength. Walter M. Doty came to teach in 1954 from his pastorate in Marion, South

Dakota. By 1955, he was providing academic leadership as dean. He had studied at Anderson College and North American Baptist Seminary in South Dakota. Doty had been burdened for a new school in the South ever since he had been pastor in Ruston, Louisiana (1945-1950), where he had heard the earliest talk of the possibility of a new school. He would be a key leader in the school's life for many years to come.

In the spring of 1955, the trustees voted to expand the curriculum to a four-year Bible college level and change the name from South Texas Bible Institute to Gulf-Coast Bible College. The school was repositioning itself for eventual accreditation. GBC was a member of the Texas Association of Church-Related Colleges by 1958. The Veterans Administration approved the program for the education of military veterans. In 1956 the first international students came, including Rolando Bacani of the Philippines, Felipe Merioles of Guam, and Kresten Norholm of Denmark. Early Hispanic graduates, both from Mexico, were Enrique Cepeda and Luz Gonzales.

Also in 1956, the school's host congregation in Houston built a new educational building, a great boost for the school. Traveling musical groups were now on the road representing the school among the churches across the nation. Joining the faculty in 1957 were Robert A. and Juanita Adams who would lead the campus music ministry for more than three decades. The 1980 doctoral dissertation of Robert Adams remains the most extensive study to date of the musical heritage of the Church of God movement.

In the early years of the school, the possibility still existed that its location might be moved. Max R. Gaulke and Walter M. Doty made occasional trips to places like Oklahoma City when offers of land and money were received. Nothing firm developed and Houston appeared increasingly to be the college's permanent home. Doty would serve at Gaulke's side for many years as professor of theology and dean (1955-1969 and 1973-1981).

As the college grew, it continued to deal with the issues of being understood, accepted, and supported by the Church of God movement at large. President Gaulke was very clear about the distinctive educational philosophy of Gulf-Coast Bible College (*Tidings*, August 1959). It was specifically a "college of the Bible." There was an important difference, he explained, between it and a Christian liberal arts college, such as his own alma mater in Anderson, Indiana. At GBC every student was required to have a major concentration in biblical studies and do required Christian service. The focus was on "training for a life of Christian service." By contrast, according to Gaulke, the Christian liberal arts college provides a liberal arts education under Christian influence, but with very little Bible or related subjects required of all students. Most students select "secular majors and Christian service is voluntary." The choice for a student, he concluded, is whether to attend "a college of liberal arts which makes available some Bible subjects, or a college of Bible that concentrates in that field, but also requires a substantial amount of liberal arts."

The drawing of this sharp contrast between types of schools, when coupled with the assertion that it was obvious which type better prepared Christian leaders and served the church more adequately, brought both students and controversy to the campus. Sometimes congregations became known as GBC or Anderson College or Warner Pacific churches. There was some understandable tension between a Bible college and the church's seminary with its graduate curriculum oriented to a liberal arts undergraduate background.

In February, 1958, President Max R. Gaulke felt keenly the need for a broader base of support for GBC and wished for a wider acceptance of the college. Anderson and Warner Pacific Colleges were the only two institutions of higher education supported by the national church budget. Gaulke wrote to the Commission on Christian Higher Education, calling for a national educational budget that would include "all of our colleges on some kind of a family relationship basis." He asked that "*all* of our functioning colleges" be recognized in Church of God periodicals and that, to give "a sense of acceptance," World Service credit be given to churches sending money to Arlington College and Gulf-Coast Bible College.

The Texas Ministerial Assembly sent a similar request, as did the GBC board of trustees, to the Executive Council of the Church of God in March, 1958. The school's trustees asserted that such moves would enable "a larger spirit of harmony" in the national work and would make it easier for GBC graduates to promote the national budget of the Church of God movement in their churches. It was an attempt to gain recognition, acceptance, and dollars for the college. The assertion was that a more official status for the college would contribute to the health of the church's life generally.

The Executive Council referred these requests to the Commission of Christian Higher Education which, on April 10, 1959, stated its judgment that World Service credit should not be given for funds directed to GBC. Why? Because GBC was not a World Service agency and had not met the necessary requirements for agency status. Those requirements included General Ministerial Assembly election of members of the governing board and ratification of the chief executive officer, and the assumption that an institution seeking agency status "should be expected to demonstrate wide acceptance and approval by the church and have some history of success in achieving stability and purposes consonant with the policies and program of the other general agencies of the Church of God. . . ." GBC was judged not yet qualified in these areas.

Time, however, would bring change. By 1964 the college had made a full presentation of its program to the Commission, which in turn reported to the Executive Council its own perceptions of the college's strengths and weaknesses. Progress definitely had been made, but fundamental weaknesses in facilities, faculty credentials, library holdings, etc., were still noted. The college had not yet done a comprehensive self-study or "exposed itself to the systematic view of any accrediting agency." The Commission concluded that a "qualitative comparison with other colleges of comparable aspiration is the most appropriate means of evaluation." That meant pursuing and achieving formal accreditation by the appropriate body, the American Association of Bible Colleges.

The following years were to be eventful indeed. The Commission on Christian Higher Education and the Division of World Service pondered the questions related to World Service credit for funds given to a non-agency college and to the criteria for and implications of the possibility of another agency college. Meanwhile, GBC worked toward formal accreditation. A self-study developed in 1966 recounted the college's origin, purpose, and curricular development. It reported a student enrollment in the a fall 1965 of 143 full-time and 65 part-time students, most of whom were affiliated with the Church of God movement. There were no doctoral degrees held by the nine full-time faculty members.

The several programs offered sought to combine a strong Bible/theology emphasis, with a range of "general education" offerings (language preferred over "liberal arts"). The five-year Bachelor of Theology degree was identified as the college's "most important project" since most Church of God ministers did not become seminary graduates and thus "required this strong undergraduate program which includes a basic foundation for the ministry." The assumption was put forward that "if GBC continues to merit the confidence of the church-at-large, it may be assumed that some method will be found in future years to undergird the financial structure of the institution." That assumption was well-founded.

In April, 1968, Gulf-Coast Bible College received accreditation from the American Association of Bible Colleges. In 2000 this accreditation was dropped by school choice since it then was seen as unnecessary and burdensome—regional accreditation was in place and there were few if any advantages to maintaining dual accreditation. Also in June, 1968, GBC became a general agency of the Church of God by action of the General Assembly and was granted representation on the Executive Council and membership in the Commission on Christian Higher Education. Finally, the college had become a formal part of the general church family.

Major milestones had been reached, but a long road yet lay ahead for a small, young college. A real sense of acceptance of the college by the

Church of God movement was still not a reality for many persons. Academic respectability was still questioned widely. Finances still presented a major problem. Even so, progress had been real and a solid foundation had been built, one on which the future could stand.

A Maturing Campus

The young school in Houston, Texas, already had come a long way. President Max R. Gaulke was honored in June, 1970, by his alma mater, Anderson College, with the honorary Doctor of Divinity degree. Donald E. Smith became vice-president for academic affairs of Gulf-Coast Bible College that same year. He was a trained educator who brought an increased professionalism to the faculty and enhanced the general education emphasis in the curriculum. The achievement of the doctorate by Walter M. Doty in 1971 was a powerful symbol of personal sacrifice and an institutional commitment to excellence. The purchase in 1973 of thirteen thousand volumes from the library of a closed college was a real step forward.

In 1975, an historic year, the college bought property from the First Church of God in Houston, constructed a fine new facility for student housing, and saw the retirement of its founding president, Max Gaulke, after twenty-two years of service. Gaulke had carried the vision in the early and difficult years. He was known as an excellent pastor and preacher, and clearly a man of action. He had served as president until 1967 on a part-time basis and without salary. He finally resigned from the pastorate to be a full-time, salaried president. The college under his leadership had come from being merely a dream and a fragile experiment to an established and accredited agency of the Church of God movement. The year 1975 was the end of the initial era of the college's existence and the beginning of another.

John W. Conley, Church of God pastor and member of the board of trustees of GBC, became executive vice-president of the college in July, 1973. He was faced with the continuing financial problems of a young school. Bills were pending, salaries were low, and the campus was located in a less-than-ideal social area of the city of Houston. But ways were found to do what was necessary to survive. In 1975 Conley became the college's second president. He left the pastorate for this challenge, saying that he had seen young ministers come from limited backgrounds and nonetheless do so much in little churches after having been trained "at struggling little GBC." A stronger college, in his judgment, could do so much more!

Eleven years later, in 1986, President John Conley reported that the keynotes of his administration since 1975 had been: (1) To press faculty to complete advanced degrees; (2) To keep the college in the Church of God (some friends of the college still wanted a separation); (3) To prove to the Church of God "that GBC was worthy of respect"; (4) To strengthen general curricular requirements so that the typical student completes a double major, with Bible/theology always being one (Biola University was used consciously as a model); and (5) To achieve regional accreditation to assist the placement of graduates because "many in the church saw a Bible college as substandard education." President Conley was sensitive to anything he thought carried a hint of his school being considered "substandard."

Accreditation by the American Association of Bible Colleges was reaffirmed in 1978. The required self-study of 1977 reported sixteen full-time faculty members (five with earned doctorates), and thirteen programs of study leading to the Bachelor of Theology (five-year program) and Bachelor of Arts, Science, and Sacred Music degrees. There now were thirty thousand volumes in the library, renamed in 1971 as the Charles Ewing Brown Library in honor of a prominent editor, writer, and historian of the Church of God movement. In 1977-1978 there were 314 full-time equivalent students, ninety-five percent with Church of God affiliation. Facilities were improving, particularly with the completion in 1978 of a new administration/library building.

Then came 1979, a milestone year. The college had held candidate status with the Southern Association of Colleges and Schools since 1973. In

1979 the school became the first Bible college to be accredited by the Southern Association, the regional accrediting body. It was hoped that this achievement would bring real respect and advantages for graduates. This process had necessitated a further strengthening of the "general education" requirements. In its 1984 self-study for reaffirmation by the Southern Association, GBC stated the following about its educational programs:

> Each student is broadly educated in the arts and sciences, commensurate with a general education germane to much of American higher education of today. A Christian biblical perspective is maintained in the foundational education of the curricula. All baccalaureate degree programs have a second major in biblical studies as supportive of the major or concentrations selected by the student in fulfillment of vocational and career objectives.

With SACS accreditation reaffirmed in 1985, there already was talk of the school moving the campus out of Texas. Thus, a new relationship with the North Central Association of Colleges and Schools was initiated to address this eventuality.

Obviously, by the 1980s the college was attracting students with a widening range of career goals and had accommodated its programs to their needs and to generally accepted standards in American higher education. For example, it had developed a cooperative program of professional study in nursing with Houston Baptist University. While GBC appeared increasingly to be a church-related, liberal arts college, it had intentionally avoided being the typical "liberal arts" part, both in name and by the requirement of a second major in biblical/theological studies for all students.

A New Beginning in Oklahoma

Gulf-Coast Bible College had begun in 1953 in Houston, Texas, as a temporary Institute. The assumption had been that a permanent and more central location would be found elsewhere in the Southwest region. However, the school had remained in its original location for more than three decades. Even so, the Texas location was not permanent. In 1983 the school's board of trustees bought thirty-five acres of land on the edge of Oklahoma City for a new campus. This was prime land, undeveloped, situated across from a public golf course and near major arteries of ground and air transportation. Subsequent land purchases increased the amount available for development to one hundred and forty-five acres

The reasons for the major land purchase were several. Houston, Texas, was not central to the constituency being served. The campus in Houston was in an undesirable and even unsafe neighborhood, with expansion possibilities limited by the high cost of local property. Particularly as President Conley saw it, the college had an opportunity to lose "the Houston connection" and the negative perceptions of the college as narrow, substandard, in bad surroundings, little more than the extension of a local congregation. While a campus move would be difficult and costly, the decision was made.

In the summer of 1985, the college moved its operations to Oklahoma City, occupying brand new facilities designed for its needs. The college established a new relationship with the North Central Association of Colleges and Schools (it had left the Southern Association's jurisdiction), and assumed the new name, Mid-America Bible College. Moving a college is an unusual and difficult task. Doing so in a way that alters accreditation jurisdictions is unusual and most demanding. Accomplishing such things, including being accepted by North Central with no immediate visitation requirement, was a real achievement.

Such a total campus move was not without its considerable problems, however. Some students and staff remained in Houston for personal reasons. The dean, Odus K. Eubanks, left the college. There was concern that the economy of Oklahoma City might not provide student employment the way Houston had done. Student enrollment dropped the first year the school was in Oklahoma City, down from three hundred to two hundred. The acting dean, Kenneth E. Jones, suffered a heart attack during the transition. Most of all, the college's property in Houston did not sell as expected, creating a financial crisis for the college that now had major financial obligations for its new facilities that cost 7.5 million dollars. The oil market in Houston had hit bottom and prospects for selling the old property suddenly appeared bleak.

Nonetheless, morale was high on campus during the first years in Oklahoma City. Emphasis was placed on student retention as uncertainty remained because of the troublesome failure to sell the old campus property. Rigorous academic self-examination was undertaken in preparation for the regional reaccreditation visit in 1988. A good foundation had been laid by the sacrificial service of long-term persons like academic leader Walter Doty, librarian Ruth Kirks, trustee Robert Pumpelly, and faculty members Robert and Juanita Adams, Donald Brumfield, William McDonald, Gene Miller, Nelson Trick, and others. Melva W. Curtis followed Kenneth E. Jones as dean. She was an internal stabilizing person with her knowledge of faculty, curricula, and the standards and procedures of accrediting agencies. The school was in a new setting, had a new image, and hoped to flourish with this fresh beginning. The governor of Oklahoma had personally welcomed the school to Oklahoma City in 1985. In 1986-1987 the teacher education program had been accredited by the Oklahoma State Department of Education.

Unfortunately, the new beginning was heavily clouded by a serious financial situation. So much was this the case that the school's very survival was in real question. The Church of God movement in North America rose to emergency action by launching a "Giant Leap" campaign that managed to reduce the school's debt by $3 million. The unsold Houston property, deteriorating and even vandalized as it sat empty, was transferred to the church's Board of Church Extension and Home Missions in Anderson, Indiana. The debt now became manageable for the school—which literally had been saved by a caring and generous national church.

In the midst of the painful process of the college finding financial stabilization in the new campus setting, John W. Conley resigned the presidency in 1988. Forrest R. Robinson, a graduate of the school who was serving on the board of trustees, was named interim president in 1989. In 1991 he was elected and ratified by the church's General Assembly as the school's third president. Among the new president's several interests was athletics. He began working to expand the school's athletic programs and facilities.

The "Evangels" teams compete regularly in the NCCAA: Division I. There was great success at the national level in both men's and women's sports. For example, the men's basketball team won the national championship in 2004, as did the Lady Evangels in 2006. Recently, the university has added membership in the National Association of Intercollegiate Athletics (NAIA): Division I. All teams now compete in both associations, with home basketball and volleyball games located in the Gaulke Activity Center that was competed in 1997 and named in honor of the founder of the institution, Max R. Gaulke. President Robinson was the catalyst for this major construction.

The University Today

Following the retirement of president Forrest R. Robinson in 1999, John D. Fozard was elected the school's fourth president. Effective in June, 2003, while celebrating its fiftieth anniversary, the name of the institution was changed to Mid-America Christian University. President Fozard said that this change "positions us for another fifty years of Christian education."

Removal of the word "Bible" from the name in no way lessened the central role of biblical studies in the curriculum of all students. The new name did shed the earlier identity of "Gulf Coast" originally occasioned by the Houston, Texas, location. It also made clearer that the school was doing much more than ministerial education and, when functioning internationally, did so beyond the high school level.

With a student body now reaching nearly 900, the university is offering over twenty-eight major fields of undergraduate study and two master's degrees. In addition, there is an adult degree completion program, and undergraduate classes carried through Interactive Educational TV broadcasting in three states. Recently, a master of business administration degree program has been launched. There is a liberal arts core to the undergraduate degree programs that is taught from a Christian perspective. Issues are intentionally explored from a Christian worldview. Programs are supported by the campus library that is named to honor a former and beloved historian-editor of the Church of God movement, Charles E. Brown.

May 7, 2006, was the day of the 51st commencement exercises of Mid-America Christian University. The speaker was the mayor of Oklahoma City, with the invocation delivered by a state senator. The graduating class included 178 persons, the largest in school history. Among them were 47 Christian ministry students, continuing a central purpose of the institution. Ages of the graduates ranged from 21 to 64, reflecting the significance on campus of the adult degree completion program. The College of Adult and Graduate Studies now offers majors in Management, Criminal Justice, Management of Information Systems, and Behavioral Science. Since 1999, the campus has been offering courses via the internet.

Of major importance in 2006 was the fact that the burdensome debt of the school was eliminated, a major, even miraculous financial turn-around. The significance of this for all aspects of school life can hardly be overstated. MACU is expanding its partnerships with businesses to make higher Christian education accessible throughout the world. There now is the Toler Leadership Center training church and community leaders, and the Thomas School of International Studies offering cross-cultural training. This broadening of programming and constituencies frames the vision of the university's future.

The Campus at a Glance

Institutional Names:

1953-1955	South Texas Bible Institute
1955-1985	Gulf-Coast Bible College
1985-2003	Mid-America Bible College
2003-	Mid-America Christian University

Accreditations:

1968-2000	American Association of Bible Colleges
1978-1985	Southern Association of Colleges and Schools
1985-	North Central Association of Colleges and Schools

State/Professional

The Department of Teacher Education is accredited by the Oklahoma State Department of Education

Chief Executive Officers:

1953-1975	Max R. Gaulke
1975-1989	John W. Conley
1990-1999	Forrest R. Robinson
1999 -	John D. Fozard

Chief Academic Officers:

1953-1955	Gerald L. Erickson
1955-1969	Walter M. Doty

1969-1970	Gene Miller (acting)
1970-1973	Donald E. Smith
1973-1981	Walter M. Doty
1981-1984	Odus K. Eubanks
1984-1986	Kenneth E. Jones
1986-1992	Melva W. Curtis
1992-	Ronald N. Roddy

Mission Statement

Mid-America Christian University equips students to impact their world for Christ through achieving Bible-based academic excellence in a Christian environment, so that students professionally serve their chosen vocation/ministry.

Campus Alumni Publication

Tidings

Contact Information

Mid-America Christian University   Phone: 405-691-3800
3500 SW 119th Street   Email: info@macu.edu
Oklahoma City, Oklahoma 73170   Web Site: www.macu.edu

MID-AMERICA
CHRISTIAN
UNIVERSITY

NCCAA

NATIONAL CHAMPIONS
BASKETBALL
WOMEN DIVISION II
2006

GAULKE ACTIVITY CENTER

CHAPTER 9

The Stories of Warner Memorial University and Midwest (Gordon) Bible School

One school evolved within the life of the Church of God movement, served well for a limited time after its 1919 founding, and then passed from the scene. It was Kansas City Bible Training School. Two other schools developed a little later, passed out of existence, but led to still another school that would be permanent. These two, the subjects of this chapter, became the background from which one day would be founded South Texas Bible Institute (now Mid-America Christian University). These schools are stories of vision, risking, and educational service, even if they were relatively short-lived. One was in Texas and the other in Nebraska. The one in Texas was founded by the same man who launched Anderson Bible Training School. The one in Nebraska was led by persons associated earlier with the school in Kansas City.

Warner Memorial University

Although other schools have now become known as such, there has been only one institution founded as a "university" within the life of the

Church of God movement. This university was born in Texas and appears to have been largely the lengthened shadow of one man. He was Joseph T. Wilson who earlier was centrally involved in the founding of Anderson Bible Training School (later Anderson University) in Anderson, Indiana. The new school in Texas, unfortunately, was characterized by a high aspiration that was strangled by severe financial problems from almost its very beginning.

The frustration of Warner Memorial University is symbolized well by the experience of young Kenneth E. Jones, who years later would play a significant role in three institutions of higher education in the Church of God. As a boy of seven in Oklahoma, Jones already was dreaming of going to college to prepare to be a minister and teacher. He heard talk that a university was going to be founded in his area by the church. He was excited by this and determined that he would attend. But long before he could complete high school, it had been founded, lived its short life, and closed its doors.

Anderson Bible Training School was ten years old in 1927. Joseph T. Wilson, its founding principal, had visited Moody Bible Institute in 1917 as the Anderson school was beginning. He learned there that Dwight L. Moody once had stood on the undeveloped property of the future Institute and envisioned men and women going from that place carrying the Christian gospel to the ends of the earth. The new school in Anderson, Wilson also envisioned, would be such a place. By 1927 it was maturing quickly into an outstanding Christian institution, but with Wilson having moved on.

Wilson had resided in Dallas, Texas, since 1924, serving there as a church planter assigned by the national Board of Church Extension and Home Missions of the Church of God. He had been replaced as general manager of the Gospel Trumpet Company and now was starting a new congregation—and still dreaming educational dreams. Two 1924 graduates of Anderson Bible Training School, John Batdorf and Dora Gerig (later the wife of John), had joined Wilson as his assistants. But Wilson had more in mind than church planting. He hoped for the founding of a liberal arts institution of higher learning in the church.

Joseph T. Wilson told *Gospel Trumpet* readers (January 16, 1930) that he had stood on the undeveloped land soon to host the facilities of Warner Memorial University and again had remembered Dwight L. Moody's vision. He had prayed: "Please God the day will come when, from the institution being established here, men and women will go forth to bless the world by taking their place in the ministry, in the schoolroom, in the lawyer's office, in the bank, in the factory, on the farm, in the mercantile establishment, in the legislative halls, and in every walk of life." The pursuit of this hope at first had led Wilson to correspond with President John A. Morrison of Anderson College about broadening the curriculum of that school into the liberal arts arena—beyond the bounds of its original Bible school curriculum.

Morrison was open in principle to the possibility proposed by Wilson, but he was not quite ready to implement it—mostly for political reasons, it would appear. The idea of the "liberal arts" was a matter of considerable debate in the Church of God movement, with many ministers judging that such a move in Anderson was not cost effective and would constitute an undercutting of the primary need for ministerial education (see Barry L. Callen, *Guide of Soul and Mind*, chap. 4). The Anderson campus would broaden its curriculum to the liberal arts in the late 1920s, but Wilson was not prepared to wait. He turned his attention to talk in Texas of the possible founding of a new institution of higher learning, one that he conceived could have a liberal arts curriculum in place from its founding. This possibility was well beyond his ministry assignment from the Board of Church Extension in Anderson. Even so, it was central to Wilson's vision for ministry, so he proceeded to explore the possibilities. He was a man of vision and action.

At the annual assembly of the Church of God in Texas, held in Gorman in August, 1927, Joseph T. Wilson made an enthusiastic recommendation. The result was a successful resolution favoring the establishment in the Southwest of a college of "Class A" rank. He was appointed promoter of the dream and member of a small committee named to review possible sites for the school's location. Both John Batdorf and Pearl Bailey, wife of the eventual dean of the new institution, recalled active contact between Wilson and John A. Morrison in Anderson during this time. The founding of a new college apparently was being discouraged by Morrison. Anderson was moving rapidly toward a liberal arts curriculum. There was no need nor adequate resources for another college in the life of a small church movement like the Church of God. But personal and regional momentum could not be stopped. Wilson was an entrepreneur.

On December 6-8, 1927, the Texas assembly met again, this time deciding definitely that the Church of God in Texas, in cooperation with the church in Louisiana and Oklahoma, would establish a new institution of higher learning. Eastland, Texas, was chosen as the site, primarily because of a gift of sixty acres of land just outside of town. The school was chartered on December 30, 1927, under the name Warner Memorial University. The first meeting of its governing board included nine members, five from Texas and two each from Louisiana and Oklahoma. Joseph T. Wilson was chair of the board's executive committee, and soon he also was named the university's first president. The stated purpose of this new corporation was:

The establishment and maintenance of an institution of learning of University rank, for higher learning, including education in all branches for general diffusion of knowledge, and under Christian influences, with authority to confer all University degrees. The said educational institution is to be forever owned, maintained, and controlled by the Texas Ministerial Assembly of the Church of God.

Wilson explained to the Church of God constituency at large the critical reason for investing in such a venture (*Gospel Trumpet*, Jan. 9, 1930, 22): "What is all our religious teaching in the home and Sunday school worth if we must send our youth to some godless institution where they

shall become modernists, materialists, evolutionists, or atheists?...
Thousands of children have been carefully taught in the home and Sunday
school, only to lose their faith during their college life." In Wilson's view, the
church needed to be engaged "in all branches" of knowledge and in the
preparation of the church's young for service to all segments of society.

The school in Anderson, Indiana, had been named after its city of
location. The new Texas school, however, was given the name of the primary
pioneer of the Church of God movement, Daniel S. Warner (1842-1895).
Even so, strong ties were built with the city of Eastland, Texas. For instance,
the groundbreaking event for the new school's main building was attended
by most of the prominent leaders locally. Speakers included heads of the
chamber of commerce, the Rotary club, and a major bank.

The first classes of the new Warner Memorial University were held on
September 19, 1929, in rented facilities in downtown Eastland, Texas, while
the school's facilities were being built on its own property just outside of town.
The headline on the front page of the *Eastland Telegram* (Sunday, Sept. 15,
1929) was: "Eastland Citizens Extend W. M. U. Welcome." A photograph of
president Joseph T. Wilson appeared, with this next to it: "Founder of
Eastland school believes it is his greatest undertaking and believes it is destined
to become one of the outstanding educational institutions in the country."
Wilson's vision was large and local enthusiasm was obvious.

President Wilson struggled from the school's first day to find the
needed dollars to build and operate a university campus. He urged the
Board of Church Extension and Home Missions in Anderson, Indiana, to
extend a $15,000 loan so that the new building could be completed. Finally,
the loan was made, although with some reluctance. Coming financial events
nationwide were to prevent the university from repaying any part of this
loan. The proud building (pictured below) was completed in 1930. Beyond
the school's life, the building was used otherwise by the area churches,
burned in 1956, and then was torn down in 1958.

Faculty and students, Warner Memorial University.
President Joseph T. Wilson stands in the back row, right of center.

Main Warner Memorial Facility, Eastland, Texas

The 1929-1930 catalog of the university announced proudly that the "curricula of many of the best institutions of our land have been examined, and the courses of study outlined in this announcement will be found to be in line with those of the best Class A colleges of the South." During its first year of operation, the university was organized into a School of Music, a

College of Science and Liberal Arts, and a Preparatory School. The curriculum included designs for both Bachelor of Arts and Bachelor of Science degrees, with courses projected in a wide range of fields. Resources for initial implementation were meager, to say the least, but the educational vision was quite expansive.

The inaugural Warner Memorial faculty was heralded as unusually strong and promising for a new and very small institution. It was comprised of twelve persons, two holding masters degrees, Paul Breitweiser in music and Frellsen Smith in history. The other persons were: Ernest Bailey, dean; Edgar Barnett, Bible; Nettie Campbell, superintendent of preparatory work; Cressie Nelson, art and violin; John Neuman, mathematics; Harry Reynolds, government and Spanish; Lenora Reynolds, voice; Louis Smith, physical science; Beatrice Smith, English; and Hutchins Ward, economics and physical education. It was a venture of faith, a daring dream, a pioneering work. The quality of the faculty exceeded their formal credentials.

Paul Breitweiser, a graduate of Chicago Musical College, had met Joseph T. Wilson when Wilson was speaking at a youth convention at Moody Bible Institute in 1928. Breitweiser was playing the organ on that occasion. Arrangements were made for him to become the first "dean of music" in the new Texas school the following year. Ernest Bailey, a University of Minnesota graduate in agriculture, read about the new Texas school in the *Gospel Trumpet* and wrote to Wilson to express interest. He and his wife Pearl Bailey then moved to Texas in 1929 so that he could teach biology and be the university dean (even though he had no previous administrative experience in education). Harry Reynolds also had written to Wilson in 1928 to ask about the university since both he and his wife were college graduates with teaching interest. They were both granted teaching positions. These and the others came to Eastland, Texas, with strong belief in the cause of church-related higher education. As the circumstances of Warner Memorial University clearly required, faculty members came prepared to make significant personal sacrifices.

The city of Eastland, Texas, had a population of about ten thousand at the time. It was proud of the new school and hoped very much for its success. It was a county seat, located on a major highway, and had been a prosperous oil town. But the prosperity was mostly in the past and the idea of a new university in its midst was an attractive thought. Unfortunately, the former prosperity was about to lessen even more. Only weeks after the school first opened its doors, the great stock market crash of 1929 occurred! From then on, things moved from difficult to desperate for the school. There was little student employment. Faculty members gardened and shared what they had.

The Reynolds family was typical. Harry and Lenora supplemented their small cash income from the school with the milk and butter from their own cow. They raised chickens and had a garden. Congregations in the area helped as they could. The educational and ministry visions were large, but the challenges being faced were quickly becoming overwhelming. John Batdorf traveled extensively to raise funds. During 1930 he drove several thousand miles to visit churches and tell the story of the new school. While in California, he learned that the Church of God congregation in Eastland, Texas, had called him to be its pastor. So he left the road and came home to minister to the faculty, staff, and students of the new school.

Between 1929 and 1933, and despite the great financial difficulties, a series of persons later to be prominent in the Church of God movement came and went as either faculty members or students. Aubrey Forrest was later to be president of Taylor University. Carl H. Kardatzke was later to be a long-term and beloved faculty member at Anderson College. Elmer Kardatzke would pursue a long and prominent pastoral career. Irene Smith Caldwell, who began her distinguished teaching career in 1931 at Warner Memorial University, would later share her teaching skills at Warner Pacific College, Anderson School of Theology, and Warner Southern College. Lester Crose and Kenneth Crose were brothers who returned with their missionary parents from Beruit, Lebanon, in 1930 to begin college at

WMU. Lester later would become a prominent leader in Church of God missions, and Kenneth would pursue a distinguished teaching career at Warner Pacific and Anderson Colleges. Paul Breitweiser would enjoy a long career in music education at Anderson College. And there were others who pastored churches and did missionary work for decades after their Texas alma mater was no more.

Whatever the institutional dream, and despite many quality persons and much personal sacrifice, 1932-1933 was to be the last year for Warner Memorial University. The name was altered to Warner Memorial College, symbolic of an institution having to scale back its vision. Tuition charges were reduced by one-third to $30 per semester. But restricting the scope of operations and level of student charges was not enough. The time was wrong. The dollars needed to survive a major economic depression were just not there. Money which had been pledged could not be paid. The school had fallen victim to economic circumstances beyond its control. Many persons believed that the need was real and the institution valid—if only the time and place had been different.

The school's debt, however, reflected awkwardly on all of the national work of the Church of God movement. President Wilson received a letter dated March 22, 1933, from the Board of Directors of the Gospel Trumpet Company in Anderson, Indiana. Since Wilson was president of the company and people in the church assumed that the financial obligations taken on by Wilson in Texas were the responsibility of the company, the company judged that it had to act in a public way to clarify the true situation. Its action, reported in this letter, was to ask Wilson "to resign as president, and as a member of the Gospel Trumpet Company, and that we also advise that he resign from membership in all other general church organizations whose headquarters are at Anderson, Indiana." Although painfully taken, this action by the Gospel Trumpet Company was thought necessary for the well being of the church at large. It was a blow to a very proud man and dedicated church leader.

Some persons, like Lester Crose, left when Warner Memorial University closed and went on to graduate from Anderson College where his WMU credits were accepted in transfer. Several others finished at Abilene Christian College and other institutions outside the Church of God movement. Only Lucille Kardatzke ever graduated from Warner Memorial University. Many persons who had invested money in the new university dream eventually lost part or all of what they had entrusted to this cause. Elver Adcock and Carl Kardatzke used the old Ford truck of Anderson College to retrieve the university's library. The Board of Church Extension and Home Missions received title to the property by buying it for $2,000 at public auction in 1935, after attorneys in Eastland had foreclosed. The Board then sold the school's property and facilities to the Church of God in Texas in 1946. The area church's Camp Inspiration then functioned on this site, celebrating its twenty-fifth anniversary in 1986. The property was sold to a non-church party in 2004.

It was a sad end for an educational vision held initially by a proud and venturesome man like Joseph T. Wilson. He truly was a visionary and promoter of a dream in which he had believed deeply. He had worked hard, welcomed progressive ideas, and planned big. In 1931, he had still believed the university could make it. In 1933, however, he left his post as president for a pastorate. But even after the school closed, Wilson worked to find ways to pay some of the bills in Eastland that had to be left behind. It was a painful process of saving face and maintaining integrity in difficult circumstances.

Harry Reynolds, faculty member who had left in 1932 to complete a graduate degree at Northwestern University, was invited by the Warner trustees to return as president following Wilson's resignation. But such was not to be. The university was unable to continue. Ernest Bailey, dean throughout the school's brief existence, returned to Minnesota to work with the Federal Land Bank, never again to be involved in Church of God higher education. His wife, Pearl Bailey, later served on the staff of Anderson

University and retained many of the University's academic records. Unfortunately, they were destroyed prior to her death (on the assumption that they were no longer of value to anyone). John Batdorf, who traveled for Warner Memorial University through the summer of 1930 and then pastored many of its faculty and students in the Eastland church until 1933, also came back north. From retirement in Anderson, Indiana, he later said, "We enjoyed our time in Texas; we got started in ministry." Harry Reynolds became a businessman and then a teacher for many years in Racine, Wisconsin. He later recalled the Texas years fondly, saying that he and his wife "came away much stronger and better fitted for things ahead."

Warner Memorial University at least got started in its educational ministry, but the start was fragile and short-lived. Attempts to revive it failed and the pain left in its wake was great for many persons. Not until about twenty years later did serious talk begin again about the need for a college in the Texas/Oklahoma area. That talk eventuated finally in the founding of South Texas Bible Institute in Houston, Texas, in 1953 (later to be Gulf-Coast Bible College and then Mid-America Christian University in Oklahoma City, Oklahoma). This later school was to represent an educational vision and philosophy somewhat different than Warner Memorial's, but it was a continuation of the concern to have a Church of God institution of higher education located in that part of the country.

Midwest (Gordon) Bible School

Another school existed for a time in the Midwest region of the country and also was part of the path that led finally to South Texas Bible Institute. What became known as Midwest Bible School in 1944 began as Gordon Bible School in 1934. According to the Gordon *Bulletin* for 1953-1954, at the time of its founding, "there were no other institutions serving the Church of God except the one college and seminary in Anderson, Indiana, and no Bible schools in the Midwestern area. Educational opportunities were fewer and meager finances made it impossible for many consecrated young people to study and prepare themselves for Christian service." Therefore, a group of young ministers began to meet each day for Bible study. The pastors of the Church of God congregation in Gordon, Nebraska, beginning in 1929, were R. A. and Nellie Germany. Soon they were giving sacrificially of their time to help equip these young persons for gospel work.

The Gordon church, although having fewer than 100 members, was the largest Church of God congregation in Nebraska, North and South Dakota, Wyoming, Montana, Utah, and Idaho. The town, in northwest Nebraska near the South Dakota state line, had about 2,000 residents. While it had good rail and bus service, it was a relatively isolated town site, agricultural in nature, with little opportunity for student employment. The school classes met in the church, with homes serving the housing needs of out-of-town students.

Both R. A. and Nellie Germany had been associated with the Kansas City Bible School when it was in existence—R. A. as a student and Nellie as a teacher. They now saw the need for a similar venture in their area of pastoral ministry. An anti-Anderson sentiment was strong in 1933—for instance, the 1933 Toledo resolution of the Ohio State Ministerial Assembly was supported by the Nebraska Ministerial Assembly in 1934. Such concern may have added to the impulse for a new school locally—operated more economically and by more known and trusted leaders.

In 1940-1941 there were twenty-five full-time and three part-time students enrolled. The 1953-1954 *Bulletin* of the school listed R. A. Germany as president, Nellie Germany as vice-president, and Beulah Lawrance as registrar. The curriculum was not intended "to compete or conflict with the existing secular institutions of learning or Christian colleges, but rather to precede and augment ordinary educational pursuits with a sound, comprehensive, and all-permeating concept of Bible doctrines and moral principles which impel Christian living."

Eight faculty members are named, teaching in the fields of theology, Revelation and Daniel, Bible doctrine, Bible, English, art, and music. Textbooks judged indispensable were F. G. Smith's *What the Bible Teaches* and *Revelation Explained.* Says the 1953-1954 *Bulletin,* a central school aim was "to emphasize the doctrines of the [Church of God] Reformation, so students can lead people they contact into the clear light of the unity of God's people." The school's focus was quite regional: "We afford Midwestern students Midwestern teachers in a Midwestern environment and train them to work with those whom they know best—Midwestern people" (22).

Rarely did a teacher at the school have a collegiate education. Many lectures were sermonized and the spiritual life of students was a key emphasis of the curriculum and social life. Nonetheless, most students were well satisfied with the practical usefulness of their training. One student, Viola Phillips, later earning two academic degrees elsewhere, observed: "The Gordon Bible School did not help me earn my degrees. But neither do my degrees give me what I got at the Gordon Bible School. . .its leaders helped

Faculty and students, Gordon Bible College, 1943-1944

Host Congregation in Gordon, Nebraska

us to awareness of God. The healings and other answers to prayer were testimonies to us all that God works today" (essay, in Church of God Archives, Anderson University, 17).

The enrollment and influence of the school peaked in the early 1940s and was never the same after World War II. Young people had more educational opportunities by then as the country prospered in its new post-war economy. The Nebraska ministers wanted the school to come under their corporate control, a wish that was resisted by President Germany. Student enrollment dropped and was almost entirely female, even when higher education was growing nationally, especially with male enrollments because of the post-war GI Bill—resources not available to an unaccredited school. The school survived largely because of the passion of R. A. Germany, but not beyond the 1950s.

A helpful historical essay on the Midwest Bible School was written in April, 1957, by Charles E. Nielsen, then a graduate student at Anderson University's School of Theology. It now is housed in the Church of God Archives at Anderson University. Also available in the Archives is a copy of the 1953-1954 *Bulletin* of Midwest Bible School.

CHAPTER 10

The Story of
Warner Pacific College

Interest in Christian education and ministerial training among Church of God leaders in the Pacific Northwest was evident as early as 1905. Formal classes began to be offered in different cities. One educational center that developed early was the missionary home in Spokane, Washington. It was under the guidance of George W. Bailey, a returned missionary from India. These classes began in 1907, soon were supervised by the Inland Empire Ministerial Assembly of the Church of God, and were formalized into the Spokane Bible Institute. Rev. O. A. Burgess functioned as principal from 1916-1918, and George Bailey from 1918-1920. Bailey announced this in the *Gospel Trumpet* in 1919: "The first object of this school is to help those who feel the call to the ministry or some other branch of gospel work, such as teaching God's word.... Come expecting to work hard, to be criticized, and to be instructed and encouraged in the divine life" (*Gospel Trumpet*, Sept. 4, 1919, 23).

This educational effort, affected negatively by World War I, found two more years of life when it relocated to Boise, Idaho, in October, 1920. This city was thought a more central and advantageous location for the Church of God constituency in this section of the country. Under the new name of Pacific Bible Institute, and now with Albert F. Gray as principal, the Northwest Ministerial Assembly of the Church of God became the guiding body. But low enrollment (never reaching thirty students), poor facilities, and lack of adequate student employment caused leaders to move the school again in 1922. This time it went to the facilities of a local congregation in Seattle, Washington. Even though the curriculum was expanded and the new setting had many practical advantages for students, enrollment remained low. Reluctantly, the decision was made in January, 1928, to close the school, at least temporarily.

For the next fourteen years the church in the region was left with an educational void and a persistent hope that someday a school would again become a reality in the Northwest. Despite low enrollments, there had been widespread appreciation of the Institute in several states. It had been one of the three schools of the Church of God movement then existing in the United States, the others being Anderson Bible Training School (later Anderson University), begun in 1917, and Kansas City Bible Training School, begun in 1919. Albert F. Gray was a member of the governing board of the college in Anderson for more than twenty years beginning in 1925 (serving as chair for more than a decade) and was recognized with an honorary doctorate from Anderson College in 1932. He was influenced by Church of God thinkers and writers like D. O. Teasley, A. D. Khan, and G. P. Tasker. In turn, he was a great influence on the early and later development of the school in the Northwest. His 1966 autobiography is titled *Time and Tides on the Western Shore*.

Time To Begin Again

Anderson Bible Training School was destined to have a great future. The school in Kansas City would be short-lived. The one in the Northwest, eventually to locate permanently in Portland, Oregon, would join Anderson in having a long and significant future.

In September, 1935, the Northwest Ministerial Assembly of the Church of God met in the First Church of God in Spokane, Washington, that was being pastored by Henry Schlatter. The Assembly developed new enthusiasm for the hope of a re-opened school and adopted unanimously the motion of E. V. Swinehart that called for a college to again be established for educating new generations of Christian leaders. Excitement was evident and activity began.

By January, 1936, the Assembly had managed to buy back the old missionary home of the Church of God in Spokane by paying its delinquent taxes. Now the new college effort had a location and, following an election in September, 1936, it had an official board of trustees. Henry Schlatter of Spokane and Albert F. Gray of Seattle sought funds to get the college off the ground. It was a difficult time since the whole country was trying to come out of a terrible financial depression. The legal incorporation of the new Pacific Bible College occurred in February, 1937, with the corporation membership consisting of ministers of the Church of God in Washington, Oregon, and Idaho. Classes began that October with fourteen students. The two faculty members were Daisy Maiden, a retired missionary from China, and Albert F. Gray, who taught Bible, theology, psychology, Greek, and music in Spokane during the week, while commuting on weekends by train to his pastorate in Seattle. Wilbur Skaggs, a young person in the Spokane congregation who was one of the first students, watched as the old "Saint's Home" was remodeled for use as a small college.

By 1938, Albert F. Gray was again called to lead the school. He had left his pastorate to devote his full time to the college in Spokane. His wife,

Rosa Gray, served faithfully as college matron and cook, while their son Harold Gray ran the printing press in the basement and daughter Dorothy Gray took classes and did secretarial work for the school. In the fall of 1938, Rosa Gray was cooking for ten students from Washington, five from Oregon, four from California, three from Idaho, and one each from Kansas, Nebraska, and Oklahoma. The academic offerings at this school on North Ash Street were a two-year program in Christian education, a three-year ministerial program, and a four-year degree program.

Then, with the student body having outgrown the available facilities in Spokane, the vacant Mountain View Sanitorium, with about two acres of land in Portland, Oregon, was secured in 1940. This would become the long-term home of the college. The hillside structure would serve as library, dormitory, cafeteria, and administration building. The full purchase price of $14,000, a major financial obligation, was paid off in three years, even though the total assets of the college amounted to only $5,400 when it moved from Spokane! This was a compelling symbol of Gray's inspired leadership and the presence in the area churches of people who obviously were committed to the mission of the school.

For the first years that the school functioned in Portland, there were four teachers, Albert Gray, Lottie Franklin, Pearl Lewis, and John Schmuki. The college was providing training primarily in Christian ministry, missions, religious education, and music. Slowly, some adjacent properties were acquired. A residence hall for women was built in 1947 and a barracks secured as war surplus was used as a chapel. It was a modest, but a determined and good beginning. Situated on the attractive southern slope of Mt. Tabor in Portland, Oregon, the Church of God in the Northwest had begun making a significant investment in its educational vision.

The coming in 1942 of Otto F. Linn as a faculty member and the dean was one of the more significant events of the college's history. Linn was a nationally recognized biblical scholar and the first leader in the Church of God movement to earn a doctor's degree. With years of personal academic preparation at Phillips University and the University of Chicago, Linn came from a pastorate to give academic leadership to the young school. Earlier he had taught at Anderson College, but had left, in part because of a disagreement with Dean Russell Olt about the proper nature of the curriculum in a church-related college. In the years to follow, biblical study remained central in the curriculum of Pacific Bible College. The primary campus purpose was "training young men and women for definite religious service." By 1944 the Oregon State Department of Education had approved the granting of the Bachelor of Theology degree, with approval for the Bachelor of Arts to follow in 1946—the same year that Anderson College achieved full accreditation far to the east in Anderson, Indiana. The professional stature and leadership of Linn were crucial for these developments at Pacific Bible College. At this point in its history, the school was free of debt.

The General Ministerial Assembly of the Church of God, meeting in Anderson, Indiana, in June, 1947, approved the participation of Pacific Bible College in the national World Service annual distribution of contributed funds. Initially, the college was to receive about six percent of the total, or about thirty thousand dollars annually. Although question was raised about the appropriateness of the college sharing in the proceeds from general church giving when it did not function under the direct jurisdiction of the General Ministerial Assembly, it was agreed that it did function under the control of the West Coast Ministerial Assembly of the Church of God, did serve the entire church, and was prepared to function in close cooperation with the national church. On occasion, the annual sessions of the West Coast Ministerial Assembly convened on the Portland campus. By 1955, at least nineteen persons associated with the college already had or were serving on the mission fields of the world, a significant percentage of all Church of God missionaries.

With an influx of veterans on campus following the conclusion of World War II, the student body grew to about two hundred. By 1951 the campus catalog was able to list nineteen faculty members, with earned doctorates held by Otto F. Linn in Bible, D. S. Warner Monroe in philosophy, and C. Anderson Hubbard in biology. Others, like Milo L. Chapman, Louis F. Gough, Irene Smith Caldwell, and John W. V. Smith, were soon to complete doctorates and play major roles in this and other

colleges of the Church of God. A major academic accomplishment was the building in 1954 of the Otto F. Linn Library, a much needed facility and an obvious name to honor.

President Gray, naturally proud of these accomplishments and supportive of a broad curriculum of genuine academic quality, nonetheless wanted it to be clear that the college was a theological school. Its majors and minors were in Bible, theology, Christian education, and music. In the second verse of the college's alma mater

President Albert F. Gray

were words expressing clearly the vision of the college that President Gray had molded over the years: "From thy stately portals issue, Ranks of stalwart youth; Forth to tell the gospel message, Heralds of the truth." Gray reached his 50th year in Christian ministry in 1955. Pacific Bible College sponsored a special "Founder's Day" program featuring the speaking of Harold L. Phillips, editor of the *Gospel Trumpet*. The school unveiled a brick and marble marker highlighting the entrance to the campus and honoring the service of the beloved President Gray. The school was now well established and serving the church effectively.

A detailed presentation of the life of the Church of God movement in the Northwest was researched and written by Donald D. Johnson (thesis, Anderson School of Theology, 1955). This church life is what gave birth and nurtured a significant school.

Years of Major Change

Arriving during the 1950s was the end of an era and the beginning of another in the history of Pacific Bible College. Because of failing health, the beloved Otto F. Linn offered his resignation in 1955. He was succeeded by Milo L. Chapman, a faculty member in Old Testament and theology. Then in 1956, while completing a men's residence hall, the college formally became a national agency of the Church of God movement. Although the college had been receiving World Service funds since 1947, agency status meant, among other things, that elections to the presidency of the college would require ratification by the General Ministerial Assembly. Also, college trustees, formerly elected by the West Coast Ministerial Assembly, would be elected by the national church body. President Gray then announced his retirement in 1957 after fifty-two years of ministry in the Church of God. Dean Chapman assumed the presidency, and faculty member Leslie W. Ratzlaff became dean. Faces changed, but the mission continued.

Closing out this most eventful decade was a change of public identity for the campus. In 1959 the institution's name was changed from Pacific Bible College to Warner Pacific College. According to former faculty member and church historian John W. V. Smith, "this was more than a shift of labels. The new name allowed an enlargement of the curriculum to a full-orbed liberal arts program which would improve both student recruitment possibilities and the basis for approval by the regional accrediting association" (*The Quest for Holiness and Unity*, 1980, 367-368). The college said in its *Warner World* publication (Oct. 25, 1962, 3) that the new name was to honor Daniel S. Warner, "pioneer minister of the church. . .teacher, poet, author, printer...who understood holiness in ethical terms" and who was "a fervent advocate of the restoration of the true catholic church founded by Christ." A similar breadth of functions and lofty vision was intended for the college as well.

Dean Leslie Ratzlaff completed his Doctor of Education degree at Columbia University in 1965. His thesis topic was "The Implementation of

Christian Goals in Christian Liberal Arts Colleges." He explained (p. 266):

> This project came out of the difficult task assigned to Warner
> Pacific College by its sponsoring body calling for the college to
> be genuinely Christian as interpreted by the Church of God
> and also genuinely liberal arts as interpreted by the regional
> accrediting association. The college had accepted the challenge
> knowing that its high task had better be substantiated by
> performance rather than betrayed by empty promises.

As President John A. Morrison and Dean Russell Olt had insisted at
Anderson College beginning in the 1920s, Ratzlaff reached four central
conclusions (267-287): (1) A Christian liberal arts college with deep
Christian commitments is possible; (2) The elements of the Christian liberal
arts college emerge with new dimensions in view of the Christ encounter;
(3) The incorporation of these depth dimensions into the Christian liberal
arts college calls for a program of bold, decisive action; and (4) Warner
Pacific College is called to take action in its seven major areas of operation.

President Milo L. Chapman, a well-educated biblical scholar,
experienced church leader, and educational philosopher, was able to lead a
process that would capitalize on such increasing challenges and
opportunities. New academic majors were added in history, English, and
general education. Then in 1961, after careful preparation, accreditation
was granted by the Northwest Association of Secondary and Higher
Schools. This achievement was one of the larger of many gifts of leadership
and hard work that Chapman would give to the college over the years.
Chapman, a humble man with a love of teaching, decided to return to the
classroom full-time at the end of his five-year term as president. An
outpouring of love and appreciation came to him at the conclusion of his
presidential term. His annual report of May, 1962, the last of his presidency,
carried a very positive tone. The accreditation had pleased him very much.

The new gymnasium had been in use for several months, student enrollment was edging upward, and even the treasurer's report was guardedly optimistic.

The early 1960s was a time of rapid growth in American higher education. Warner Pacific College experienced something of this momentum. Louis F. Gough became the college's third president in 1962 after serving on the faculty of Anderson School of Theology in biblical studies and then as assistant to President Chapman from 1960-1962. He launched an expansion program on the occasion of the college's silver anniversary to raise an extra $250,000 to improve faculty salaries, expand library holdings, increase student financial aid, and maintain properly the campus facilities. By 1965, with the help of $100,000 authorized as a special project for the college by the General Ministerial Assembly of the Church of God, success was declared. Enrollment had increased from 177 students in 1960 to 338 in 1965. Library holdings went from about nineteen thousand to thirty thousand volumes. There were thirty full-time faculty members, with twenty-eight percent holding the doctoral degree.

A new residence hall housing eighty-four students had been opened in 1964. Also that year, Marvin H. Lindemuth, a prominent Washington educator and layperson, was installed as the fourth academic dean. The college joined the National Association of Intercollegiate Athletics and, with Cascade and George Fox Colleges, formed the Associated Christian Colleges of Oregon. President Gough had announced at his inaugural the intent that "our college deepen and enrich its curriculum, strengthen and improve its processes of higher education in order that our campus may be characterized by academic excellence in every division of the liberal arts program." Dean Lindemuth then stated in 1964:

> The Christian college is not a church, but it is at its best when related to one. The church and its college have separate as well as shared responsibilities. The college is primarily an academic

institution with its own unique task and function of providing opportunity for a liberal arts education within the Christian context.

Respect for the college was being sought through breadth and excellence of curriculum. Service was the intended result, to be carried out in the context of the larger life of the church. It was a stretching and productive time.

Despite the volatile condition of American society in the 1960s (the Vietnam war and civil rights movement), Warner Pacific College anticipated a bright future. A long-range planning study led to the anticipation of seven hundred students by 1970 and an increasing role in the mainstream of Christian higher education in the United States. The board of trustees, judging that the Portland campus had limited expansion potential and the area was already oversupplied with colleges, was open to a new possibility. It received the offer of a gift of one hundred acres of land in San Jose, California. President Louis F. Gough and the long-range planning committee favored accepting the gift and moving the campus to this site that was more central to the West Coast constituency of the Church of God movement. The campus trustees in April, 1965, approved the recommendation to move, and it also was approved that June by the General Ministerial Assembly of the Church of God in Anderson, Indiana.

In the meantime, discussion was carried on between Warner Pacific and Arlington College, the Church of God school in Long Beach, California, being sponsored by the Southern California Association of the Church of God. The issue was a possible merger of the colleges on the San Jose site. It appeared that a merger and a new campus were coming. But the dream, at least as envisioned by the move's proponents, soon collapsed. There were many persons, some Warner Pacific alumni, some ministers, and many Portland area residents, who opposed the move. There were strong feelings and genuine concern about the level of communication, the cost involved in the move, and even the solvency of the college in Portland. This produced widespread unrest and finally precipitated a crisis situation.

On June 7, 1966, President Gough, knowing that the consensus needed for the college to make the move no longer existed, and feeling that his own influence and effectiveness as president had eroded seriously, submitted his resignation. Some people felt that he had been pushing for a new day well beyond what the college could afford. Others felt that he could have managed the move if he had been more patient. Whatever the case, the San Jose move was "temporarily" delayed and the college concentrated on raising money to cover its many unpaid bills in Portland. With a major effort and the sacrificial giving of many congregations and the national church and its agencies, the college survived the financial and relational crisis and remained in Portland.

Arlington College, disappointed, would discover another merger possibility in the greater Los Angeles area (Azusa College). Former Warner Pacific president Milo L. Chapman had left Warner Pacific to teach at Arlington in 1964. He viewed with regret the failure of Warner Pacific and Arlington to unify the educational efforts of the Church of God on the West Coast. It had been a grand dream that would never be. Instead, Warner Pacific College would have a long future in Portland, Oregon, and Arlington College would have the same, but through Azusa Pacific College (University) in Southern California.

Struggling Toward a New Future

The loss of the California merger option and the presence of new campus president E. Joe Gilliam created a difficult transition time for Warner Pacific College. The financial challenge was significant. Irene Smith Caldwell, faculty member in Christian education for fourteen years, resigned to go to Anderson School of Theology, as did Kenneth Crose en route to the history faculty of Anderson College. Dean Marvin Lindemuth himself would leave to join Anderson College's education faculty in 1968. To varying degrees, these and other changes resulted from professional and personal reasons, as well as from a range of reactions to the perceived instability and apparent direction being taken by Warner Pacific College. E. Joe Gilliam, pastor in Indianapolis, Indiana, and a Warner Pacific College trustee, had been elected as the fourth president of the institution in 1966. He invited Milo L. Chapman to return from Arlington to rejoin the faculty. There was need to bring new life to a campus which had come through some troubled waters, and probably had more still lying ahead.

In the fall of 1966, the Warner Pacific board of trustees and the Church of God movement nationally responded to a $300,000 emergency appeal for the unpaid and past-due bills of the college. President Robert H. Reardon of Anderson College, chair of the Emergency Fund Committee, reported to pastors in November that the financial position of the Portland school had improved greatly from what it had been. The regional accrediting association on the West Coast extended for only one year the school's accreditation, with a full self-study required the following year. The drive was on to re-establish confidence in college programs and personnel, and to achieve financial stability for a debt-ridden institution plagued with several internal and external problems.

A financial consultant was secured. With his help, efforts began to meet the expectations of a potential donor said to be capable and interested in making a multi-million dollar gift to the college. Stern measures were taken to find financial stability. Two of these were ending the tenure program for faculty and introducing a more restricted approach to the classic liberal arts curriculum in favor of more vocationally and theologically oriented programs. Such moves were seen by some, including the college dean, as unnecessarily dramatic and clearly detrimental to the integrity of the academic program. Dean Marvin Lindemuth left for Anderson College and Milo L. Chapman, beloved by Warner Pacific and the church, became dean. It was indeed a hard and transitional time.

Despite everything, rebuilding was soon underway. The fall 1970 student enrollment was up to a record 442. In June of that year the college requested, and the General Assembly of the Church of God agreed, to provide more special assistance, this time in the form of a guarantee of continuing World Service funding to discharge up to $600,000 of unsecured debt if the college should be unable to do so from its own resources. With creditors being reassured and President E. Joe Gilliam providing aggressive leadership, there again was a guarded optimism on campus. The Northwest Association of Colleges and Schools, recognizing appropriate progress, reaffirmed the college's accreditation without time limitation. Earl McGrath, a national leader in higher education, was the guest speaker at Warner Pacific's 1971 commencement. He praised President Gilliam for giving "leadership in this hour of crisis for all colleges."

President Gilliam sought a broadening of the base of guidance and support for Warner Pacific College. Believing that the programs and personnel of the college were to penetrate all of society and not function as an ingrown institution, he established a College Advisory Board consisting of Ralph G. Turnbull, Evelyn Egtvedt, Paul S. Rees, D. Elton Trueblood, Earl J. McGrath, and Lowell J. Williamson—persons of national prominence in education, religion, or business. With the generous assistance of the Kellogg Foundation and the Lilly Endowment, aided by the guidance of Earl McGrath, and with primary guidance from Marshall K. Christensen, the faculty designed an innovative liberal arts program known as the "Culture of Western Man." The number of academic majors being offered was reduced from sixteen to eleven, and in 1973, under the leadership of Dean Chapman, the college launched a Master of Religion degree program (expansion of the earlier five-year Bachelor of Theology degree), with pastor/writer Ralph G. Turnbull as a supporting scholar in residence. In 1974 Turnbull also was influential in launching the faculty's annual Christian Writers' Conference that was to gain national prominence in the years to follow.

Unfortunately, these program developments, constructive and innovative as they were, still were plagued by the continuing problem of the school functioning beyond available financial resources. Annual budgets were based on expected income, but expectations proved to be set unrealistically high. The long anticipated multi-million dollar gift from a private donor finally did materialize, but in the form of a long-term trust not immediately available for operational support. Business leaders were added to the advisory board, as were political leaders such as congresswoman Edith Green and Oregon's Senator Mark O. Hatfield. Even United States President Gerald R. Ford visited the campus as a commencement speaker in May, 1976. Properties adjacent to the campus were acquired for future development through a major grant from the Murdock Trust. These and other signs of progress were evident; concern continued, however, about whether the financial foundation was adequate for continued operation.

The casual observer would have judged campus progress substantial and enviable during the 1970s. The number of graduates grew. There was significant improvement in campus facilities. But there continued to be an undercurrent that was quietly ominous. Operational deficits were persistent and threatened the viability of the institution. A series of personnel and program decisions over the years had created a pool of ill will in various quarters. The visibility of the advisory board caused some ministers in the Church of God movement, and even members of the board of trustees, to feel that an informal group of hand-picked, "outside" persons was inappropriately in charge of the school's direction and destiny. Then, in 1979, all of this concern and criticism surfaced in a local newspaper article that ignited widespread discussion and turmoil (Kathie Durbin, in *Willamette Week*, Oct. 9, 1978).

This turmoil resulted in President Gilliam's decision to resign. He was replaced in the presidency by Milo L. Chapman. The national Division of World Service of the Church of God was convinced by the struggling school to suspend temporarily its normal fund-raising limitations so that an urgent

$300,000 appeal could be made directly by the college to congregations of the Church of God in the western states. Survival depended on this special privilege being extended and the resulting effort being successful.

Why the large and perennial operational deficits? Board chair Jay A. Barber, Jr., suggested that it was a pattern of smaller student enrollments than budgets were based upon, too heavy a reliance on the excellent fund-raising abilities of President Gilliam to cover whatever financial shortfalls there might be, and even an unconscious reliance on the eventual availability of that multi-million dollar trust from the private donor. The Church of God constituency in the Northwest was not large and, as President Gough had observed years earlier, the Portland area was well populated with competitive institutions of higher education. Even so, many persons believed deeply in the mission of Warner Pacific College and were prepared to help find a way for it to be viable into the future.

That future was to be guided by Marshall K. Christensen who had come to Warner Pacific as a student in 1960, then became a faculty member in 1966, Dean of the Faculty under President Gilliam, and finally president in 1981. As a former Fulbright scholar in Germany and the first layperson chosen to serve as president of any Church of God college, Christensen had great faith in the mission of a Christian college. As a highly trained scholar in the field of history, he was prepared to pursue that faith with academic integrity, considerable energy, and historical perspective. There surely was much to be done.

A three-year plan was set forth. The college had passed through a difficult transition in leadership and now looked at the decade of the 1980s as one in which the college would reach its fiftieth year (1987). During this new decade, the college would make every effort to increase student enrollment, become a leader in curriculum innovation among Christian liberal arts institutions, and be recognized as a significant educational resource in Portland, Oregon, and in the Pacific Northwest generally. Obviously, this would require much creativity and an expanding base of persons who would be challenged by this cause and motivated to give the needed financial support. A central part of the plan was to put the operating and capital budgets of the college on a path of stability and real growth. It had to be a time for a new beginning if the college were to have a viable future.

The 1984 annual report of President Marshall K. Christensen celebrated several ways in which God had been blessing the college. In that one year, Joyce Erickson, a nationally recognized educator, had come to campus as Dean of Faculty. There also had been a thirty-seven percent increase in the number of freshmen and transfer students. A new five-year plan of action had been launched. A multi-million dollar "Investing in People" capital funds campaign had been designed to bring significant reduction in the burden of continuing institutional debt and to enable a sizable increase in the small institutional endowment. The stated intent was that the new funds would "provide the margin for excellence in educational programs and facilities for Warner Pacific College." It was reported that efforts at disciplined management of resources allowed the audit for the year ending June, 1983, to be the fourth in a row to show a modest surplus in the operational budget. This was real progress.

Innovative programming, including the hearing and speech therapy program for preschool children and the Bethlehem Inn for homeless families, highlighted the campus concern for human needs locally. Such programs reflected well the college motto, "In Christ, Light." The resulting excellent media coverage of the college in the Portland area became a plus in public relations. President Christensen was becoming known and appreciated across the Church of God movement as a strong educational and church leader. Hope was growing in the viability of a long-term future for Warner Pacific College.

The Portland campus and the whole Church of God movement celebrated the college's fiftieth anniversary during 1986-1987. On one occasion in the Mt. Scott Church of God congregation's sanctuary in Portland, some 650 persons gathered to remember and give thanks. The planning committee was chaired by Arthur M. Kelly, then the Dean of Students of Warner Pacific College and later to be a national leader in the field of Christian education. During that year's annual sessions of the General Assembly of the Church of God in Anderson, Indiana, a resolution was adopted in recognition of the fifty years of the school's existence and service. It characterized these years as ones of "sacrifice and dedication in the quest for excellence, informed by the central convictions of both the Christian faith and higher learning." It also called on the church to "dedicate herself anew to the importance of Christian higher education in these troubled times."

Into the decade of the 1990s, celebration of a proud college history continued to be mixed with the anxiety of major campus challenges. Chief among the challenges was the judgment in 1992 of the Northwest Association of Colleges and Schools that there had to be a substantial addressing of annual budget deficits and accumulated institutional debt. Campus accreditation, and thus its very exisitence, was in jeapordy. Campus officials were daring and creative in their efforts, believing deeply in the history and future of the college. An infusion of cash came from a "sale and lease back" arrangement with a Japanese company. This obligated the college for thirty years and created controversy among school alumni and Church of God leadership on the West Coast. More recent years have seen increased financial stability for the college, with growth in revenues allowing adequate if not ideal support for its many educational programs. An evidence of this new stability is that institutional debt service in 2001 was about 5.7 percent of the annual operating budget, a significant improvement compared to the early 1990s. A significant portion of the accumulated debt was paid by the death of a major benefactor who had established a multi-million dollar charitable trust during the E. Joe Gilliam presidency.

The College Today

A key time of transition for the college came in 1996 when President Marshall K. Christensen left office after fifteen years and was replaced by Jay A. Barber, Jr. He brought with him fundraising experience and a long relationship with the college. He reinstated intercollegiate athletics, something sacrificed earlier in an attempt to save money. President Barber also put in place a highly qualified leadership team. A welcome circumstance early into the new presidency was a gift of $1 million that was matched by an anonymous donor. By 2005, through such generosity and careful budgetary planning, the college was able to pay off its mortgage to GEOS International, that financial arrangement made in 1989 with this Japanese-owned organization that had allowed a refinancing of very burdensome long-term debt. Implementation of this refinancing had been essential for the school's very survival during the 1990s. The early repayment, announced President Barber, was indeed the work of God.

In fact, Warner Pacific's whole academic program clearly recognizes the work of God. It is based on this question, according to Dean Cole Dawson: "What does it mean to love God with 'all of your mind'?" The campus intentionally integrates faith and learning in ways that express its belief that all of life is sacred. Currently, there are eighteen major fields of study on campus, leading to a range of associate, bachelor, and masters degree programs. The humanities core of the liberal arts program is designed to equip students to lead and serve in a world that is increasingly challenged by ethical and pragmatic dilemmas. The urban Portland, Oregon, context in which the campus is situated provides ample opportunity for engagement in cultural activities, internships, and understanding of the needs of today's world, thus preparing graduates for lives of effective service. The distinctive Humanities Core Curriculum is the cover story of the spring 2006 issue of the college's *The Experience* magazine.

As is the case of some other of the Church of God colleges and universities, Warner Pacific College is a member of the Council for Christian Colleges and Universities. By virtue of this membership, select students can qualify for participation in a range of high-quality summer programs focusing on American Studies, China Studies, Middle East Studies, Contemporary Music, etc. There also is the possibility of becoming involved in the Scholar's Semester in Oxford (England) or in the Washington Journalism Center. In addition, newly launched on the home campus are three master's degree programs, one each in education, biblical and theological studies, and management and organizational leadership.

Beyond the academic programs, another measure of campus growth and excellence is seen in intercollegiate athletics. Competing in the Cascade Conference as the "Knights," Warner Pacific College is a member of the National Association of Intercollegiate Athletics, Division II, competing in four men's and five women's sports. In 2006, both the men's and women's basketball teams claimed conference championships and competed in the NAIA national tournament.

Located in a major city with numerous institutions of higher education, public and private, Warner Pacific College recently realized that it is relatively unknown to the general public. Extensive market research was initiated, now has identified the college's distinctives, and has set in motion various new public relations efforts. Included are ads on local radio stations and on city buses and the unveiling of a new school logo shown below. This process has not been about changing the essence of the institution, but more clearly and openly articulating and living out the college's historic identity with fresh enthusiasm and joy. The distinctives of the college include its being a Christ-centered liberal arts college that engages students in transformative, seamless learning processes, all rooted in the values of the Church of God movement (Anderson). Enrollment in 2006-2007 consisted of 665 students, 353 of whom were full-time traditional students, with the others enrolled in the Adult Degree Program.

The Campus at a Glance

Institutional Names:

| 1937-1959 | Pacific Bible College |
| 1959- | Warner Pacific College |

Accreditations:

| 1961- | Northwest Association of Colleges and Schools |

Chief Executive Officers:

1937-1957	Albert F. Gray
1957-1962	Milo L. Chapman
1962-1966	Louis F. Gough
1966-1979	E. Joe Gilliam
1979-1981	Milo L. Chapman
1981-1996	Marshall K. Christensen
1996-	Jay A. Barber, Jr.

Chief Academic Officers:

1937-1942	Albert F. Gray (while president)
1942-1955	Otto F. Linn
1955-1957	Milo L. Chapman
1958-1963	Leslie W. Ratzlaff
1963-1968	Marvin H. Lindemuth
1968-1973	Milo L. Chapman
1973-1975	Curtis Loewen
1975-1978	Marshall K. Christensen
1978-1981	Thomas N. Pappas
1981-1983	Louis G. Foltz
1983-1987	Joyce Erickson
1987-1991	Edward Whitehead

1991-1993	Richard Craghead
1993-1995	Arthur M. Kelly
1995-2005	John W. Hawthorne
2005-	Cole Dawson

Mission Statement

Warner Pacific College is an urban Christian liberal arts college dedicated to providing students from diverse backgrounds an education that prepares them for the spiritual, moral, social, vocational, and technological challenges of the 21st century.... As a contemporary Christian learning community, Warner Pacific is Christ centered, people focused, excellence driven, and future directed.

Campus Alumni Publication

The Experience

Contact Information

Warner Pacific College
2219 SE 68th Avenue
Portland, Oregon 97215

Phone: 503-517-1020 or
800-804-1510
Email: admissions@warnerpacific.edu
Web Site: www.warnerpacific.edu

Anatomy of a Logo

The two "faces" represent two people with differing points of view engaged in informed dialogue, literally seeing "eye-to-eye" across the expanse of the cross.

Curved edges reflect the waves of the Pacific Ocean, and also serve as entry and exit points for the WPC education.

The academic process takes our students to the cross and equips them for dealing with the paradoxes of life and culture.

The tagline is adapted from Ephesians 3:3, which describes the mystery of Christ. It suggests the idea of paradox – central to Warner Pacific's Humanities core curriculum – because it is itself a paradox. A mystery made known is no longer a mystery. The tagline hints at academic rigor as well as the vast nature of God's love, creation, and power.

Color palette suggests the natural beauty of the Pacific Northwest.

Mysteries made known

Kardatzke

C.C. Per

CHAPTER 11

The Story of
Warner Southern College

FAITH • SCHOLARSHIP • SERVANTHOOD

A ctive conversation about the possibility of a "southern college" for the Church of God movement began in 1945 at the Jacksonville, Florida, meeting of the Southern Convention of the Church of God. Such talk was to continue for the next twenty years before a series of concrete actions finally were taken that led to the actual establishment of a new institution of higher education within the Church of God movement. The dream was for such a school to be located in the southeastern area of the United States. The early dreamers included Russell Olt, dean of Anderson College, Charles W. Cheeks, and Joseph Benson, a graduate of Anderson College and public educator in Florida.

Why was there such interest in this possibility by many church leaders in this region of the country? The interest persisted despite the many frustrating years of exploration and the difficulties involved in realizing such a dream. Why? Distance was one reason often stated. Anderson College in Indiana seemed so far away from the southern states. Travel was slow and expensive. Another reason was more of a regional concern. Young persons who did go north for college often remained in the north. So it seemed reasonable, even crucial, to many persons that there should be a southern college. It was expected that such a school would encourage the development of new leadership, particularly Christian ministerial leadership, and thereby bring increased strength to the Church of God movement in the South.

An Extension Center of Anderson College

The hope for a new school in the southeastern United States was not a critique of Anderson College as such. In fact, what originally was envisioned as a practical way to begin addressing this dream was not a new and independent institution at all. It was an extension of Anderson College. In this cooperative way, the new educational venture could, from its beginning, be an accredited and respected school connected to the larger life of the Church of God movement.

Charles W. Cheeks, a key person in these conversations from their beginning, said that "we never had a thought of starting an independent college." Cheeks, from Mississippi, graduated from Anderson College in 1945. He had worked for both the Gospel Trumpet Company (now Warner Press) and Anderson College. He also had carried a burden for ministerial education, particularly in the South and particularly to assist disadvantaged African-American young persons in the church. Returning south to pastor in Alabama in 1945, he and others encouraged the idea of an extension college. Cheeks was in an especially good position to work closely with officials at Anderson College in an attempt to realize such a possibility.

Russell Olt, dean of Anderson College, expressed interest in an extension possibility, but there were practical questions to be answered. By 1948, Cheeks was again employed by Anderson College as a development officer and soon was involved in raising money for its first major student residence hall, Morrison Hall. But his personal interest in the South remained strong. Soon he moved to South Carolina to pastor. Meanwhile, the discussions at various meetings of the Southern Convention of the Church of God about a new college had continued. Pastors Henry Johnson from Mississippi, Harry L. Harp from Georgia, Fred Vines from Alabama, and others explored and promoted the idea of a college in the South. Johnson preached in 1949 for Malcolm Rigel, then pastoring in Indiana, and shared the vision with him. Six years later, Rigel returned to the South to pastor, now also carrying this vision.

In 1953 the Southern Convention appointed a nine-member committee to study the need for a Church of God college in the Southeast. Several members were Anderson College graduates who understood the importance of education and were anxious that something be done. Progress was slow, however. By 1957, another committee was appointed. It was comprised of Charles Cheeks, then pastoring in Florida, Joseph Benson, an elementary school principal in Florida, and Arlo F. Newell, a pastor in North Carolina. These men proceeded to explore again the problems and the possibilities. Momentum was building toward some kind of action. John A. Morrison and Russell Olt of Anderson College were supportive of this process of exploration. In February, 1958, a group of the state assembly chairs of the Church of God gathered in Florida and went away promising to seek some underwriting for such a project from their states. A brochure was printed that announced the coming of the "Southeastern Extension Center of Anderson College."

Charles W. Cheeks was now pastoring in Columbia, South Carolina. In March of 1958 he hosted a meeting of forty area ministers. An important guest was Robert A. Nicholson, assistant to the dean of Anderson College. Plans were laid for a beginning, an initial summer session of the Extension Center. Operational details were worked out with Nicholson by that June. The basic design was for the Center to be sponsored by the Southern Convention of the Church of God, with Anderson College providing the academic administration, faculty, library resources, and credits.

This first summer term began on June 30, 1958, with Charles Cheeks as coordinator and Burt Coody from the Anderson campus teaching the two courses offered, one in Bible and one in psychology. The six students were housed by Cheeks. Each of them finished the summer with six hours of academic credit granted by Anderson College. Two additional summer terms were held, both in Birmingham, Alabama, one in 1959 and the other in 1960. They used the facilities of the Pinehurst Church of God congregation and the camp meeting grounds, with about fifteen students attending each term. Admission requirements and academic policies were those of Anderson College. Felix Murrell and Marie Strong taught in 1959, and Donald A. Courtney and Florence Orr in 1960. Local layperson Carl Raines hosted the teachers in his home. Robert A. Nicholson, then dean of Anderson College, was present for the launching of each term.

This mobile extension center, however, had its obvious limitations. It seemed only temporary to the students, causing them to question its usefulness for their long-term educational needs. Among some ministers, strong feelings surfaced about the appropriateness of a potentially racially integrated student body in the face of the heated racial tensions of the time. For these and probably other reasons, there was too little money pledged and too few students pre-registered to justify the Center's functioning in 1961. But the end was not yet. The next two years were ones of wrestling with the concept of the Center and a search for its most appropriate manner of functioning. The search developed into the hope for a two-year junior college tied closely to Anderson College. Three possible sites were considered, one each in the states of North Carolina, Arkansas, and Florida. Enthusiasm, frustration, and general turmoil were the end result.

A campus in Red Springs, North Carolina, became available. James C. Burchett, then chair of the Southern Convention of the Church of God, convened church leaders on the site in August, 1962. An option for the purchase of this property went before the Southern Convention that November. It lost amidst considerable emotion about a range of issues.

What was approved was a resolution naming a Southern Commission on Higher Education (including the Convention's officers) "to give direction to such programs of action and study as this Convention shall initiate, and to give direction in the soliciting and expenditure of funds for these purposes." The new commission was charged to "give continuing study to the possibility of establishing some type of college in the South." The working assumption of the Southern Convention was that "the progress and growth of the Church of God in the South lies in training and educating today's youth, and that to invest in them at this crucial point in our history is the best hope for the future."

The new Southern Commission met in Anderson, Indiana, in January, 1963. It heard and decided against a substantial offer made by the Industrial Development Committee of Eldorado, Arkansas, to host a new college. It reported to the church's national Commission on Christian Higher Education, also in session in Anderson, and tried to clarify past actions and future intent. The Southern Commission next met in March, 1963, in Jacksonville, Florida. An offer of prime land in that city had been received. Because this appeared an exceptionally attractive offer, the Southern Commission set a strategy for sharing information and building support for this option.

In November, 1963, the Southern Convention debated the Jacksonville opportunity for nearly a day. Supporters of the opportunity were vocal and strongly committed. Others, however, feared the financial obligation, or thought that the site was not centrally located, or did not want to encourage the birth of a weak and unaccredited college, or argued that the Southern Convention, a fellowship assembly, was not an appropriate sponsoring body. All agreed that a vote of at least eighty-five percent should be required to accept the Jacksonville land offer. The affirmative vote was seventy-six percent, bringing strong disappointment to many. Some of the ministers gave up in the face of the recurrent inability for the southern ministers to take definitive action together. Too many contrasting agendas were involved. Even so, the dream of a new college in the South persisted.

A New College In and For the South

W. Malcolm Rigel, who had just accepted a pastorate in Jacksonville in anticipation of the proposed school there, took his own action. He sent a letter to the ministers. It insisted that "this issue is not dead. We are going to get a structure started!" He then organized a meeting in Florida a month later so that a group could look prayerfully to the future. About twenty persons came, including Leslie W. Ratzlaff, former dean of Warner Pacific College in Portland, Oregon, and the new pastor in Fort Lauderdale, Florida. At this meeting, Ratzlaff presented his concept of a "unique Christian college." He had developed this concept extensively in his 1965 doctoral dissertation at Columbia University. Its original reference was to the particular challenges facing Warner Pacific College, but it certainly would apply to a fresh college circumstance in the South. Ratzlaff had concluded that it is possible to have a Christian liberal arts college with deep Christian commitment.

Now there was new hope that the Jacksonville option might be accepted after all. The Florida Ministerial Assembly of the Church of God set in motion a process that, in April, 1964, convened in Jacksonville about sixty persons who were burdened to see a college founded. The hope was that the Jacksonville property option might still be accepted by a grouping of Church of God leaders other than the full membership of the Southern Convention. But before the meeting convened, and unknown to those involved, the Convention chair formally rejected the Jacksonville offer and thereby ended the opportunity altogether!

This was a severe blow, but the 1964 meeting was to be significant nonetheless. What happened was the establishment of the Southeastern Association of the Church of God. It was to be chartered in Florida and exist as a legal body for the sole purpose of establishing a college. Kenneth Cleary, an attorney from Bradenton, Florida, and a new Christian, had become involved through his pastor. He prepared a proposed constitution and bylaws for the new college. They called for a board of trustees of ten ministers and eleven laypersons, all from the Southeast. The bylaws were adopted by the new Association and the first board members were elected. According to these bylaws, the coming school would be a co-educational, four-year college in the liberal arts tradition "wherein the study of religion, the arts, sciences, literature, languages, and mathematics and related subjects may be taught and advanced."

Pastor Leslie W. Ratzlaff was asked to serve as a consultant because of his considerable educational training and experience. He presented a written "Prospectus on a Southern College." His vision was of a distinctly Christian college, four-year in scope, designed specifically for area needs. It should be, he wrote, a college "in the South, that understands the South, and that supplies Christian leadership for the church in the South." Possibly because he himself had served previously in Grand Cayman and Jamaica, and certainly because of the potential of a Florida location, he also emphasized the Caribbean and Latin America as within the scope of the particular mission of such a college.

A longstanding assumption had changed. A new school did not have to be an extension campus of Anderson College in order to be viable. Many factors had brought forward the new-college option. They included the experience and particular vision of Leslie W. Ratzlaff, the major involvement of laypersons like Kenneth Cleary, the Florida setting in which the state already was committed to providing a junior or community college option to its citizens at very low cost, and the belief that Anderson College was not fully in favor of a southern college. In addition, the concern for regional church relevance and control of the proposed school was strong.

The newly constituted board of trustees soon elected two laypersons, Kenneth Cleary and Richard Smith, as chair and vice-chair. It organized into committees and continued the search for a site to locate a new college. Several were considered in different parts of Florida. Finally, the board accepted a gift of 350 acres of property in a rural area near Lake Wales in central Florida, although there was opposition to this acceptance. Pastoral trustee members Malcolm Rigel, Leroy Fulton, and Ernest Gross opposed this choice in early votes of the board. Finally, however, they decided to go along with the majority, despite concern about its rural location which, they had argued, would bring lack of school exposure, require more traveling, and provide little student employment opportunity. Even so, two highways intersected in the nearby city of Lake Wales, one connecting the two coasts of Florida and one going from Michigan to Miami. Thnking long term, development possibilities were substantial.

Board chair Kenneth Cleary went to Anderson, Indiana, in January, 1965, to report to the national Commission on Christian Higher Education of the Church of God. He shared the anticipated nature and scope of the coming college and the intention that it would function cooperatively with the whole church. What he heard in return was a series of probing questions about the wisdom and feasibility of such a venture. Even so, the decision to proceed was firm and would not be altered by the questions and concerns of many national church leaders. They worried particularly that there were not enough students and dollars in the church to support another college, at least not without undermining the ones already existing.

A call for financial support went out to the churches in the South. At a crucial meeting of the board of trustees in Cordelle, Georgia, on May 6, 1966, Leroy M. Fulton, then pastor in Sarasota, Florida, was elected new board chair. Malcolm Rigel remained secretary and Leslie W. Ratzlaff was asked to leave his pastorate and become the administrator who would actually organize and start the college in the rural setting near Lake Wales, Florida. Charles Cheeks began assisting in various ways as work proceeded to finally bring the dream to reality. In November, 1966, the Southern Convention of the Church of God went on record as favoring the recent decisions and encouraged the churches to become supportive. That was an important reversal of its earlier stance.

Work began in earnest. Property became available for a new local congregation of the Church of God. Books for a library came from one now closed in Miami, Florida, and from Arlington College in California that was merging with Azusa Pacific College. Six thousand volumes had been processed and were ready for use the day the new Church of God college opened. Nina Ratzlaff had assumed responsibility for the library's operation. Hersel and Eula Studebaker moved to Lake Wales to start a mobile home manufacturing plant so that students could have employment—crucial in that rural setting. Charles Cheeks, O. M. Richardson, and Harold White established College Park, a mobile home park adjacent to the new college site. It was hoped that it would attract Church of God retirees from the North who would become members for the new congregation, which in turn would be a convenient and compatible place for the college students to worship and serve. Also, such new residents would tend to bring with them financial resources that, at least over time, could be significant for the future support of the college.

Finally, the college got its name. In November, 1967, the school's board of trustees adopted the name Warner Southern College. "Warner" related to the Church of God and "Southern" to the region of the country to be served. This name was the suggestion of Leslie Ratzlaff who earlier had suggested "Warner Pacific College" as the new name for Pacific Bible College in Portland, Oregon. The use of the Warner name (Daniel S. Warner, 1842-1895) for a Church of God college had been pioneered decades earlier by Warner Memorial University in

Dean Leslie W. Ratzlaff

Texas. In December, 1967, the first new building on the Florida campus was under construction through the generosity of trustee Carl Raines. It would carry his name proudly.

Leslie W. Ratzlaff, an experienced academic leader, planned the new academic program and reported progress to the national Commission on Christian Higher Education of the Church of God in January, 1967. There he heard continuing reservations about the wisdom of starting another college in the church. In fact, this Commission reported to the General Assembly of the Church of God the next June that the Church of God already had enough colleges and could not support more. In the South, however, there now was no turning back.

Classes were scheduled to begin in the fall of 1968. Pastor Ero Moore (1927-2006) of Lake Placid, Florida, took a leave of absence to recruit students and raise money for the college. He gave twenty-six years to the campus, traveling widely and becoming known to many people as "Mr. Warner Southern." Malcolm Rigel moved to Lake Wales to pastor the new Kingdom Builder church. Leslie Ratzlaff worked at communicating clearly his own intention as the school's founding administrator and academic leader. He wrote: "An accredited. . .college is on the way. Accredited by God, in that it is to be thoroughly Christian; accredited by higher education in that is it to be academically sound!" Ratzlaff would serve the new school as dean until 1983 and would be honored by the college in March, 2005, at his 90th birthday.

Classes began on schedule, with twenty-seven students enrolled. Of the seventeen full-time students, thirteen were from Florida. Another one thousand volumes arrived for the library, gifts from faculty members at Anderson College who were moving their offices into mobile units so that Decker Hall could be constructed on the site of "Old Main." An excellent new faculty was assembled, all part-time, but four with doctoral degrees. One, Charles Bates, drove a long distance to teach a night class. Malcolm Rigel, the local pastor, was dean of students. Ernest H. Gross, pastoring in

Orlando, Florida, assisted in the classroom. Faculty members Charles Bates, Florence Orr, and Cecil Hartselle all had taught previously at Anderson College, the latter two having recently retired. It was a small but clearly a quality beginning.

Building on a Good Foundation

That first year of the life of Warner Southern College, 1968-1969, was characterized by a pioneering spirit and close family atmosphere. In spite of the limited scale of the beginning, a representative from the regional accrediting body, the Southern Association of Colleges and Schools, was invited to examine the situation and give direction after the first year of operation. This was evidence of Leslie W. Ratzlaff's tenacious commitment to quality in academics. He always coupled this commitment with a careful screening of faculty candidates in regard to compatibility with the Christian mission of the college. Faith and learning were to be joined, and both were to be significant.

During that first year of operation, the board of trustees offered a formal position to Charles Cheeks. There were questions about what the title would be and how the position would relate to that of Leslie Ratzlaff. It was decided that a president should be named. Consideration was given to Cheeks and Malcolm Rigel, but Rigel nominated and the board elected its chair, Leroy M. Fulton. He was the Church of God pastor in Sarasota, Florida, a graduate of Anderson College and its

President Leroy M. Fulton

School of Theology. He had been called to Christian ministry under the influence of Maurice Berquist who had served on the executive committee of the founding board of trustees of Warner Southern College. Fulton expressed the desire not to assume office until 1970, after a year of graduate study in college administration. So the board agreed to name Cheeks president for a year, with Fulton being president-elect until July, 1970. While Cheeks was considering this proposed arrangement, he suffered a heart attack. The board convinced Fulton to assume the presidency in July, 1969. Under his executive leadership and the academic leadership of Leslie W. Ratzlaff, the college grew rapidly. The beginnings, modest as they were, nonetheless were built on a strong foundation and enjoyed quality leadership.

The first graduating class received degrees in 1972. There were four graduates, with Robert Sharpless receiving his bachelor of arts degree in pastoral ministries. By 1974-1975, student enrollment had increased from the original 29 in the fall of 1968 to 187. They came from twenty states, with Florida leading the way and Ohio next. Six foreign countries were represented (eleven students, mostly from the Caribbean islands). Significant persons had joined the faculty, including P. Edgar Williams and J. Perry Grubbs in 1970, and Robert H. Clark in 1971. Charles Bates became full-time in 1972 and Harold W. Boyer, pastor and national leader in the Church of God movement, joined the teaching staff that same year. Soon there were others, including Irene Smith Caldwell who came in 1973 after retiring from Anderson School of Theology, Ronald M. Jack who came in 1974 and was to become dean when Ratzlaff retired in 1983, Sam Wellman in 1974, and Wade Jakeway in 1975. These and other skilled men and women were beginning to make major contributions.

This growth in enrollment and faculty was paralleled by program development and an expanding library of exceptional quality for a small, young college. Accreditation was a major goal and the foundation was being laid carefully. Correspondent status was granted by the Southern Association of Colleges and Schools in 1972, with candidate status to follow the next year. More buildings were built and properties improved. A quality business office operation had to be designed and implemented. All of this went forward on the east side of U.S. 27 that divided the campus property. A long-range plan envisioned the building of the main campus on the larger section of land on the west side of this busy highway. This was an unacceptable way to divide a growing campus. It would take years to address this problem.

Income and total college assets rose steadily. Finances always were a struggle, but the college managed to pay its bills and students found the necessary employment. By 1977 there were twenty-three buildings on campus, including a library of about fifty thousand volumes and several homes and mobile units. Then, in December, 1977, full accreditation was granted by the Southern Association of Colleges and Schools. The campus rejoiced and morale was high. Part of the proof offered to the Association for the quality of the academic program was the fact that a series of Warner Southern graduates had gone on to successfully pursue graduate work at Anderson University's School of Theology in Anderson, Indiana. Its dean, Barry L. Callen, had visited the Warner campus on several occasions prior to the accreditation and was pleased to provide the needed documentation for the institutional self-study. Formal accreditation was a major accomplishment for a college in only its tenth year of operation.

It was hoped that accreditation would result in a significant increase in student enrollment, but this did not happen. The college sought to be innovative by working on other fronts to build a larger financial and student base. By the end of the 1985-1986 school year, eleven academic majors were being offered, concentrating in church ministries, teacher education, business administration, social services, and international development and missions. Included in the 1987 graduating class were fifty persons receiving the Bachelor of Arts degree and eleven the Associate of Arts degree. Of these, twenty-two were in teacher education and nineteen in fields related to church ministries.

The "HEART" Institute (hunger education and resources training) is an interdenominational mission training center on campus. It is designed to prepare people for effective Christian service in underdeveloped countries.

The Institute has gained a national reputation and become linked with several Christian mission organizations. Attempts were made to organize and build a condominium community near campus, something more recently converted to student residences. Progress finally was made on the development of the new campus on the west side of the highway, with a student residence hall completed, an academic-recreational complex constructed, and other buildings soon to come. Even with all this progress, the president's report for 1985-1986 carried a basic note of continuing caution: "The concerns are always the same—students, finance, faculty, and staff."

Originally, the intent behind the existence of Warner Southern College had been the founding of an extension of Anderson College in the South. The eventual result was an independent, four-year Christian college in the liberal arts tradition, with an educational philosophy very similar to that of Anderson College. Ties with the Anderson campus remained close over these years. This was particularly true of the graduate School of Theology to which many Warner Southern graduates went for seminary education. This relationship was highlighted even further in 1983 with the establishment of an extension of Anderson School of Theology functioning periodically on the Warner Southern campus. Barry L. Callen of the School of Theology initially developed this extension program with Leslie W. Ratzlaff of Warner Southern College. The seminary's Jerry C. Grubbs and then others continued it in following years. It was a new form of the tradition of an extension relationship between these schools that went back to 1958. In 1986 the School of Theology granted six Master of Arts in Religion degrees to persons from the Florida extension. By 1988, however, the constituency for this extension had dropped to a level that led to the decision to cease its operation.

A Formal Member of the National Church Family

Warner Southern College has worked hard at being relevant to the needs of the Church of God movement, particularly in the Southeast and the Caribbean. This task was central to the school's founding purpose. The limitation of resources has been an ongoing challenge. As feared initially by the national church, the need for students did lead to serious recruitment efforts in the Midwest where the Church of God population is much larger than in the Southeast. Ohio, for instance, has been a major source of students for Warner Southern College over the years, although Florida has come to dominate the student population.

The problems faced by Warner Southern College since its beginning have tended to be seen by the school as only expected hurdles that every young college must clear somehow. Persons have been willing to serve and sacrifice over many years. Included as institutional pioneers are: Ero Moore, a key staff person beginning in 1968; J. Perry Grubbs, who began with the college in 1970 as a music faculty member and then vice-president for development; Donald Pickett; Wesley Rouse; and numerous others. Also to be highlighted, of course, are the long and distinguished tenures of Leroy M. Fulton as president, Leslie W. Ratzlaff as founding administrator and dean, and Nina Ratzlaff in library services. School pioneers eventually pass from the scene. For instance, the opening of the 1987-1988 school year saw several significant faculty persons absent because of retirement. Included in this one year were Harold W. Boyer, Robert H. Clark, Deryl Johnson, Fred Morgan, and Malcolm Rigel. Clearly, it was a challenging time of transition.

The college over the years has remained closely tied to the Southern Convention of the Church of God and was represented regularly in the national Commission on Christian Higher Education prior to its disbanding in the 1990s. In its early years, Warner Southern College did not become a "national agency" college like Anderson, Mid-America, and Warner Pacific. This status was not sought actively for several reasons. In part, it was a matter of keeping faith with the school's early promise that the church at large would not be asked to take responsibility for the new college once it was founded. Eventually, however, interest was expressed by President Leroy M. Fulton that this possibility be given some objective consideration. Some persons outside the college suggested that the limitations imposed by agency status might be to the college's disadvantage. Some were concerned that one more college agency might overbalance higher education's share of the national World Service budget, and thus trigger an entirely new way for all of the colleges to relate to this budget of the general church—maybe to the disadvantage of all of them.

By a formal action taken in June, 1997, the General Assembly of the Church of God admitted Warner Southern College into the coveted category of national agency schools. The action recognized that the school had served the Church of God since 1968, had formally applied for such status, had addressed satisfactorily certain matters earlier called to its attention as concerns, and now had been recommended for such recognition by the Commission on Christian Higher Education of the Church of God. Beginning in 1997-1998, then, the Florida school would have a share in the national budget of the church. It was financially solvent, competently led, and had demonstrated itself as a valuable team player in the church's larger life.

President Leroy M. Fulton tended to speak for the many faculty and staff members of the college over the years when he recalled:

> My happy times have been seeing students graduate and go on to be involved in ministry. A short time ago I ran across my roll book for the freshman Church of God doctrine class for 1972-1973. Of the 55 in the class, fifteen now work in missions or church ministry, nine are wives of pastors, six are teaching, some are in social work. It is a real joy to see persons involved in ministry around the world.

By 1987 the college had graduated a total of 633 persons who were serving in Argentina, Bermuda, Brazil, Canada, El Salvador, Grand Cayman, Grenada, Haiti, Honduras, Japan, Kenya and, of course, the

United States. That same year was the one in which "Year 20" was celebrated and the highest enrollment in the college's history was enjoyed. The future would not be easy, but neither was the past. Already, so much had been accomplished against great odds. Doors of opportunity were wide open.

The College Today

The decade of the 1990s saw student enrollment at Warner Southern College rise sharply from about 400 to more than 800 students, and on to 1,035 by 2006. With Gregory V. Hall installed in 1991 as the school's new president, and with the regional accreditation by the Southern Association of Colleges and Schools reaffirmed the following year, significant developments came in facilities, infrastructure, financial resources, and academic programs. The adult degree completion program began, the first off-campus site was opened in Orlando, Florida, a computer skills component was added to all majors, and a music technology lab was created. Teaching sites now are located in nine Florida cities. In 1997 the campus became a formal ministry agency of the Church of God movement—a clear sign of institutional maturity and church acceptance nationwide.

Warner Southern College competes as the "Royals" in nine intercollegiate sports. The school is a member of the National Association of Intercollegiate Athletics and the Florida Sun Conference. It enjoys new sports venues for baseball, softball, and soccer.

The early years of the new century have been filled with memories, honors, crises, and dramatic new growth for Warner Southern College. In 2002, William M. Rigel, Jr., the current dean and executive vice president of the college, was honored for thirty years of service. In 2004, the prestigious publication *U. S. News and World Report* included Warner Southern as among the top ten southern comprehensive colleges for campus ethnic diversity. In spite of the $3.8 million of damages received from hurricanes in 2004 and flooding in 2005, significant natural disasters in

Florida, the campus has been fully repaired and significantly improved. Since 1991, gift income has totaled over $33 million.

In 2005, Arthur Tetrick retired as Director of the Pontious Learning Resource Center after thirty years of service to the college. The book collection had grown to 87,000 volumes, now supplemented by access to numerous online journal and databases. Also in 2005, the spring commencement saw one hundred and forty four students receive their degrees. One hundred and twenty one received the bachelor of arts degree, now available with twenty-seven different majors, fifteen the master's of business administration, and eight the associate of arts degree. Newly available that year was a Master of Arts in Education degree program and a web-based Master of Science in Management. Also available to church leaders is an online church ministry major in Transformational Christian Ministries.

The physical plant of the campus has grown dramatically in recent years, primarily on the west-campus side of Highway 27. Prominent on the 380-acre campus are the Michael W. Crews Memorial Clock Tower and Carillon, new student housing, the Turner Athletic Center, the Rigel Student Center, the Ratzlaff Ministry Center, and the pride of the campus, the Pontious Learning Resource Center that opened in 2001. These fine facilities help enable the college's ongoing work of offering a Christ-centered academic curriculum, supplemented by quality chapel experiences, Bible studies, and service opportunities.

The Campus at a Glance

Institutional Names:

    1968-   Warner Southern College

Accreditations:

    1977-   Southern Association of Colleges and Schools

Chief Executive Officers:

1968-1969	Leslie W. Ratzlaff
1969-1990	Leroy M. Fulton
1990-1991	Robert B. Hayes
1991-	Gregory V. Hall

Chief Academic Officers:

1968-1993	Leslie W. Ratzlaff
1983-1991	Ronald M. Jack
1991-1992	Robert B. Hayes
1993-	William M. Rigel, Jr.

Mission Statement

Warner Southern College seeks to provide excellence in Christian higher education through a curriculum and community that consciously integrates, models, and promotes Christian faith, scholarship, and servanthood.

Campus Alumni Publication

The Journal

Contact Information

Warner Southern College   Phone: 863-638-7261
13895 Hwy. 27   Email: advancement@warner.edu
Lake Wales, Florida 33859   Web Site: www.warner.edu

RATZLAFF
Ministry Center

Pontious Learning Resource Center

CHAPTER 12

Schools Around the World

From almost its beginning in 1880, the Church of God movement has had a world vision of its own nature and mission. This vision took the form of evangelism and education wherever opportunity presented itself. The movement became larger outside North America than inside many years ago. Accordingly, a history of higher education in the Church of God needs to include information about various educational programs around the world, even though its primary focus is North America.

The first World Conference of the Church of God was convened in Fritzlar, Germany, in 1955. In recent years, there have been convened in this same city annual gatherings of administrators and instructors of various schools associated with the Church of God around the world. Prominent among the participating schools, other than those in North America, have been Christliche Bildungsstätte Fritzlar (Fritzlar Bible College) in Germany, Kima International School of Theology in Kenya, and Mediterranean Bible College in Lebanon. Brief histories of these three schools follow.

Christliche Bildungsstätte Fritzlar (Fritzlar Bible College)

Fritzlar Bible College traces its history back to a mission center in Kassel, Germany, in 1932. World War II brought to Germany massive social disruption and physical destruction. Leaders of the Church of God movement in Germany began to rebuild as quickly as possible. A key part of the rebuilding was the beginning of the Bible School in Fritzlar in 1948. The school had begun that October, with thirty-five students doing a five-week course in a room of the local Church of God congregation. Ernst Kersten, the Church of God pastor in nearby Kassel, was soon the only full-time teacher. The purpose was preparing leaders for the German churches. The first school building was completed in 1952, built mostly by the students. A second building was completed in 1979.

The first World Conference of the Church of God movement was convened in Fritzlar, Germany, in 1955, in part to gather church leaders from around the world in an effort to accomplish new acquaintances and continue the process of reconciliation. Under the dedicated leadership of Wilhelm Link, beginning in 1961, and then Helmut Raschpichler, beginning in 1982, the school grew. Brother Raschpichler was a member of the first class and then a longtime teacher and principal. He reported in 1996 that he had served the school for forty years, with the last fourteen as dean (*Church of God Missions*, July/Aug., 1996).

In the early 1970s the school proudly published a booklet celebrating its 25-year history (1948-1973). A new name was recently adopted, Christliche Bildungsstätte Fritzlar. It means the Christian Institute of Education in Fritzlar. Located in the heart of Europe, this now is the longest serving Bible school of the Church of God movement located outside North America. Some five hundred former students are serving the church in at least fifteen countries in Europe, North America, the Caribbean, and the Middle East.

Offering a one-year curricular plan for those intending to work in a local church, the school features a five-year course for those seeking formal ministerial status. By 2000, the school was offering a biblical correspondence course already completed by thirteen people in Bulgaria. Fritzlar's main purpose is finding ways to enable students to share biblical truths and their own faith with others from all walks of life. Jesus Christ is the school's center as it seeks to convey necessary theological knowledge and educate students to become people living in the image of God. Being a small educational community, while a limitation in some ways, is an advantage in others. In 2005, the Fritzlar school began cooperating with another German theological institute, enabling the possible completion of a Bachelor of Theology or even Master of Theology degree by select students.

Most pastors of today's German congregations of the Church of God have studied at Fritzlar and built lifelong relationships. In recent years, Church of God leaders in theological education from around the world have gathered in Fritzlar to do strategtic planning.

The current administration of Christliche Bildungsstätte Fritzlar includes Eckhard Bewernick, president, and Rainer Klinner, dean. Today's student body of about thirty persons comes from Germany, Bulgaria, Brazil, Argentina, and elsewhere.

Kima International School of Theology

By 1901, the railroad between Mombasa and Nairobi had reached Kisumu on Lake Victoria. Various Christian missions soon began in this newly opened western province of Kenya, East Africa. They came to include the Church of God movement in the vicinity of Kima, a local word meaning anything with life in healthy condition. Over the century to follow, Kima would become the center of a very large Church of God population in East Africa. The "healthy condition" of this new Christian work soon came to feature a program of Christian education. Missionary historian Lester Crose reports that it was in 1945 that the first teacher training class was started at Kima to provide qualified teachers for a growing number of Church of God elementary schools (*Passport for a Reformation*, 116).

Kima Bible School began in 1954. Its first students had no more than a second-grade education; this would change dramatically over the years because of a rapid advance in the education of young people generally in Kenya. While the Kenyan government was anxious to assist churches in providing schools to educate young Africans, it was not willing to subsidize a theological school. Therefore, the Missionary Board in Anderson, Indiana, U.S.A., became a primary supporter of this school for educating church leaders in East Africa. By the commencement of 1967, the school name had been changed to Kima Theological College. Celebrated that year were six graduates who received the Certificate in Christian Ministry. They were awarded by Douglas E. Welch, chair of the board of directors, with Richard Yamabe of Alberta Bible Institute in Canada (now Gardner College) delivering the address. The principal was P. Edgar Williams.

A key step in the school's quest for accreditation occurred in 1985 when Nelson K. Obwoge was principal. At the time, Barry L. Callen, then vice president for academic affairs and dean of Anderson College, conducted an on-site visit and provided practical counsel and assistance. A follow-up resolution by the Anderson board of trustees stated, "Anderson

College has supported Kima Theological College for many years through the practical work of faculty/student TRI-S groups, the professional services of retired professors, and now the on-site consultation of its vice-president for academic affairs." Recognizing the school's upgrading to a post-secondary instructional level, Anderson College authorized a transfer-of-credit policy and expressed "best wishes to Kima Theological College as it seeks to gain full accreditation and thereby increase its important role of providing education for Christian leadership in contemporary Africa."

While formal accreditation did not come quickly, the hope did not die. The school was newly conceived as Kima International School of Theology (KIST), freshly committed to being a school serving the church's need for leadership throughout English-speaking Africa. The new principal was Steve Rennick and the dean Mary Ann Hawkins. Campus development now did come quickly. In November, 1999, two new facilities were dedicated, the Fellowship Community Conference Center and the New Life Computer Center, the only such center in a seminary in East Africa at the time. The largest theological library in East Africa had been built on the Kima campus in 1997. The student body has grown from 27 in 1995-1996 to over 100 in 2007. By the turn of the century, KIST had thirteen faculty members coming from six countries. In November, 2006, it proudly dedicated its new Chapel of the Nations.

The current president is Donald Smith from the United States and the dean is Kenyan John Ochola, who holds a Ph.D. in educational administration and intends to lead the school to full accreditation with the Accrediting Council for Theological Education in Africa (ACTE) and the Kenya Commission for Higher Education. Johnson Kitetu, soon to receive his Ph.D. in business administration, is the new director of KIST's Extension and Research Center. The school currently offers a range of two-year certificates and a four-year bachelor of theology degree.

Mediterranean Bible College

The Mediterranean Bible College began as a dream in the 1970s. God stirred the heart of Fouad Melki, pastor and key leader of the Church of God in Lebanon and Syria, to establish a Bible training school in the region. After a pivotal meeting in Cyprus in 1980, including church leaders from Lebanon, Egypt, Greece, Cyprus, Italy, and the United States, the dream became reality in 1984. The school's beginning was in Beirut, Lebanon, in the midst of a raging civil war. With Rev. Fouad B. Melki as founding president, the school originally shared facilities with the Ashrafieh Church of God in Beirut. It has since moved to a new campus with some 2,000 square meters of educational, residential, and recreational space.

Located in Beirut, Lebanon, strategic in the Middle East region, the college provides a traditional Bible college education in residence. It has member status with the Middle East Association for Theological Education and the European Evangelical Accreditation Association. It participates actively in cooperative training efforts with two other Bible colleges within Lebanon, the Arab Baptist Theological Seminary and the Christian Alliance Institute of Theology. The school's board of directors adopted the following mission statement in 1998:

> The Mediterranean Bible College exists as an institution of higher education to help fulfill the Great Commission by enabling its students to carefully study God's Word, commit to a lifestyle of discipleship, and become effective in practical ministry. The central task of the College is to raise up servant leadership for the church in the region, particularly churches from a Wesleyan/Holiness tradition.

In its relatively short life, MBC has educated about 300 students, many of whom have graduated and are now pastors or lay Christian workers in Lebanon, Syria, Jordan, Ethiopia, Egypt, Switzerland, France, and the Bahamas. The school's primary purpose is to equip lay and full-time church planters, pastors, disciple-makers, and missionaries for ministry and service in the name and style of Jesus Christ, especially within the 10-40 window. Its curriculum currently makes available a one-year Certificate of Ministry, a two-year Diploma of Ministry, and the standard four-year Bachelor of Theology degree. B. Th. graduates may qualify for a fifth-year at Warner Pacific College, leading to the Bachelor of Arts degree.

A wonderful day came in September, 2002, when the school relocated. On October 13, 2002, the eighth commencement exercises were held in the newly-dedicated Fouad Melki Building. The chair of the governing board was Franco Santonocito of Italy and Egypt. That year's graduating class included five Certificates in Ministry (students from Lebanon and Syria), two Diplomas in Ministry (students from Lebanon and Sudan), and two Bachelor of Theology degrees (both students from Lebanon).

After President Fouad Melki's death in 1997, school leadership was provided by the new president, John M. Johnson, and then, beginning in 2004, by the current president, Camille Melki. The current dean is Don Deena Johnson. Of special note is the thesis of John Johnson (Ashland Theological Seminary, 1999) titled "Enhancing the Quality of Christian Leaders Developed by the Mediterranean Bible College, Beirut, Lebanon, Through Discipleship."

CHAPTER 13

Church in Partnership with Higher Education

A History of the Commission on Christian Higher Education

T he early period of pioneer activity in the Church of God movement (1880s and 1890s) was characterized by a strong aversion to almost anything that resembled the organized life of the divisive denominations. "Man-rule" in God's church was constantly identified as an evil to be shunned vigorously. Even in Daniel S. Warner's lifetime (d. 1895), however, it had become evident to various movement leaders that "perhaps as much as 40 years more may elapse ere the Judge of all shall proclaim the end of time" (*Gospel Trumpet*, Jan. 3, 1895). The urgency that had helped fuel the fires of anti-institutionalism lessened somewhat because of the delay in the Lord's return. Some institutional organizing of church life became necessary. Eventually, even some long-range planning came to be seen as justifiable.

Institution building in the life of the Church of God movement was well underway by the 1920s, including the founding of Anderson Bible Training School in 1917. Institutions were launched with reluctance, however, fearing that the full governance of the Holy Spirit in church life might be usurped. Accountability to divine headship in all things always has been a prominent concern in this movement. Disciplined stewardship of time, talents, and financial resources has been valued highly. What also has been valued is the freedom of God's Spirit to work in the church's midst apart from the complications of formalized human control.

Institutions of higher education did emerge over the decades, as did the question of their relationships to each other and the church. What constitutes a responsible relationship between this church movement and her institutions of higher education? As sovereign corporations in their own right, the schools would be required to conform to various academic and institutional standards in the larger world of North American higher education. Would enhancing student minds jeopardize a parallel enhancement of their spirits?

Beginning Guidelines and Procedures

In the decades that followed the death of Daniel S. Warner in 1895, the concern for the effectiveness of evangelistic outreach and the stewardship of available resources necessarily led the young Church of God movement to certain adjustments in its initial anti-organizational stance. By 1898, the growing demand for "pure literature" had brought the prayerful conclusion that "God has moved that the publishing work be placed upon a firmer basis by the formation of a stock company, under the laws of the state of West Virginia" (*Gospel Trumpet*, Oct. 13, 1898, 4). Increasingly, congregations were becoming local property owners with residential pastors, something that Warner once had seen as "a snare to entangle God's flying messengers" (*Gospel Trumpet*, Mar. 10, 1892).

Missionary activity broadened across the world, sometimes in such a haphazard way that the Ministerial Assembly in 1909 chose seven brethren as a missionary committee with the duty of "advising, instructing, encouraging, or restraining those who feel called to the foreign missionary field" (F. G. Smith, *Look on the Fields*, 1920). This Ministerial Assembly of the Church of God was itself formalized at the Anderson Camp Meeting of

1917, partly to increase participation in cooperative ministries and partly to give general direction to the increasing business of the church. It was becoming obvious to most thoughtful people that the urgent work of the Lord needed some careful coordination and even regulation so that it could be implemented effectively over an extended period of years in a highly organized society.

With this new understanding came the founding of such program agencies as the Board of Church Extension and Home Missions (1920) and the Board of Christian Education (1923). By 1928 it had become so apparent that these agencies needed to have their separate fundraising efforts coordinated that the General Ministerial Assembly established the Associated Budgets. Not long after came additional steps of coordination which eventually evolved into the Executive Council of the Church of God, a separately incorporated body coordinating the budget askings of all general agencies and the long-range planning of these cooperative ministries. Such functions now are in the hands of Church of God Ministries, Inc., in Anderson, Indiana.

This pattern of ministry coordination and institutional development was the result of responses to obvious needs in the life of the church. It evolved slowly and usually with reluctance in the face of the Church of God movement's early reaction against nearly all forms of typical denominational life. According to sociologist Val Clear, the Church of God might be seen as having passed through several standard phases, arriving only after decades of ministry to a "sophistication" level that saw the need and accepted the legitimacy of the establishment of institutions. With the rise of multiple institutions came recognition of the need to formalize in some manner the coordination of their many activities (*Where the Saints Have Trod*, 1977).

As early as 1918, with Spokane Bible School, Kansas City Bible School, and Anderson Bible Training School in existence, there already was some need to discuss the most appropriate relationship among the schools developing within the boundaries of the Church of God movement. The

General Ministerial Assembly of 1918 addressed this need and appointed D. O. Teasley, J. W. Phelps, Robert L. Berry, Albert F. Gray, and R. H. Owens to comprise a committee to explore "the school question." As Gray later recalled (*Time and Tides on the Western Shore*, 1966, 91), the committee's discussion involved some significant disagreement.

> As the Spokane school was so far away, it would be expected to draw students and support from its own territory. The Kansas City school was expected, so someone thought, to draw its students and support chiefly from Missouri, whereas the Anderson school would serve the church in general and be entitled to general support. Brother Berry opposed this conclusion vigorously. He declared the Kansas City school benefited the whole church, and if it was not entitled to general support neither was Anderson. He said that Missouri could support the Kansas City school by itself, if need be, but this would lessen its giving to other causes.

Finally, the committee concluded that any work of a general nature was entitled to general support. All existing schools thought of themselves as "general" in nature and came to be recognized as such.

The General Ministerial Assembly then proceeded to pass a resolution creating an "Education Fund" to be held by the Missionary Board of the Church of God and distributed "to the existing Bible training schools in proportion to the number of enrolled students" (*Gospel Trumpet*, July 4, 1918, 4). Here was the earliest attempt on record to raise and distribute proportionately general church support for institutions of higher education. As Robert L. Berry had argued for the national status of Kansas City Bible School, and thus no regional limitation on its recruitment or fundraising boundaries, so did the managing committee of Anderson Bible Training School (later Anderson University) in regard to its own prerogatives. The

September 19, 1921, minutes of the Anderson board of trustees state "that we should not be barred out of the territory west of the Mississippi River in soliciting school funds."

Clearly, each school saw itself as serving the whole church and was opposed to the imposition of a system of limitations. Some general coordination and widespread support were seen as desirable by the schools and the church. However, centralized control of the actual ownership and operation of the several institutions was judged inappropriate and clearly would not have been accepted by the institutions.

Steps Toward a Permanent Commission for Higher Education

The modest pattern of educational oversight, first set up around 1920, functioned essentially unchanged for the next two decades. Schools were founded and died with little church-wide consultation and virtually no conscious coordination, and certainly no centralized control. Limited financial support was distributed. The circumstance was still one of local initiative and control. An ambitious venture like Warner Memorial University in Texas from 1929 to 1934 was justified by area ministers as a regionally necessary enterprise, but its demise was hurtful financially to many persons across the United States who had invested in it. There was the inevitable afterthought—was it a legitimate venture for the church, short-lived only because of the Great Depression, or was it the unexamined and unchecked dream of one man? Would it ever have come into being if there had been some formal means of coordinating the church's total investment in higher education? Should there be such a formal means?

A young minister named Mack M. Caldwell, a graduate of Anderson Bible Training School and dean of Southern Bible Institute in Georgia (an educational dream that survived for only two years in the mid-1920s), became acquainted with the systematic way the Church of the Nazarene denomination was handling its institutions of higher education. While a student and teacher at Trevecca College in Nashville, Tennessee, from 1928-1930, Caldwell learned that the Church of the Nazarene had established a General Board of Education. By 1919 it also had issued a document explaining a system of "educational zones" within the church, each designed to support only one college within its bounds, with no college making systematic efforts to raise funds or recruit students outside its own zone. In contrast, Mack Caldwell observed that the Church of God movement was going about this business very inefficiently, with things too centralized in the Midwest. Being a dreamer and activist himself, he began to seek ways to do something about this concern.

The years during and immediately after World War II brought increasing unrest in the Church of God movement. There was a considerable amount of independent action. The scene was crisscrossed by the proliferation of church-related programs being started by individuals or groups. Activities often were competitive and uncoordinated. Being understood as Spirit-inspired ventures in a Spirit-led church, they generally hoped to draw upon the resources of the whole church. Rumors were abroad that more new schools were on regional or even local drawing boards.

The large majority of pastors in those years were not college educated and had few resources to support expensive programs of continuing education. So a minister in Oklahoma, Horace Hathcoat, began offering ministerial degrees by correspondence. He called the program Berean Bible College. The national Board of Christian Education also saw the need. On September 12, 1945, its executive committee issued the following directive: "To meet the rising need and demand on the part of pastors for courses they can study individually at home, the secretary [T. Franklin Miller] was instructed to explore the possibilities of promoting our second series leadership training courses for the study of ministers."

Otto F. Linn, former Bible professor at Anderson College (University), became dean of Pacific Bible College (Warner Pacific) in Portland, Oregon, in 1942. In June, 1944, he found himself before the annual meeting of the national Board of Christian Education presenting a case for the establishment of an "educational commission to study the field of higher education in the Church of God and to discourage many of the attempts in the field." The Board agreed with Linn and, according to its minutes of June 16, 1944, decided to appoint two board members to meet with the presidents of Anderson College, Pacific Bible College, and Alberta Bible Institute (Gardner College) "to consider the possibility of setting up such an advisory committee on higher education." E. E. Perry and Walter S. Haldeman were so named.

Each June between 1945 and 1948, an ad hoc group of concerned ministers met "under the trees" at Anderson Camp Meeting. T. Franklin Miller agreed to be the secretary because he was the only one in the group who had access to a general agency office and could provide some clerical support. He recalls that Mack Caldwell continued to be a "moving force" in this group. A. Leland Forrest and John W. V. Smith were in the earliest conversations. Soon they were joined by men like A. T. Rowe, John A. Morrison, and William E. Reed. In a letter dated March 7, 1979, John W. V. Smith recalled what prompted their concern:

> Several sections of the country were discussing the possibility of launching new institutions. Ever since the failure of Warner Memorial University at Eastland, Texas, there had been repeated expressed interest in starting another school in the South Central Plains area. Specific sites had already been proposed in Texas, Oklahoma, and Kansas for the opening of such a school. There was also some preliminary discussion in the wind about a school in Southern California, a discussion which eventuated in the founding of Arlington College a few years later. There was also a considerable interest in getting a college started in the Southeastern states, with some proposals for specific locations. There were likewise rumors to the effect

that Pacific Bible College was going to ask for participation in the World Service Budget and that possibly they would be expanding their program to offer a full three-year seminary course above the college degrees they were already offering. Dr. Otto F. Linn had stated this dream on many occasions.

William E. Reed, in a letter dated February 5, 1979, recalled that Horace Hathcoat was strongly promoting a correspondence school education for ministers. He observed that "some of us did not want to give any encouragement to that type of development."

The talk about educational coordination finally turned to action in 1948. In an attempt to stimulate discussion and precipitate action by the General Ministerial Assembly, a petition was circulated on the Anderson Camp Meeting grounds among persons concerned about such issues. Thirty-six ministers attached their names to the petition, including Maurice Berquist, Mack M. Caldwell, Charles Cheeks, I. K. Dawson, Harry L. Harp, William E. Reed, Herschell D. Rice, Hillery C. Rice, Warren C. Roark, John W. V. Smith, and E. E. Wolfram. It was significant that most of the signers were not from the educational "establishment." The concern was deep and from across the church. In the form of this petition, the concern found its way to the agenda of the 1948 General Ministerial Assembly. It was adopted in principle by a voice vote, with the chair of the Assembly being instructed to proceed in the naming of members to a new "commission." The petition read:

> We, the undersigned, petition the business committee to bring before the General Ministerial Assembly the question of setting up an educational commission of fifteen or more members, two-thirds of whom shall not be officially connected with present institutions of higher learning. The purpose of this educational commission is to be: 1. To survey the needs and resources for higher education in the Church of God; and 2. To

plan an adequate national program of higher education. The findings and suggestions of which commission shall be presented to the General Ministerial Assembly.

There was a sense across the church of needing to pull together in a time when fragmentation seemed to be everywhere. In this same 1948 Assembly, for instance, the Committee on Revision and Planning reported progress in its work "towards more satisfactory methods of nominations to the boards, more direct control of the boards by the ministers, and toward a more representative ministerial assembly" (*Gospel Trumpet*, July 24, 1948, 19). A few weeks later, Robert L. Berry announced in the August 21, 1948, issue of the *Gospel Trumpet* that "unity of action is imperative." He insisted that showing "the most hearty loyalty to the Church of God world program" is essential if the Church of God were to make an impact on the needs of the world. Keenly aware of the independent and critical attitude of some church leaders, he concluded somewhat scoldingly: "Are some of us wanting to be dictators? Do we want things to go just as we think best? Is our judgment so perfect that we throw over a church program because we think some things could be better? Let us analyze our minds and hearts in this matter, lest we be found dictators in heart, persons who will not play at all unless the Church plays as we want it to."

That 1948 General Ministerial Assembly had been especially active. It authorized the preparation of a manual on ministerial ordination in the hope of making more uniform the procedures used across the country. It adopted a pension plan for ministers, something that had been discussed for twenty years. It also adopted a record-breaking budget totaling $785,000, with higher education represented by amounts of $126,650 to Anderson College and $50,700 to Pacific Bible College (a total of 22.59 percent of the budget devoted to higher education). It had also taken the first small step in attempting to bring some conscious coordination to the higher education enterprise of the Church of God.

The Commission on Higher Education, authorized for a three-year period in 1948, was chaired initially by Mack Caldwell. At the end of this initial period, its life was extended by one year at the request of the commission itself. When the extension expired in June, 1952, a Study Committee on Christian Education was appointed by that year's Assembly to serve for three years. In May, 1953, this Study Committee elected as its officers: Adam W. Miller, chair; Samuel C. Sharp, vice-chair; and T. Franklin Miller, secretary. These were significant church leaders attempting to accomplish a significant task.

Exploration and Frustration

The early years of educational coordination, 1948 to 1955, might be described as ones of general exploration and philosophical frustration. First came the exploration. A series of preliminary surveys were conducted by the new committee because it was evident that so little was actually known about many significant matters. These surveys were reported in 1950 as revealing:

1. That there is an undetermined number of our young people who are entering college each year, only a small percentage of whom attend Church of God schools. A more complete survey for ascertaining the accurate number and vocation of these students is necessary for further guidance in reaching them.

2. There is considerable sentiment in certain areas in favor of establishing new schools in those areas. As yet there has been no adequate study for determining the specific educational needs of each area.

3. We have an indication that there are qualified teachers for the college level whose services are not being used in Church of God institutions, and there is a growing number of people now in training for teaching on the college level. The exact number and qualifications of most of these prospective teachers is not yet known.

It was concluded that "a definite program for providing adequate opportunity for training and a system of maintaining contact with the young people should be inaugurated." Otherwise, it was feared, the church likely would lose many of its youth.

With this exploration of the issues came the philosophical frustration. Exactly what was the status and future of the Study Committee and what should it be empowered to do about anything it discovered? How much regulation of higher education was needed and could be justified? The Study Committee had begun in 1949 by aggressively putting before the General Ministerial Assembly the following substantive guidelines—which the Assembly accepted:

1. We recommend that the General Ministerial Assembly go on record as discouraging the practice of our ministers either granting or receiving theological or academic degrees given solely on correspondence work. However, we do not wish to see the General Ministerial Assembly discouraging home study courses and reading courses not offered for degrees.

2. We recommend to the General Ministerial Assembly that, for the sake of coordinating the educational work of the church, individuals or groups desiring to establish institutions of higher learning seek the counsel of and avail themselves of the resources of the Commission on Higher Education of the General Ministerial Assembly.

3. We recommend to the General Ministerial Assembly that all ministers be encouraged to avail themselves of the existing avenues of furthering the education of ministers and lay leaders, such as ministers' institutes, the first, second, and third series courses offered through the Board of Christian Education, study courses at camp meetings, etc.

4. We recommend to the General Ministerial Assembly that it urge pastors who live near institutions of higher learning to

make and maintain contact with Church of God students in these schools, either through a campus fellowship group or by integrating them into the local church youth fellowship.

In 1952, when it was making its case for a new three-year lease on life to continue its exploratory work, the Study Committee argued that "before any constructive planning can be done, before the structuring of a total educational program in the church can be accomplished, an intensive study and survey of the whole church ought to be made." In view was a "resultant structuring of a total educational program" in which the study committee would serve as follows:

1. Be the medium through which the faculty of the various colleges or seminaries are interchanged, library books are shared, and other services of mutual benefit are shared, such as assisting one another in dealing with accrediting agencies, sharing findings of faculty committees and other academic matters;

2. Be the sponsoring agent in keeping contact between the student bodies of the various schools;

3. Define spheres of activity, of enlistment, of student fieldwork, of financial appeal, and other activities carried on by the colleges;

4. Give counsel and guidance to brethren who contemplate the establishment of institutions of higher learning;

5. Act as the medium through which the interaction between the actual pastoral, teaching, and missionary situations, and the training given for each, is registered, studied, and recommendations made to colleges concerning curriculum, equipment, and procedure;

6. Be alert to areas of duplication or neglect and report any of such to the colleges;

7. Stimulate the colleges to aggressive efforts to provide guidance, incentive, and information to local pastors, state and district Christian education and youth leaders, in the enlistment of our youth for service needing college and seminary training, and to act as a coordinator of these promotional and recruiting activities;

8. Make available to the various educational institutions of the church, on the basis of careful study, certain necessary information and shared experience pertinent to the establishing of theological seminaries of graduate study, colleges, or Bible schools.

By 1952, membership of the Study Committee had come to include Mack M. Caldwell, Ronald Joiner, John W. V. Smith, Ida Byrd Rowe, T. Franklin Miller, and Carl H. Kardatzke. These persons saw a big need that could be met only with coordinated action. But they were only a temporary committee supposed to be exploring, among other things, the need for a permanent body. Given the non-authoritarian nature of the general work of the Church of God movement, the rather independent free-church mentality, the regionalism, and the autonomous nature of institutions of higher education within the church, the chances of successfully introducing a carefully controlled educational plan were not good. In fact, the several functions which the study committee projected for itself in 1952 (listed above) were very aspirational indeed given the magnitude of the problems and the inherent limitations of a tradition strongly opposed to "man-rule" in the life of the church.

The need was real and the persons involved were determined. In June, 1953, the General Ministerial Assembly received the following report:

The present thinking of the committee is that such a commission should think of itself as an agency of the church rather than as an agency of educational institutions, and must have sufficient authority to carry out its functions. Such a commission should think of itself as a planning commission for the educational program of the church and, as such, ought to develop the long-range program of educational development.

While the commission was announcing that it should be established "as an authoritative body," it also was conceding that "maintaining the true cooperation of the several institutions of higher education must be by request and consent, and any benefits or penalties for cooperative endeavor or refusal of such be referred to the Assembly for action."

As stated in the commission's June, 1953, report to the Assembly, the suggested goal was to balance the privilege of being a recognized center of planning and coordination and the limitation of being such only "in terms of fraternal guidance" without attempting "to legislate or enforce any rule upon the institution." Commission members now included institutional representatives Milo L. Chapman (Pacific Bible College), John A. Morrison (Anderson College), Adam W. Miller (Anderson School of Theology), Gordon A. Schieck (Alberta Bible Institute), and T. Franklin Miller (Board of Christian Education). Members appointed in 1953 by the Assembly chair were Harry L. Harp, James Wade, W. I. Plough, Samuel C. Sharp, and Harold W. Boyer.

A Permanent Commission on Christian Higher Education

The Association of the Churches of God in Southern California announced in 1954 the decision to establish a four-year Bible college in southern California, with the doors to open that fall. In a resolution directed to the 1954 General Ministerial Assembly of the Church of God, the Association defended its move. Southern California was said to be an ideal location for a school. Students in the Los Angeles area likely would not go to Anderson College, Pacific Bible College, or South Texas Bible Institute because of the distance. Further, the churches of southern California "have repeatedly expressed their eagerness to operate within the framework of the general agencies of the church." This resolution, submitted by C. Herbert Joiner and Albert J. Kempin as officers of the Association, was received by the Assembly and apparently shifted for discussion to the future agenda of the Commission on Christian Higher Education.

By June, 1954, the Commission had developed a statement of "recommended criteria for the establishment of institutions of higher education." It reported to the General Assembly that year that these criteria had formed the basis for consultation with representatives from the southeastern states, the World Evangelism Institute, Arlington College of Southern California, and Gulf-Coast Bible College of Houston, Texas. As usual, the report concluded by noting that the "high interest evidenced in the establishment of institutions of higher education would seem to indicate the desirability of a strong, permanent Commission on Higher Education." The criteria of the Commission are found in full in Barry L. Callen's *Preparing for Service* (1988, 196-199). In brief, they were: (1) The adequate establishment of the need for a new institution; (2) Making sure of the availability of the financial resources necessary to insure continuance of a new institution; (3) Intending that a new institution would operate within the general principles established by the church; and (4) Being sure that there is full cooperation with structures and institutions of the Church of God movement.

The California development helped spark even more concern that the Commission was needed permanently. In successfully proposing to the 1955 General Ministerial Assembly a three-year extension of its life, the Commission had argued:

> As educational institutions grow, they come to find that the
> sectional and regional support which once maintained them is
> no longer sufficient and, in view of the service they render to

Commission on Christian Higher Education, 1959

Commission on Christian Higher Education, 1978

the church at large, these educational institutions would naturally look to the church at large for financial support. This fact further underscores for us the need for a permanent Commission, not only to serve in a coordinating capacity, but which will also be prepared to advise and counsel with such groups as contemplate setting up additional institutions of education. Such services rendered by the Commission would enable us to avoid setting up more institutions than the church could adequately maintain.

Finally, in 1957, the Commission came forward with a formal proposal for its own existence on a permanent basis, by-laws and all. When the discussion died away, it seemed best for the ministers to think about it for a year. Then, on June 17, 1958, the issue was taken from the table and passed. After a decade of exploratory activity, it finally was ordered by the General Ministerial Assembly that the Commission be a standing body within the Church of God movement. Its responsibilities included:

1. To awaken the entire church to the conviction that true religion and true education complement each other, and that education highly conceived is Christian education, and that the promotion of Christian higher education is a proper activity of the church;

2. To lay plans for and to guide the development of the total higher education program of the church;

3. To establish and recommend criteria for the development of institutions of higher education in the Church of God;

4. To act as a connection link between the institutions and the church, urging the church to help the schools, and helping the schools to better serve the church.

Now the Commission existed on a firm and long-term basis. It was hoped that it could bring effective coordination, even though it lacked authoritative powers over the institutions involved. Within this framework, the exploratory period was over and the real work was to begin.

Many significant leaders within the Church of God movement and its institutions of higher education have been involved in the work of the Commission. Given the stated purposes for its existence, the Commission functioned from year to year in a central, changing, and sometimes troubled arena of the church's life. There was a constant mixture of aspiration, accomplishment, and frustration. It became the Commission's annual practice to receive and review reports from the several colleges, the School of Theology, and the national Board of Christian Education. These reports contained information about each school's enrollment, personnel, finances, programs, and facilities. In addition, the Commission addressed a wide range of important matters of common concern to these schools, including their nature, existence, funding, programs, and their relationships to each other, the Church of God, and the larger community of higher education.

A review of these years of Commission activity demonstrates the important role played by such a body, and stimulates appreciation for the seriousness with which the Commission approached its tasks. Throughout, however, there was a persistent dilemma. As T. Franklin Miller stated it in a January, 1980, interview, the big issue has always been a philosophical one. Do we want in the Church of God a body that will "facilitate conversation" or one that has power and authority over existing and new institutions? The frustration has come, he noted, from the limitations of the obvious choice of facilitator. It probably is the inevitable impasse given the church's approach to organization and Holy Spirit leadership. Institutional anarchy, Miller concluded, is the risk we have chosen rather than the risks inherent in becoming burdened with the creation of standard denominational machinery.

This limited facilitator role was meaningful and worthwhile, as a review of the Commission agendas clearly shows. But the felt need for more coordination and even some control in the church's higher education efforts has been voiced often. In 1980 interviews, Milo L. Chapman and Frederick G. Shackleton, each with long-term involvement in Church of God higher education, expressed this need. According to Shackleton, "the total enterprise of higher education in the Church of God would have been much stronger if from the beginning a total plan could have been developed that had the official approval and support of the church at large." Chapman observed that the church has needed "responsible leadership" in higher education, but instead "we formed a discussion group with little power to act. We talk mostly at superficial levels and do not try to formulate policy for higher education in the church."

Mack M. Caldwell, very influential in the beginnings of the Commission, shared a similar perspective in 1979. He said, "We need the commission now even more than earlier in our history." Why? There was an inequitable distribution of funds, too much power lying with the larger institutions, too much vested interest resident in the commission's membership, and too little church control over the whole scene. "Instead of the church running its colleges," Caldwell concluded, "the colleges are running the church!" Such perennial concerns, plus events in the early part of the 1980s, set the stage for an extensive reconsideration of the composition and work of the Commission.

A New Beginning for the Commission

In the sessions of the 1980 General Assembly of the Church of God convened in Anderson, Indiana, there was sharp criticism voiced from the floor about a particular set of curricular and instructional circumstances at Anderson College. This public criticism dramatized an apparently deep division on a series of issues and began a difficult year in the church. As one way of helping, the board of directors of the Executive Council of the Church of God convened in January, 1981, a "dialogue on internal unity." Thirty church leaders from across the country met and decided that the issue of biblical authority was probably the most central issue to be discussed. These leaders came to consensus on a set of affirmations on this issue and proceeded to make recommendations in other areas of concern. One recommendation was: "A serious concern is expressed that our colleges are essentially unrelated and competitive. Some initiative should be taken to speak to this major problem."

By the General Assembly of June, 1981, the board of trustees of Anderson College had prepared a major report in response to the issues about this campus that had emerged in the General Assembly the year before. Beyond speaking clearly to the issues, the report identified "two major and yet unresolved concerns which deserve responsible and church-wide attention." One of these, the relationship of the church to its colleges, reads:

> Historically, the relationship of the Church of God to its colleges has been largely informal and undefined. There has been the relationship created by the election of trustees, the ratification of chief executive officers, budgetary support and general reporting. However, there is little clarity regarding the church's expectations of its colleges, and there has not been a widespread understanding of what constitutes a responsible relationship between a church body and its institutions of higher learning. We urge an exploration of this subject.

In December, 1981, a second dialogue on internal unity was convened. It involved a new group of thirty church leaders from across the nation chosen by the Executive Council office. Again, the issue of higher education was singled out for attention by the group. This group reported "a great deal of frustration over the competition and independency of action on the part of our educational institutions, and other problems relating to the need for overall coordination and supervision of our higher educational process." It recommended a study of how other church bodies handle these things and called for some action "for the corporate structuring of our approach to higher education."

In January, 1983, the commission considered these matters and decided on a path of action. It called for a meeting of the presidents, deans, and board chairs of the schools in the United States that were predominantly maintained and governed by the Church of God (Anderson College, with its School of Theology, Bay Ridge Christian College, Mid-America Bible College, Warner Pacific College, and Warner Southern College). The purpose was to "initiate candid conversation regarding the overarching goal of serving and advancing the Church of God through its ministries of higher education and to work deliberately at enhancing that which is mutually supportive and minimizing that which is combative." This group met in Kansas City, Missouri, in November, 1983, established its own agenda, experienced candid and fruitful conversations, judged the meeting historic, and established a possible agenda for a second such meeting. One item on that next agenda was to be clarification of the possible future role of this ad hoc group in relation to the Commission on Christian Higher Education.

By this time, many straws of change were blowing in the wind. The national Division of World Service developed a "higher education scenario" in a brainstorming session during its 1984 spring meeting. Concerns about general church budgeting and fundraising made up the immediate context. This scenario was sent by the Executive Council office to college boards of trustees for review and reaction. Partly because the scenario called for a "board of regents" with governance functions over the colleges and a regional concept for college fundraising, reaction was negative. The December, 1984, response of the Anderson College board of trustees was representative:

1. The scenario takes for granted that the problems likely to arise in the more centralized system proposed are preferable to the present problems. This may not be the case.

2. The scenario appears to move in a direction counter to a central characteristic of the heritage of the Church of God, i.e., a resistance to centralizing power and authority in human hands.

3. The concept of "regionalism" is unacceptable to colleges which, by tradition and mission, serve the national church.

Apparently, the scenario was destined to play only one role, that of stimulating additional exploration of less dramatic alternatives.

Where, then, would a new beginning come from? If not this more centralized approach, then what? The answer was to come initially from the proposed second meeting of the presidents, deans, and board chairs, this time in November, 1984, at the site of the new Mid-America Bible College campus under construction in Oklahoma City, Oklahoma. It was agreed by this gathering of higher education leaders that the following assumptions were significant considerations in any recommendations for change:

1. As servants of the Church, the colleges should be responsive to the evolving needs within the Church and society.

2. The Church deserves proper accountability from the colleges it supports.

3. The diversity among our colleges is real and valued, and healthy forms of competition are appropriate and effective.

4. There is need for raising awareness about the value of Christian higher education within the Church; there will be long-term deterioration of the Church if increasing numbers of students are educated in institutions other than our own.

5. The present loose affiliation of colleges lacks the means to effectively guide and promote the cause of Christian higher education within the Church.

6. The financial needs of Church of God colleges will continue to outpace the growth of World Service resources in basic budget through the end of this century.

7. The pool of prospective traditional students is shrinking and Church of God colleges are presently attracting only a small percentage of these, even though these colleges have the capacity to serve a greater number.

8. Financial support for private education from non-church sources is likely to decrease.

9. The character of Christian higher education is being endangered through legal challenges and the imposition of external criteria.

With these considerations in mind, and remembering the value experienced in its two meetings, the group developed and proposed a model for reconstituting the membership of the Commission on Christian Higher Education. The basic idea was for the commission to be comprised of this ad hoc group, plus a few at-large members elected by the General Assembly. It was thought that such a model would strengthen the commission, without adding the negatives of centralized control over sovereign college corporations.

This new commission model was reviewed by the commission in January, 1985, and, with only slight modification, was forwarded to and approved by the Executive Council that May and the General Assembly that June. Therefore, beginning on July 1, 1985, the commission was enlarged to comprise twenty-eight members, including the "key decision makers in higher education." This had been determined to be the best way to "further facilitate cooperative efforts while minimizing unwholesome competitive activities." The new membership now included:

Anderson University president, dean, and board chair	3
Warner Pacific College president, dean, and board chair	3
Mid-America Bible College president, dean, and board chair	3
Bay Ridge Christian College president, dean, and board chair	3

Warner Southern College president, dean, and board chair   3
Anderson University School of Theology dean   1
Azusa Pacific University president   1
Executive Council representative (staff director)   1
Elected representatives (General Assembly)   6
Board of Christian Education executive secretary   1
Gardner Bible College president, dean, and board chair   3

Total   28

From Commission to Covenants

Annually, the Commission of Christian Higher Education of the Church of God had sought to be a constructive force on behalf of the whole enterprise of higher education in the Church of God movement. One means of accomplishing this goal was the addressing of pressing issues. Another was the collecting of comparative information from the institutions and sharing it with the schools and the church. The major issues addressed by the commission from 1970 to 1988 are found in Barry L. Callen's 1988 book *Preparing for Service.* Also found there are the church leaders who served from 1958 to 1988 as chair, vice-chair, and secretary of the commission. Robert A. Nicholson of Anderson College and Milo L. Chapman of Warner Pacific College were prominent among them. Included in the 1988 publication are examples of significant information gathered annually by the commission. There are total enrollments and numbers of students affiliated with the Church of God movement in the Church of God colleges and seminary.

With the major reorganization of the North American ministries of the Church of God movement authorized by the General Assembly in June, 1997, the commissions of the former structure were disbanded. This ended the life of the Commission on Christian Higher Education that had been active in one form or another since the 1940s. Recognizing the need for some continuing venue for higher education leaders to share problems, resources, and act and speak together, ad hoc meetings began on an annual basis. Some were on an international scale, convening at Fritzlar Bible College in Germany. Others were North American only and usually involved school leaders being hosted in Anderson, Indiana, by Ronald V. Duncan of Church of God Ministries.

In addition, a new pattern of formal relationships was established between the church and its institutions of higher education. The center of this pattern involves the categories of Endorsed and Affiliated Agencies. Through Church of God Ministries, covenant agreements are formally established and periodically reviewed with each of the schools. The intent is to foster unity of ministry, provide ongoing monitoring, encourage collaborative ministries, and facilitate positive dialogue. In short, drawing language from the covenants themselves, the intent is to "lessen the risk of isolation in agency ministry and enhance effective and interdependent work on behalf of the church."

The colleges remain separately incorporated and not-for-profit corporations with their own governing bodies. Those in the "endorsed" category are more closely held by the church in certain ways and share in the World Ministries budget of the church. The church and schools, while in covenant relationship for mutual ministry purposes, disclaim responsibility for each other's financial obligations. The basic understanding of these covenants is exemplified by the biblical one between David and Jonathan (1 Samuel 18:1-4). It is characterized by mutual respect, shared goals for the greater good, and cooperative efforts wherever possible. As of 2007, here are the schools involved:

Endorsed Agencies	Affiliated Agencies
Anderson University	Azusa Pacific University
Anderson School of Theology	Bay Ridge Christian College

Mid-America Christian University   Gardner College
Warner Pacific College
Warner Southern College

Books Detailing Key Aspects of
Higher Education in the Church of God

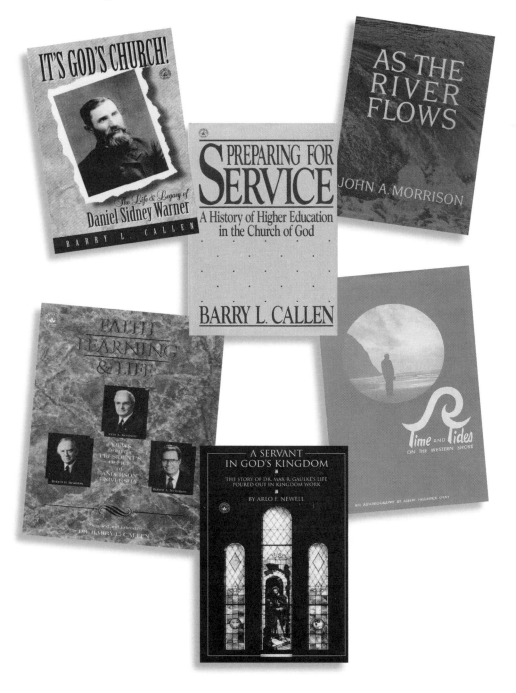

CHAPTER 14

Issues That Have Made a Difference

Higher education in North America was born in the womb of the Christian faith. Time, however, has made a large difference for many of the institutions involved. Most higher education in the United States now is state sponsored and, at best, religiously neutral. Even many of the schools that remain church sponsored are merely "church-related" and not "Christian" in any substantial sense.

There is a significant question. What makes a church-related institution of higher education deeply "Christian"? Students often look only on the surface, thinking that being made to go to chapel regularly or hearing a professor pray in class on occasion distinguishes the school as Christian. But it goes much deeper than that. The meanings of "higher" in higher education have been explored, with this careful affirmation:

> The Christ-centered college aspires to be truly "higher" by introducing sympathetically the claim of Christ as the final authority and the ultimate end of life…. The ultimate questions of life, meaning, and destiny will be addressed in such an institution of higher learning and will be viewed finally in light of the highest we know, the light of God shining in the face of Jesus Christ. Opening oneself to that light is indeed

going back to basics in the "highest" way possible! (Barry L. Callen, in *Faculty Dialogue*, spring, 1991, 14:67-78).

Anderson University Press published a booklet in 2004 containing a lecture given on the Anderson University campus that year by Richard T. Hughes. It is titled "What Makes Church-Related Education 'Christian'"? The summary statement of Hughes is:

> The truth is, the gospel is a *radical message*. It is radical in its call for discipleship and radical in its promise of grace. But grace apart from discipleship can be "cheap," and discipleship apart from grace can quickly degenerate into legalism. This is why sanctification *and* justification are the two indispensable poles of the paradox of the Christian gospel, and the two indispensable dimensions of Christian higher education. When the board, the administration, and the faculty of a church-related college or university can embrace this paradox and orient the institution squarely in the context of these imperatives, that institution ceases to be merely church-related. It becomes, instead, deeply and profoundly *Christian*.

The several schools associated with the Church of God movement, each described in this book, have honestly sought to be profoundly Christian. They have faced many issues, as all institutions do. They have done so, however, in the context of their commitments to the Christian call to serious discipleship and the promise of divine grace. What follows are brief presentations of the several issues that have been faced.

The Pivotal Issues for the Church of God Schools

The following are general observations, concerns, and projections that arise from a review of the whole history of higher education in the Church of God movement. These issues root in issues that have proven pivotal and perennial. These issues deserve careful reflection by persons wishing to learn from the past so that informed and thoughtful decisions can be made about the future. Many of these issues address in various ways the central question of what it means to be profoundly Christian, and particularly so in the context of the Church of God movement.

1. Oriented Around Spiritual Experience. The general approach of the Church of God movement to matters of Christian theology and discipleship has been to be oriented strongly toward spiritual experience. This approach has not been creedal, propositional, or institutional in nature. It has fostered a repudiation of formal education as a means to salvation, and sometimes a distrust of education as the best way to go about the discovery of truth or maturing in faith.

The most important truth has been understood to be theological in nature. It is best attained by the joining of divine revelation and spiritual discernment. Through the inspired text of the Bible, the Spirit of God will lead an obedient believer into the light of truth. Therefore, understandably, formal education has not always been given high priority in the life of the Church of God movement. When such education did become prominent, its nature and goals were still influenced significantly by the general orientation to the higher value of spiritual experience. The school slogan of Anderson University, in its earliest years, was "Where spirituality predominates." This was a clear reflection of the sponsoring church body.

Dean Marvin H. Lindemuth of Warner Pacific College put it clearly in 1964: "The Christian college is not a church, but it is at its best when related to one. The church and its college have separate as well as shared responsibilities. The college is primarily an academic institution with its own unique task and function of providing opportunity for a liberal arts education within the Christian context." The Church of God movement often has worried that a "liberal arts" education is a threat to the priority of Christian spirituality.

2. Continuing Openness to New Truth. Countering somewhat the church's tendency to devalue institutions of formal education has been a central conviction about the necessary openness to the guidance of the Holy Spirit. It has been believed consistently within the Church of God movement that God continues to reveal truth and that no person or denomination has arrived at a full understanding of that truth. Creeds have been viewed as formalized and necessarily flawed articulations of divine truth. They too easily limit the need for continuing quest, and they provide convenient tools for groups of Christians to divide from each other and thus weaken their mutual witness to the world.

Over the history of the Church of God movement, therefore, there has been an emphasis on the importance of questing after and discovering truth—not only proclaiming and protecting it. The biblical revelation is unchanging, but our grasp of it should be ever growing. Truth is both received and achieved. Awareness of this has contributed to a diminishing of the earlier assumption, held by many movement leaders, that persons who increase in knowledge can be expected to decrease in spirituality. The colleges, universities, and seminary of the Church of God have been accepted increasingly as appropriate centers of learning, research, and renewal in the church. Even so, the hesitancy and sometimes even the suspicion remain.

3. Forces of Group Conservatism. The spirit of genuine openness to learning and growth has been very real in the Church of God movement, especially when focused on spiritual maturing and skill development tied directly to effectiveness in Christian witness and mission. However, openness to learning has faced a persistent opposition. In the Church of God, despite its non-creedalism, there have been influential ministers, "standard" literature, and controlling group perspectives on many subjects. These have provided group identity and cohesion. They also have been a conservative force which on occasion has resisted free exploration and individual thought.

There has been tension between an honestly proclaimed openness to all truth and the controlling influence of the consensus view on various subjects among movement leaders. There has been the establishment or threatened establishment of various schools that promised to be more loyal than the existing ones to the truth that was seen as foundational to the life of the Church of God movement. There have been tense times when a school was perceived to have "strayed" into unacceptable teaching territory—most often this has been the Anderson campus since it is the oldest, largest, and most prominent.

Despite the stress on Christian unity and a "movement" identity, such "sectarian" impulses have persisted. On occasion, these conserving impulses have sought to clarify the movement's identity and distinctive teachings by embodying themselves in the life of a college (usually a "training" center at first). This has provided some tension, not always unhealthy, with the parallel impulse toward openness and innovation.

Once institutions of higher education did develop within the life of the Church of God movement, there also developed a pattern of concern about how to control and coordinate their work. While openness to truth has always been an honored virtue, the more dominant mandate usually felt in the church has been a championing of the biblical truths perceived to be foundational to this church reform movement. To preach and train in the known truths has been the central task. There is a very special heritage that all educational institutions have been expected to affirm and even herald.

4. How "Church of God" Should They Be? When an institution of higher learning became strong and attracted constituencies beyond the Church of God movement, some important questions began to come into focus. How "Church of God" should a Church of God college, university, or seminary be? Is it appropriate for faculty members, administrators, trustees, or a significant percentage of the student body to not be associated directly with the Church of God movement? How wide a range of theological belief and lifestyle should be permitted? Without question, part of the impetus for founding and maintaining the Church of God institutions of higher education was to enable persons to learn, grow, and make vital decisions under the movement's influence and with direct exposure to its teachings. But there are realities of growing educational communities that counter the movement's influence on students. For instance, the consumer-oriented student marketplace of today and the lack of available faculty members with specialized preparation and Church of God affiliation brings tension with the concern for an institution's "Church of God" identity. Sociological realities can easily conflict with church ideals.

What about a merger arrangement, such as that of Arlington College with Azusa College, or close program ties, such as that of Gardner College with Camrose Lutheran, Anderson University with Purdue University, or the proposed ecumenical relationships attempted by Anderson School of Theology and Jamaica School of Theology—both rejected by the church? What percentage of a faculty, student body, or board of trustees should (must) be "Church of God?" Should the Commission on Christian Higher Education have been given any real power over the colleges? Is the circumstance weakened now that the commission no longer exists? How much church control of its colleges is essential or even possible? These are central questions that often have and will continue to be raised.

5. Diversity of Educational Missions and Philosophies. The missions of the several colleges, universities, and seminary that have developed within the Church of God movement are diverse in several ways. While the origins of the diversity were many, each a story in itself, eventually there has evolved a tendency to see richness more than threat in the diversity. Individuals with their own personalities and agendas certainly have added to the diversity. So have regional needs and special opportunities that have appeared in different settings. The issues contributing to the diversity have included whether a college should go beyond the original task of training church leaders for church vocations, whether "training" and "educating" are the same or different goals, and whether the "liberal arts" is something to be sought or shunned in curricular range and design.

The diversity is very real and is quite understandable given the variety of needs to be served, the personalities involved, the particular concern and needs of geographic regions, and the limited availability of resources. Healthy forms of institutional competition are inevitable and can be constructive, although this has not always been the case among the schools of the Church of God movement.

6. A Bias Against Church Institutions. The time of the beginning of the Church of God movement provided a negative atmosphere in which to evolve movement-related institutions of higher education. In the late nineteenth and early twentieth centuries, orthodox Christianity and the emerging trends in American higher education were increasingly in conflict. The Church of God movement, if not anti-intellectual in its attitudes, at least tended to put its priorities elsewhere. When it came to what was judged more important to enhance, sometimes only two choices were presented. The movement's initial mentality clearly chose the spirit over the mind— although serious Bible study and skill enhancement for effective ministry were always seen as critical.

Given the "liberal" colleges and seminaries its early leaders knew something about, the Church of God movement began with suspicion. It was suspicious of scholars probing difficult faith-related questions and openly testing ideas previously unacceptable within the thinking of the movement or even within orthodox Christianity in general. Preaching and evangelism rested on firm convictions, not theoretical questions. Such probing and testing did not seem the place to put precious energy and time. Colleges and seminaries usually were classified with the evils of denominationalism. In fact, they often were judged to be little more than hotbeds of heresy and tools of denominational self-perpetuation.

While creativity was common within the Church of God movement, and several persons prominent in the movement's earliest life pursued active intellectual lives of their own, institutions of higher education were not to begin appearing within the movement for several decades. They had low priority on the agendas of "flying" ministers who were opposing church-related institutionalism in general. Accordingly, when colleges eventually were founded, the usual circumstance was one of an outstanding individual's initiative and/or a concern for the health of the church in a given geographic region that refused to be stopped by widespread reluctance, even opposition from the larger church body.

7. **Lack of an Educational System.**   Even after decades of institutional development in the area of higher education, there has been reluctance to legislate some form of educational establishment that has the power to coordinate and regulate the institutions. Such regulation would run counter to the "freedom in the Spirit" mentality of the Church of God movement. The hesitant and even haphazard approach to organizational matters in the Church of God movement has had a dramatic impact on the development and inter-relatedness of all of its institutions, including its colleges. Especially since the 1990s, such haphazardness has been addressed with increasing effectiveness.

The emphasis on local autonomy and the bias against the controlling ability of central organizations or persons has meant that colleges have had maverick-like beginnings, often have been the lengthened shadows of one man or regional agenda, and have benefited from very little effective coordination of their efforts or the available resources. While the Commission on Christian Higher Education sought some modest role in this area (until it was disbanded as part of a major reorganization in the late 1990s), what typically has prevailed has been the impact of charismatic persons and regional or other special interests. The result has been a general lack of effective coordination, let alone direct control by the church. There have been periodic times of crisis management by the church as a given school has been challenged on an issue or fallen into serious economic trouble.

This lack of coordination has been judged by some as a strength inherent in a free and creative fellowship; by others it has been seen more as a weakness that has spawned unhealthy competition and a poor stewardship of scarce resources. However judged, it is what one would have expected. It is the reflection of the church movement itself as it has struggled to evolve necessary and effective institutions in all areas of its life and mission—without such institutions coming to duplicate the "man-rule" evils decried in denominationalism. The circumstance remains a central challenge for the future.

8. Being in Covenant Relationship. Edward L. Foggs spoke wisely in his 1988 report to the Commission on Christian Higher Education:

> . . .our church colleges must be clear about their mission and their relationship to the church…. [The circumstance] calls for a covenant relationship between our colleges and the church setting forth mutual expectations and commitments. The impact of all other trends will, in some measure, be mitigated by the extent to which we embrace this trend and allow it to become mutually operative.

The major reorganization of the North American ministries of the Church of God movement in the late 1990s included creation of the categories of "Endorsed" and "Affiliated" agencies, each with differing levels of relationship and responsibility to the North American organization, Church of God Ministries. For the Endorsed agencies, including Anderson University, Mid-America Christian University, Warner Southern College, and Warner Pacific College, formal and renewable covenant agreements came to be required.

A clear pattern of accountability and mutual expectations had been introduced, even while these schools remain sovereign corporations. A sampling of this covenant accountability is seen in the following from the current Warner Pacific College covenant, which is virtually duplicated for Anderson University, Mid-America Christian University, and Warner Southern College. Warner Pacific College (Portland, Oregon), as an Endorsed Agency of the Church of God, covenants with the General Assembly, acting through Church of God Ministries and its Ministries Council, to serve the church by:

1. Being a quality center of learning that will provide opportunities for student challenge and growth.
2. Offering programs of study that are based in the historic mission and vision of the Church of God.
3. Playing an active role in the development of future generations of church leaders.
4. Partnering with the Church of God in the use of their facilities for educational purposes.
5. Operating prudently in financial and business affairs.

In turn, the Church of God movement covenants to provide various benefits to Warner Pacific College, including:

1. Use of the name and goodwill of the Church of God, Anderson, Indiana.

2. Listing in the Church of God *Yearbook* as an Endorsed Agency.
3. Recognition as an extended ministry of the Church of God.
4. Eligibility for budgetary gifts from Church of God Ministries.
5. Access to and [non-voting] participation in the general session meetings of the Ministries Council by invitation of the General Director of Church of God Ministries.

9. The Influence of Time and Place. Colleges associated with the Church of God movement obviously have been impacted greatly by the particular times and places of their foundings. The manner of their origins and the lack of general church control of their lives have contributed to their adaptability and vulnerability to localized circumstances.

The impact of the Great Depression on Warner Memorial University, the volatile influence of the civil rights scene in Mississippi on Bay Ridge Christian College, the favorable results of the central location of Anderson University within the distribution of Church of God people, and the problems caused by the geography and politics of the islands of the West Indies on the Caribbean colleges are clear examples of the influence of time and place. Less obvious but no less influential have been the subtle pressures of American culture and accrediting associations. College policies and programs have influenced college programs toward equipping students to be "successful" in professional and "materialistic" terms, terms sometimes standardized outside these colleges and the Church of God movement. No church or college lives in a vacuum and the histories of these colleges provide dramatic examples of this truth.

Church historian Merle D. Strege stresses the way that *place* shapes institutions, with place thought of geographically, socially, culturally, and within a given church tradition. He argues for a college allowing its given theological tradition to influence significantly its social life and academic curriculum. With the Church of God movement particularly in mind, he reflects on holiness, experience, community, and vocation as potential contributors to the schools associated with this movement (in the *Wesleyan Theological Journal*, 32:1, spring, 1997). There are riches to be recovered, important locations to be reclaimed, and stories out of which institutions should be living. Place can be a limiting factor; it also can be greatly enriching. Church of God schools have sought to champion their *places* for the enrichment of general church life.

10. Leadership for the Church. The colleges that have developed in the life of the Church of God movement have functioned with great influence on the church's life. They often have been the centers for leadership development and major users of the dollar resources available. They also have influenced significantly alterations in traditional beliefs and attitudes within the church at large. They have been objects of high praise and the occasional targets of sharp controversy. Anderson University in particular has played a dominant role in all of these regards, given its central location, leadership, and relative size.

The movement's Visioning Conference in 1998 identified leadership development as a central priority for the Church of God movement. It said that there was urgent need to "broaden the existing leadership base." Included in the perceived need were concerns "for distance learning, clergy care, mentoring, and assistance for students in Church of God higher education." For decades, the schools have been about this central task of preparing people for leadership. The future requires an enhancement of this task.

The colleges, universities, and seminary have led the way in minimizing the intellectual and relational isolation characteristic of the Church of God movement in its earliest years. They have had a broadening effect that, in the main, has brought increasing maturity to the movement. At times they have also raised the question of who should have priority in church authority, the pastor or the professor. This question has found no final answer. Probably, it will not and should not be answered in favor of either, since there is creativity and corrective in the ongoing tension between the two.

11. Inadequate Funding Levels. Funding for higher education in the Church of God movement always has been a major problem. Some colleges have not survived, including Warner Memorial University and Jamaica School of Theology. Others would not have survived apart from crisis intervention on the part of the national church. Some have been taken into the official family of national agencies, thereby sharing in revenues collected from the general church and distributed by formula. In more recent years the colleges, primarily through state and federal student aid programs, have developed an unwanted but real reliance on such indirect assistance. Since Church of God colleges have relatively small or no endowments, any loss of such external assistance to their students, whose tuition dollars represent a high percentage of total institutional incomes, would be critical. Any such loss cannot be expected to be recovered by major increases in church funding through allocations from the national budget of the Church of God movement.

Dollar allocations from the church to higher education have been significant in the past, particularly when compared with the level at which other church bodies have supported their institutions of higher education. But giving levels in the Church of God have not been increasing rapidly, other national ministries also are in great need of increased funding, and not all of the colleges benefit directly from this national budget. Additional sources of endowment and current giving for operational purposes must be found. New constituencies outside the Church of God movement are being identified to speak to the enrollment challenges, and thus the income levels of these schools.

In 1948, the institutions of higher education received 22.59 percent of the total annual budget of the national church. In the decade of the 1980s, that percentage stabilized at about 25.75 percent. The 2007 World Ministries Budget of the Church of God includes $2,763,725 for higher education, 21 percent of the total. This is generous, but the church's giving represents only 2.8% of the total combined budgets of the four schools supported in 2007.

12. Possible Loss of Institutional Autonomy. The Church of God institutions of higher education in North America are legal corporations governed by their own articles of incorporation and bylaws. They voluntarily have granted some prerogatives to the church with which they are affiliated, like the right to ratify the election of their institutional presidents and members of their boards of trustees. There have evolved affiliations other than the church. Sometimes these organizations expect a measure of leverage in the institution. Church-related schools have missions and worldview stances that they consider essential to their integrity. Therefore, there is obvious concern when there appears to be some threat to such stances.

The potential loss of full institutional autonomy has appeared on the legal, accreditation, and other fronts. Many of the laws of the United States have placed an increasing number of restrictions on private, church-related colleges. In addition, Church of God schools have sought regional and specialized accreditations. The resources expended in this process, and the resulting influence on the schools have been substantial. Presumably, such influence in the main has been wholesome and in the direction of educational quality and fair employment practices. Without doubt, however, some directions have been forced that otherwise would have been judged of low priority or not desirable by the institutions themselves.

Beyond the legal and accreditation fronts, student enrollment patterns have followed national trends for the most part. Recently they have shifted toward increased numbers of part-time and older, non-traditional students. This shift has increased the diversity of student interests, needs, church affiliations, and often life-styles, lessening the tolerance for campus regulations designed for younger, full-time, Christian, residential students, and "distance" online learners. There even has developed a sense of being engulfed in a tide of student consumerism when the dollars brought to campus by such students are needed to enable institutional survival. It has not been easy to maintain institutional autonomy and integrity in the midst of these conflicting forces. In general, however, Church of God institutions appear to have managed rather well despite all that they have faced.

13. A Decreased Loyalty by Constituencies. Vital to the well being of church-related colleges is the degree to which they are valued and supported by their own constituencies. Colleges and universities in the Church of God movement have been relatively small, of recent origin, and populated by persons of limited wealth. Thus, they have not been able to build large, loyal alumni bodies or significant numbers of affluent friends. Although the schools have become major centers of activity and cohesion for the life of the Church of God movement, commitment to them has lessened in recent years. Church of God young persons, not traditionally a strong college-going group in the first place, have been showing less commitment to Church of God institutions just because they are "our colleges." Rather, they and/or their parents have been influenced by the availability, quality, lower cost, and prestige of particular programs, often of state-supported schools closer to home.

The Commission on Christian Higher Education conducted parallel studies in 1969 and 1979 to determine the college-going patterns of Church of God young persons. It learned in each instance that about fifty-three percent of the church's high school graduates went immediately to college, and that only twenty-five percent of those going to college chose a Church of God institution. There is fear of this trend increasing. This gives urgency to the long-standing concern that somehow families in the church be sensitized to the inherent value of Christian higher education, value worth the extra money required (a primary reason why this present book was written). It also raises the questions of whether and how the church should identify and serve the largest percentage of its college-going young people, most of whom are studying in state-sponsored institutions.

14. God Has Been at Work! The Church of God movement, with its strong anti-sectarianism, always has been committed—at least in principle—more to the work of God than to any church-related institutions set up to try to get that work done. This has not always made for the strongest institutions within the movement, but it has kept an important perspective before all institutions that have come along. The movement increasingly has accepted the premise that God works *through institutions* as well as through gifted individuals. Strong institutions can provide a means for effective, cooperative ministry, as well as create the danger of centralized and largely non-divine control of church life. The colleges, universities, and seminary that have developed over the years certainly have not been all that God might have wanted. They often have been fragile organizations guided by very human persons in less than ideal circumstances. Nonetheless, *God obviously has been at work*, using what has been imperfect, honoring the dedication of gifted servants of Jesus Christ, and adding to the reign of Christ in our troubled world through the work of higher education.

Higher education in the Church of God movement has taught and learned from students, led and followed the church, and profited from and been a friend to various constituencies outside the campus and church communities. The alumni of these Church of God institutions now number in the tens of thousands. They have been prepared to serve the church's mission and address the many urgent needs of today's society. The scope, quality, and magnitude of this service is well worth all the investment that has been made! The Church of God movement, which has made much of the investment, in the process has wrestled with its own most fundamental premises. As church historian John W. V. Smith has summarized (*The Quest for Holiness and Unity*, 1980, 253):

> Believing as strongly as they did in divinely called and Holy Spirit-directed leadership, the [Church of God] pioneers rejected all human efforts to "produce" leaders in the church. Yet they quickly learned that the skills of leadership did not

necessarily come in the same package with a divine "call." The pilgrimage through the apprentice method, the missionary homes, the training schools, the Bible colleges, the liberal arts colleges, and later a graduate seminary, represents a long struggle with the question of how to provide for leadership that is both divinely empowered and humanly efficient.

The journey has been long, still continues, and always has been accompanied by the gracious and generous God who both calls and equips.

15. Hope for the Future. Since the early 1970s, perceptions of the prospects for American higher education have been influenced strongly by volatile and sometimes gloomy economic and demographic realities. In general, however, the results have proven more favorable than the forecasts. Higher education has been tenacious and found ways to adjust to the circumstances. In the particular setting of the Church of God movement, too much could not be said about the pioneering courage of men like Joseph T. Wilson, John A. Morrison, Max R. Gaulke, Carlton T. Cumberbatch, and J. Horace Germany. Consult the "Who's Who" section of this book for detail on these and dozens of other pioneering leaders.

Church-related higher education has seemed particularly vulnerable for the various reasons listed above. But it also has been creative in seeking means to face the negative circumstances. It has been forced to clarify its nature and justify its particular mission. It has had to improve its programs of planning and become aggressive in institutional development, particularly the seeking of operational and endowment dollars. It has had to become more conscious of the needs of its immediate constituents—and to find new ones. It has become more accountable to sponsoring church bodies, the many organizations to which it relates, and individuals whom it serves and relies upon. And it has dedicated itself anew to the concept of service. Finally, it has networked nationally in bodies like the *Christian College Coalition*.

Creativity, courage, and faith appear to be very much alive. Therefore, the future, laden with problems as always, is by no means without a sturdy hope! The call is still the same, to prepare persons for service in the light of the work and commission of Jesus Christ. To do so necessarily involves the enhancement of both mind and spirit.

CHAPTER 15

A Vital Resource for Today's Church

In June, 2006, the presidents of the four endorsed-agency colleges of the Church of God movement stood together before a session of the General Assembly. They were there to present a shared report of pivotal information and concern about the urgent importance of Christian higher education in the church's life. They were Jay A. Barber, Jr., of Warner Pacific College, James L. Edwards of Anderson University, John D. Fozard of Mid-America Christian University, and Gregory V. Hall of Warner Southern College. Their report was based on several recent studies of higher education in the United States that brought sobering information. To neglect the schools of the church is to jeopardize the church's future!

The college years are crucial to the faith development of the young. The context chosen for the college experience is key to the nature of the personal shaping that arises from the education received. Those church youth who attend colleges that are not Christ-centered, where faculties are typically "a most liberal lot," experience decline in religious values, attitudes, and behaviors. Therefore, attending Christ-centered colleges is vital to the mission of the church. The university and college presidents called for the church to invest in Christian higher education at this most challenging time.

Many youth of the Church of God movement are not attending a Church of God institution of higher education, often because of not being adequately aware of the church's schools, or having mis-information about what they offer or whether they can be afforded. It is time to get informed and be encouraged. Usually, what is so valuable can also be afforded!

Enhancing the Historic Partnership

The General Assembly, the most representative deliberative body in the Church of God movement, received with appreciation the view of the church's Visioning Conference convened in Chandler, Arizona, in 2002. The view was that leadership development must be seen as a high priority in the church's life. The General Assembly also had been informed in June, 2005, of a "case statement" on behalf of Christian higher education that had emerged from the May, 2005, Consultation on Higher Education in the Church of God convened in Anderson, Indiana. In light of the compelling impact of this statement, the 2005 Assembly gave attention to a resolution presented to it by John D. Fozard, president of Mid-America Christian University, on behalf of the presidents of the other endorsed-agency schools of the church. It overwhelmingly adopted the following resolution:

> WHEREAS, since 1917 institutions of higher learning have served the Church of God movement well and continue to function in a supportive and interdependent manner with other ministries of the movement; and
>
> WHEREAS, these schools have demonstrated willingness to be appropriately accountable to the church and are exercising careful stewardship of their human, physical, and financial resources; and
>
> WHEREAS, with one voice in 2005, these colleges, universities, and seminary, have reaffirmed their commitment to provide excellence in Christian higher education that promotes Christian faith, scholarship, and servanthood in the world—and to do so while respecting each other and valuing

their church relatedness; and

WHEREAS, the current visioning effort of the Church of God movement in North America has highlighted five priority goals, with all of them, especially leadership development, being addressed significantly by these schools; and

WHEREAS, in today's highly competitive world of higher education, those few schools truly committed to the church need every possible encouragement and support; therefore,

BE IT RESOLVED, that the General Assembly of the Church of God, convened in Anderson, Indiana, June, 2005:

1. AFFIRM AND CELEBRATE with its colleges, universities, and seminary the significant partnership that has prevailed between them and the larger life of the Church of God movement for many generations; and

2. RECOGNIZE that the maintenance and enhancement of this historic partnership is crucial for the mentoring of a new generation of pastors and other church leaders who understand and embrace the nature of the Church of God movement and its distinctive mission in the Body of Christ; and

3. CALL ON present pastors and youth leaders in Church of God congregations to:

   A. Promote the Church of God movement's need for higher learning and an appreciative awareness of the particular schools now serving the church so well; and

   B. Recruit and encourage persons to choose as the place for their own educations one of the church's schools; and

C. Turn increasingly to the exceptional human resources
resident in these schools to assist with their own
teaching, preaching, evangelizing, and leadership
development needs.

The Church of God movement marked its 90th year of experience
with its schools of higher education in 2007 (having begun with the
founding of Anderson Bible Training School in 1917). The church's attitude
toward higher education had changed considerably over these decades.
Initially very cautious about all human organizing of the church's life,
including programs of learning that might supplant the generous gifting of
God's Spirit for ministry, the year 2007 saw the movement with a different
attitude. The church still put the highest value on God's directing and
gifting; but now the church was also aware of the complimentary importance
of disciplined learning. It now was proud of its several schools of higher
learning and appreciative of the key resource that they are for the life of
today's church. What is so valuable must be well understood and supported.

Expanding the Church's Mission

Higher education in the Church of God movement began as efforts
to prepare sincere Christians to better serve the church's mission in the
world. These efforts continue on its college and university campuses. In
addition, the schools now have grown in size and strength adequate to allow
them to expand the range of their programs offered and the constituencies
served. On the church's behalf, so many people have observed, the schools
now are the church's largest mission arm.

All Christians are called into Christ's service, whether or not they
function as clergypersons. Programs of ministerial and teacher education
have been central in the curricula of the church's schools historically.
Numerous other fields of professional pursuit now have evolved, including
pre-law, pre-medicine, nursing, graphic arts, music industry,

communications, computer science, business, and more. Technology has opened the doors to on-line degree programs. Demographic developments in the society and shifting employment needs have put emphasis on degree completion programs for working adults. The continuing educational need of baccalaureate graduates has encouraged the development of masters and doctoral programs in Christian ministry, education, business, and other fields. The schools of the church have been responding to the changing needs of the thousands of people seeking their services.

Anderson University has served the mission of the Church of God movement in numerous ways, including through many of its prominent alumni. For example, heralded widely in the gospel music world are three Anderson graduates, each now honored by their alma mater with honorary doctorates: 1959 graduate William J. Gaither (Doctor of Music, 1973); 1965 graduate Gloria Sickal Gaither (Doctor of Letters, 1989); and 1979 graduate Sandi Patty (Doctor of Music, 1991). In the international arena, the TRI-S program (study, serve, share) of the Anderson campus began in 1964 and was led from 1964 to 1998 by Norman Beard, and since then by Willi Kant. Every year hundreds of Anderson students have gone around the world for cross-cultural exposure and hands-on Christian ministry. Many of them have found this experience life-changing and have dedicated their lives to the mission of the church. Other campuses have had similar programs, with the HEART program at Warner Southern College prominent among them.

Recently it has become clear that the campuses of the church are vital to the church in more ways than personal enhancement and leadership development. The 2006 annual report of the General Director of Church of God Ministries, Ronald V. Duncan, to the General Assembly celebrated an important move forward. He said: "Because of some extraordinary gifts received by all of our endorsed educational institutions and Church of God Ministries, Inc., the financial positions have improved dramatically over the past eighteen months." The campuses were now capable of attracting significant funding into the church's life, and they were willing to expend their resources for the church's good. A prime example of this generosity was seen in the 2006 General Assembly sessions.

Warner Auditorium for decades had housed the major worship services of each North American Convention convened in Anderson, Indiana. It had been closed in May, 2005, because of the health danger from the presence of friable asbestos in the internal air of the building. Whatever solution would be chosen to address this crisis, a staggering number of dollars would have to be expended. Anderson University stepped forward and offered a generous solution, one benefiting itself and the whole church. It would purchase 37.7 acres of land owned by Church of God Ministries, Inc., adjacent to the campus, including the closed auditorium. The University was willing to pay a price above the appraised value of the property, continue to make this land and its own facilities available for use by future North American Conventions of the Church of God, and be responsible for the costly razing of the auditorium.

This willingness of Anderson University, and its ability to make this purchase through private gifts to the school, would relieve the church of significant liabilities. The church would be relieved of much of its debt, freeing it for fresh ministry initiatives. The sale of the church property was approved overwhelmingly by the General Assembly, and a letter of sincere appreciation was sent to James L. Edwards, president of the University, and to the school's board of trustees. Schools birthed by the church had grown into great resources vital for the church's future—sometimes in ways totally unexpected.

A Wonderful Investment for the Future

The Church of God movement has been supporting Christian higher education for ninety years, confident that this is a valuable investment for the individual students and the church itself. For example, the 2007 World Ministries Budget of the Church of God in North America includes the following line items for higher education—a major investment indeed.

Anderson University	$707,800
Anderson School of Theology	$319,675
Seminary Tuition (ASOT)	$160,350
Mid-America Christian University	$800,500
Warner Pacific College	$316,200
Warner Southern College	$459,200

Total: $ 2,763,725

Observed Ronald V. Duncan, General Director of Church of God Ministries, in the 2006 publication *A Guide to Financing Christian Higher Education* (Board of Pensions of the Church of God, 2): "Christian higher education is one opportunity to invest in the lives of young people. The foundations being formed during the developmental years of young adulthood carry over for decades. Christian higher education seeks to positively influence men and women from all walks of life in such a way as to build within them a solid foundation of Biblical values." In the same publication, Jeffrey A. Jenness, Executive Secretary-Treasurer of the Board of Pensions of the Church of God movement, shared personally (1): "Both my wife and I have been blessed to have an education from a Church of God institution of higher learning. I have a parent who attended a Church of God institution and now have a child benefiting from that same experience. To say my life has been enriched by the Church of God's commitment to Christian higher education would be a vast understatement." He added this important note about costs: "The difference in cost between a Church of God institution and a state institution is likely not as much as you might think. This guide [the publication] will help you to navigate the financial hurdles that are a part of financing an education today."

For individual students, the substantial cost of attending a church college or university must be seen in light of some very important facts.

Studies regularly show the lifetime income for a college graduate is increased considerably because of the education. Further, the Church of God schools, beyond qualifying their students for most state and federal programs of financial aid available to students in state institutions, have numerous scholarship funds, loan programs, and employment opportunities on campus. For most potential college students from church homes, there is a way to afford the costs if there is academic ability and genuine desire to receive a quality education in a church-related institution.

Anderson University

"The Christian college or university offers higher education at its best, with outstanding Christian faculty in a campus culture committed to the virtues of the Christian faith. All of this is a priceless benefit to the student seeking the challenges of academic and Christian discovery."

Dr. James L. Edwards

ANDERSON UNIVERSITY

Mid-America
Christian University

Dr. John D. Fozard

MID-AMERICA
CHRISTIAN UNIVERSITY

"When choosing a college, be sure to list all the costs! Sometimes parents only evaluate tuition and fees. What about the school's influence on their child's life? We would have preferred to keep our daughter nearer to home. Yet, we asked ourselves, 'Which is harder, having your daughter attend an out-of-state college where her faith is nurtured, or sending her to a state university where professors may destroy her faith?' We realized that cheaper tuition packages may also mean a more dangerous environment for your child!"

Warner Pacific College

Dr. Jay A. Barber, Jr.

"College choice is among the most important of life decisions — the investment families make in Christian higher education will pay dividends throughout a lifetime. Life decisions one often makes during the college years—choosing a spouse, selecting a vocation, and owning faith—set the course for the rest of life. I believe the context we provide at Church of God colleges will best challenge and support the values of the church and your family."

Warner Southern College

Dr. Gregory V. Hall

FAITH • SCHOLARSHIP • SERVANTHOOD

"Institutions of Christian higher education offer students opportunities for both a quality education and discovery of purpose for their lives. Church of God colleges are here to help students discover a biblical Christian worldview and to equip them to express their faith in whatever walk of life they choose. To help shape the intellectual and spiritual lives of young people is a great calling for all of us — Christian college presidents, faculty members, and staff alike. What better educational community is there for a son or daughter than a Christian college?"

Who's Who
In Church of God Higher Education

The history of the Church of God movement has been influenced greatly by the ministries of prominent and gifted leaders. This has been true partly because of an abundance of such individuals and partly because of the movement's emphases on the significance of divine gifts and the evils of institutionalism in church life. Nowhere has the crucial role played by outstanding personalities been more obvious than in the history of the movement's activity in the arena of higher education.

What follows is the identifying of selected Christian educators through whose gifts and dedication the several institutions of higher education of the Church of God were founded and led in their significant avenues of service. While some of these persons pursued significant ministries in addition to higher education, and sometimes in higher education outside the institutions of the Church of God, only those roles associated with higher education in the Church of God have been noted. Earned degrees have been identified for each person as information was available. Dissertation and book titles have been included only if their subject matter relates directly to Church of God higher education or is an autobiography of or biography about the person.

These educational leaders have made a real difference by God's grace! Many generations of young persons have learned and grown, both in mind and spirit, because of their dedication to the calling of God for service in higher education. Most of the names in this Who's Who are or have been administrative or academic leaders of the colleges, universities, and seminary of the Church of God movement in North America, the Caribbean, Africa, Europe, or the Middle East. Hundreds of others have brought their expertise to the classrooms, sharing their wisdom and lives with thousands of students. All deserve honor, whether or not their names appear in this select listing.

Deans of the Anderson School of Theology (taken May 10, 1997)
L. to R.: Drs. David L. Sebastian, James Earl Massey,
Jerry C. Grubbs, Barry L. Callen, and Gene W. Newberry

BAILEY, Ernest O. (1895-1951)
Dean and Registrar, Warner Memorial University, 1929-1933. B.S., University of Minnesota.

BARBER, Jay A., Jr. (1941-)
Vice President for College Advancement, Warner Pacific College, 1981-1985; Executive Vice President, WPC, 1985-1988; President, WPC, 1996 to the present. B.A., Warner Pacific College; M.A., University of San Francisco; L.H.D., Anderson University.

BELL, Dewayne B. (1920-1988)
President, Arlington College, 1963-1969; Assistant to the President, Azusa Pacific University, 1968-1975 and 1976-1977; Vice President, APU, 1975-1976. B.A., Anderson University; L.H.D., Azusa Pacific University.

BELTER, Siegfried (1945-1984)
Faculty member, Gardner Bible College, 1971-1984; Dean, GBC, 1975-1984. B.Th., Gardner Bible College; B.A., University of Alberta; D.D., Gardner Bible College.

BENGTSON, F. Dale (1934-)
Faculty member, Anderson University, 1960-1995; Dean, School of Arts, Culture, and Religion, AU, 1983-1995. B.S., Anderson University; M.Mus., University of Wichita; D.M.A., University of Missouri, Kansas City.

BRUNEAU, John (1940-)
Faculty member, Gardner College, 1999 to present; Dean of the Faculty, GC, 2006 to present. B.A., University of Toronto; M.Div., Regent College.

BUEHLER, John A. (1916-1981)
Faculty member, Anderson University, 1947-1962; Dean, Bay Ridge Christian College, 1960-1970. B.A., University of Pennsylvania; B.Th., Anderson University; Ph.D., Indiana University.

BYRUM, Russell R. (1889-1980)
One of the founders and first faculty members of Anderson Bible Training School (now Anderson University) in 1917. Author of the

influential book *Christian Theology*. Resigned in 1929 from the faculty because he feared the negative impact on the college and the church of the criticism of some ministers about aspects of his teaching. D.D., Anderson University.

CALDWELL, Carl H. (1944 -)

Vice President for Academic Affairs, Dean, Professor of History, Anderson University, 1996 to present. B.A., Anderson University; M.A., Ohio University; Ph.D., Indiana University.

CALDWELL, Irene Smith (1908-1979)

Faculty member, Warner Memorial University, 1930-1932; faculty member, Warner Pacific College, 1945-1966; faculty member, Anderson University School of Theology, 1966-1973; faculty member, Warner Southern College, 1969, 1973-1979. B.A., Northwestern State Teachers College, Oklahoma; M.A., University of Oklahoma; B.Th., Anderson University; M.A., Oberlin Theological Seminary; Ph.D., University of Southern California.

CALDWELL, Mack M. (1897-1981)

Dean, Southern Bible Institute, 1925-1927; faculty member, Warner Pacific College, 1944-1964; faculty member, Warner Southern College, 1969-1970. Played significant role in the establishment of the Commission on Christian Higher Education. Min. Dip., Anderson University; B.A., Whittier College; B.Th., Pacific Bible College; M.Ed., University of Oregon; Ed.D., Oregon State University.

CALLEN, Barry L. (1941-)

Faculty member, Anderson University, 1966 to 2005; Director, Center for Pastoral Studies, Anderson University School of Theology, 1972-1974; Acting Dean, School of Theology of Anderson University, 1973-1974 and 1988-1989; Dean, School of Theology of Anderson University, 1974-1983; undergraduate dean, Anderson University, 1983-1988; Vice President for Academic Affairs, Anderson University, 1983-1990. Founding Editor, Anderson University Press, 2000 to present. Editor of the Church of God historical volumes titled *The First Century* in 1979. M.Th. title: "Church of God Reformation Movement (Anderson, Indiana): A Study in Ecumenical Idealism" (Asbury Theological Seminary).

Ed.D. dissertation title: "Faculty Academic Freedom in Member Institutions of the Christian College Coalition" (Indiana University). Compiler and editor of *Following the Light*, 2000 (contains General Assembly actions related to higher education). Author of *Preparing For Service: The History of Higher Education in the Church of God* (1988), *Faith, Learning, and Life: Views from the President's Office of Anderson University* (1991), *Guide of Soul and Mind: The Story of Anderson University* (1992), and *Staying on Course: A Biography of Robert H. Reardon* (2004). B.A., Geneva College; M.Div., Anderson University School of Theology; M.Th., Asbury Theological Seminary; D.Rel., Chicago Theological Seminary; Ed.D., Indiana University.

CHAPMAN, Milo L. (1915-1996)
Faculty member, Warner Pacific College, 1950-1954; Acting President, WPC, 1954-55; Dean, WPC, 1955-1957; President, WPC, 1957-1962; faculty member, WPC, 1963-1964; faculty member, Arlington College, 1964-1967; faculty member, WPC, 1967-1968; Academic Vice-President, WPC, 1968-1973; faculty member, WPC, 1973-1979; President, WPC, 1979-1981; Provost, WPC, 1974 to present. Chair, Commission on Christian Higher Education, 1972-1978. B.Th., Anderson University; B.D., Th.D., Pacific School of Religion; L.H.D., Anderson University.

CHRISTENSEN, Marshall K. (1941-)
Faculty member, Warner Pacific College, 1966-1975; Academic Vice-President, WPC, 1975-1978; President, WPC, 1981-1996. B.A., Warner Pacific College; M.A., Texas Christian University; Ph.D., University of Oregon.

CONLEY, John W. (1932-)
Member, Governing Board, Mid-America Bible College, 1969-1973; Executive Vice-President, MABC, 1973-1975; President, MABC, 1975-1989. Member, Executive Council, American Association of Bible Colleges, 1984-1989. B.A., Asbury College; M.Th., St. Thomas University; D.D., Asbury College.

COURTNEY, Donald A. (1929-1986)

Faculty member, Anderson University, 1958-1961; faculty member, Anderson University School of Theology, 1961-1966; Executive Secretary-Treasurer, Board of Christian Education of the Church of God, 1966-1986; member, Commission on Christian Higher Education of the Church of God, 1966-1986, chair, 1985-1986. M.Div. thesis title: "A Study of the Development of the Sunday School in the Church of God." Ph.D. dissertation title: "Some Relationships Between Environmental and Institutional Factors and Observed Differences in Classroom Practices in 36 Protestant Church Schools." B.S., University of Pittsburgh; M.Div., Anderson University School of Theology; M.Ed., Ph.D., University of Pittsburgh.

CROCKETT, Isom R. (1921-1996)

Dean, Bay Ridge Christian College, 1959-1960. Member, Governing Board, Anderson University, 1962-1982. B.S., B.A., Anderson University; M.A., Xavier University of New Orleans.

CUMBERBATCH, Carlton T. (1921-)

President, West Indies Theological College, 1959-1988. Thesis title: "The Role of Leadership Training in the Development of the Church of God in the English-speaking Caribbean." B.A., Anderson University; M.A. Rel., Anderson University School of Theology, M.A., Ball State University.

CUMBERBATCH, Theodosia (1926-2001)

Faculty member, West Indies Theological College, 1962-1999, President of WITC, 1989-1999. B.A., M.A., Anderson University and School of Theology.

CURTIS, Melva W. (1928-)

Faculty member, Mid-America Bible College, 1982 to present; Dean, MABC, 1986 to present. Member, Commission on Christian Higher Education of the Church of God, 1986 to present. B.A., California State University, Fresno; M.A. University of San Francisco; Ed.D. candidate, Oklahoma State University.

DAVIS, David W. (1943-   )

President and Dean, Gardner Bible College, 1974-1975. B.S., University of British Columbia; M.Div., Anderson University School of Theology.

DAWSON, Cole (1949-   )

Faculty member, Warner Pacific College, 1977 to present. Vice President for Academic Affairs and Dean of the Faculty, Warner Pacific College, 2005 to present. B.A., Anderson University; M.A., Ph.D., Miami University.

DENNISTON, Charles G. (1939-   )

Faculty member, Bay Ridge Christian College, 1972-1982 and 1987 to present; Dean, BRCC, 1976-1977; President, BRCC, 1982-1987; Director of Development, BRCC, 1987 to present. A.A., Long Beach Community College; B.Th., Bay Ridge Christian College.

DODGE, Harry L. (1914-2003)

Dean, Gardner Bible College, 1953-1957. B.A., University of Cincinnati; B.D., Oberlin Graduate School of Theology; B.Ed., University of Alberta; M.A., University of Akron.

DOTY, Walter M. (1916-   )

Member, Governing Board, Mid-America Bible College, 1955-1966; Dean, MABC, 1955-1969; faculty member, MABC, 1969-1973; Vice-President for Academic Affairs, MABC, 1973-1981; faculty member and Dean of External Studies, MABC, 1981-1983; Dean, Bay Ridge Christian College, 1987 to present. Ed.D. dissertation title: "Factors Which Influenced the Selection of Academic Deans in Thirty-One Texas Public Junior Colleges." B.A., Anderson University; B.D., North American Baptist Seminary; M.Ed., Ed.D., University of Houston; L.H.D., Anderson University.

DRAKES, Frank (1937-   )

Dean, West Indies Theological College, 1974-1988. Dip. Theo., West Indies Theological College; B.A., M.A., University of the West Indies.

EDWARDS, James L. (1943-)

President, Anderson University, 1990 to present. B.A., Anderson University, M.Div., School of Theology of Anderson University. Ph.D., Ohio State University.

ERICKSON, Gerald L. (1915-1997)

Dean, Mid-America Bible College, 1953-1955. B.Th., Anderson University.

ERICKSON, Joyce Q. (1939-)

Dean of the faculty, Warner Pacific College, 1983-1987. B.A., North Central College; M.A., Ph.D., University of Washington.

EUBANKS, Odus K. (1933-)

Faculty member, Mid-America Bible College, 1975-1981; VicePresident for Academic Affairs, MABC, 1981-1985. B.S., Southeast Missouri State University; M.R.E., Southwestern Baptist Theological Seminary; M.Div., Anderson University School of Theology. Ed.D., Texas Southern University.

FOLTZ, Louis G. (1947-)

Faculty member, Warner Pacific College, 1976-1981 and 1983 to present; Dean, WPC, 1981-1983. A.A., Napa College; B.A., M.A., Ph.D., University of California, Berkeley.

FOZARD, John D. (1952 -)

President, Mid-America Christian University, 1999 to present. B.A., Southern Illinois University; M. Min., Anderson University School of Theology; Ph.D., Trinity College and Seminary.

FROESE, Donnalyn (1952 -)

Member/chair of board of trustees, 2001 to present; Comptroller/Registrar, 1979-1986; Administrative Assistant, 1981-1986; President, 2007 to present. B. Th. Gardner College.

FULTON, Leroy M. (1931-)

Member, board of trustees, Warner Southern College, 1964-1969, chair, 1966-1969; President and faculty member, W.S.C., 1969-1990. B.A., Anderson University; M.Div., Anderson University School of Theology; D.D., Anderson University.

GARDNER, Harry C. (1894-1961)

Principal, Gardner Bible College, 1933-1945; President, GBC, 1945-1953, 1957-1961; Dean, GBC, 1933-1950; chair, governing board, GBC, 1933-1950. B.Th., Anderson University; D.D., American College.

GAULKE, Max R. (1910-1992)

President, Mid-America Bible College, 1953-1975. B.A., Anderson University; B.D., Chicago Theological Seminary; M.A., University of Houston; D.D., Anderson University. His biography by Arlo F. Newell is titled *A Servant in God's Kingdom* (1995).

GERMANY, James Horace (1914-2001)

President, Bay Ridge Christian College, 1959-1982, Dean, 1970-1971, 1975-1976. B.Th., L.H.D., Anderson University. His autobiography it titled *At Any Cost* (2000).

GILLIAM, E. Joe (1929-)

President, Warner Pacific College, 1966-1979. L.H.D., Anderson University.

GOUGH, Louis F. (1910-1978)

Faculty member, Warner Pacific College, 1952-1956; faculty member, Anderson University School of Theology, 1956-1960; assistant to the president, WPC, 1960-1962; President, WPC, 1962-1966. B.Th., B.S., Anderson University; B.D., Duke University; Th.D., Princeton Theological Seminary.

GRAY, Albert F. (1886-1969)

Faculty member, Anderson University, 1929-1930; President, Warner Pacific College, 1937-1957; faculty member, WPC, 1957-1960, 1963-1969; chair, governing board, AU, 1931-1948. D.D., Anderson University. Autobiography *Time and Tides on the Western Shore* (1966).

GRUBBS, Jerry C. (1940-)

Member, governing board, Warner Southern College, 1972-1974; faculty member, Anderson University School of Theology, 1973-1988; Director, Center for Pastoral Studies, AU-SOT, 1980-1984; Dean, AU-SOT, 1983-1988; Vice-President for Student Life and Human Resources, AU, 1988 to present. Ed.D. dissertation title: "A

Study of Faculty Members and Students in Selected Mid-Western Schools of Theology to Determine Whether Their Education Orientation is Andragogical or Pedagogical." B.A., Northeast Louisiana University; M.R.E., Anderson University School of Theology; M.S., Ed.D., Indiana University.

GUNPATH, Linda (1970-)
Vice President for Academic Affairs, West Indies Theological College, 2005 to present. B.A., West Indies Theological College; M. Sc. (cand.), University of the West Indies.

HALL, Gregory V. (1951-)
President, Warner Southern College, 1991 to the present. B.A., State University of New York. M.Ed., Ed.D., University of Pittsburgh.

HASTINGS, Raymond E. (1917-)
Faculty member, Mid-America Bible College, 1965-1970, Dean of Students, MABC, 1965-1967; faculty member and Dean, Bay Ridge Christian College, 1971-1974. B.A., Anderson University; M.Div., Anderson University School of Theology.

HAYES, Robert B.
President, Warner Southern College, 1990-1991; Dean, W.S.C., 1991-1992.

HAZEN, Robert J. (1923-2005)
President, Gardner Bible College, 1977-1989. B.Th., Anderson University; D.D., Warner Pacific College.

HOWARD, John Alan (1949-)
Faculty member, Gardner Bible College, 1982 to present; Dean of the Faculty and Chief Operating Officer, GBC, 1984 to 2006. B.A., Anderson University; M.R.E., M.Div., Anderson University School of Theology; S.T.M., University of Winnipeg.

JACK, Ronald M. (1934-)
Faculty member, Anderson University, 1958-1959, 1971; faculty member, Warner Southern College, 1974-1999; Vice-President for Academic Affairs, WSC, 1983-1991. B.A., Anderson University; M.Div., Anderson University School of Theology; M.S., Ph.D., Purdue University.

JANUTOLO, D. Blake (1952-)

Faculty member, Anderson University, 1977 to present; Dean, School of Theoretical and Applied Science, AU, 1985 to present. B.S., West Virginia University; Ph.D., Virginia Polytechnic Institute and State University.

JOHNSON, Donald D. (1929 -)

President of West Indies Theological College, 1957-1959, dean 1959-1961. Faculty member, Anderson School of Theology, 1965-1968. Member of the board of trustees of Warner Pacific College, 1988-2003. Consultant to the Mediterranean Bible College, 1984 to present. B.A., Warner Pacific College; M. Div., Andeson School of Theology; S.T.M., Christian Theological Seminary; Pacific School of Religion.

JOHNSON, Don Deena (1953-)

Dean, Mediterranean Bible College. B.A., Warner Pacific College; M.Div., Anderson School of Theology; M.A., Ball State University.

JOHNSON, John M. (1958-)

Dean, Mediterranean Bible College, 1996-1997; President, MBC, 1997-2003. Faculty member, Warner Pacific College, 2006 to present. B.A., Anderson University; M.Div., Anderson School of Theology; D.Min., Ashland Theological Seminary.

JOINER, C. Herbert, Jr. (1918-1974)

President, Arlington College, 1954-1960. B.A., Anderson University; M.Div., Louisville Presbyterian Seminary.

JONES, Kenneth E. (1920-1999)

Dean, Gardner Bible College, 1950-1951; member, governing board, Jamaica School of Theology, 1960; Principal and faculty member, Jamaica School of Theology, 1962; faculty member, Mid-America Bible College, 1963-1965; member, Commission on Christian Higher Education, 1963-1965, 1985-1986; faculty member, Warner Pacific College, 1965-1974; faculty member, MABC, 1974-1987; Dean, MABC, 1985-1986. B.Th., Anderson University; B.D., Oberlin Graduate School of Theology; M.Th., Winona Lake School of Theology; Ph.D., International Institute for Advanced Studies; D.D., Warner Pacific College.

KELLY, M. Bruce (1937-)

Director, Alumni and Church Relations, 1980-1987, and Assistant to the President for Development, 1998-2001, Warner Pacific College; President, Gardner Bible College, 1989-1997. B.A., D.D., Warner Pacific College.

KEMPIN, Albert J. (1900-1974)

Dean, Arlington College, 1954-1956. B.A., Taylor University; M.Th., University of Southern California; Ph. D., Los Angeles Baptist Theological Seminary.

LINDEMUTH, Marvin H. (1923-2003)

Acting Dean, Warner Pacific College, 1963-1964; Dean, WPC, 1964-1968; faculty member, Anderson University, 1968-1988; assistant to the dean, AU, 1968-1971. B.S., Seattle Pacific University; M.Ed., University of Washington; Ph.D., University of Michigan.

LINN, Otto F. (1887-1965)

Faculty member, Anderson University, 1932-1937; Dean, Warner Pacific College, 1942-1955. B.A., B.S., M.A., Phillips University; Ph.D., Divinity School, University of Chicago.

LOEWEN, Curtis E. (1927-)

Dean, Warner Pacific College, 1973-1975. B.S., Ed.M., Ed.D., Oregon State University.

MACHOLTZ, James D. (1926-1985)

Faculty member, Anderson University, 1953-1985; Dean, School of Theoretical and Applied Science, AU, 1983-1985. B.S., Anderson University, M.S., University of Michigan; M. S., P. E. D., Indiana University.

MARTIN, Earl L. (1892-1961)

Faculty member, Anderson University, 1930-1950; Dean, Anderson University School of Theology, 1950-1953; faculty member, Anderson University, 1953-1957; vice-chair, Commission on Christian Higher Education, 1958; visiting professor, West Indies Theological College, 1958; Acting President, Arlington College, 1960-1961. B. Th., Anderson University; M.A., Northwestern University; B.D., D.D., Anderson University.

MASSEY, James Earl (1930-)

Principal, Jamaica School of Theology, 1963-1966; faculty member and campus pastor, Anderson University, 1969-1977; chair, Commission on Christian Higher Education, 1969-1971 and member, 1987 to present; faculty member, Anderson University School of Theology, 1981-1984. B.R.E., B.Th., Detroit Bible College; M.A., Oberlin Graduate School of Theology; D.O., Asbury Theological Seminary.

MELKI, Camille (1966-)

Dean, Mediterranean Bible College, 1978-1996, President, MBC, 2004 to present. B.A., Anderson University, M.Div., Anderson School of Theology.

MELKI, Fouad B. (1928-1997)

Founding President of Mediterranean Bible College, 1984-1997. B.A., Haigazian University; D.D., Anderson University.

MILLER, Adam W. (1896-1994)

Faculty member, Anderson University, 1941-1962; chair, Study Committee on Graduate Ministerial Training (led to establishment of Anderson University School of Theology); Dean, AU-SOT, 1953-1962. B.A., Anderson University; M.A., Butler University; D.D., Anderson University.

MILLER, E. Darlene (1940-)

Faculty member, Anderson University, 1965-2001; Dean, School of Social and Professional Studies, AU, 1983-2001. B.S., Anderson University; M.A., Ed.D., Ball State University.

MILLER, Gene (1929-)

Faculty member, Mid-America Bible College, 1968-1985; Acting Dean, MABC, 1969-1970; faculty member, Anderson University School of Theology, 1985-1994. B.A., Anderson University; M.Div., Anderson University School of Theology; Ph.D., Duke University.

MILLER, T. Franklin (1910-2004)

Executive Secretary, National Board of Christian Education, 1945-1966; vice-chair, Commission on Christian Higher Education, 1965-1966; faculty member, Anderson University School of Theology,

1950, 1975-1980; Director, Center for Pastoral Studies, 1976-1980. B.A., Gordon College of Theology and Missions; B.D., Butler University School of Religion; D.D., Anderson University. Autobiography titled *Life is the Journey* (2003).

MORRISON, John A. (1893-1965)

Faculty member and Assistant Principal, Anderson University, 1919-1923; Principal, AU, 1923-1925; President, AU, 1925-1958; member, governing board, AU, 1925-1954. D.D., Anderson University.

NEWBERRY, Gene W. (1915-)

Faculty member, Anderson University, 1946-1950; faculty member, Anderson University School of Theology, 1950-1980; Dean, AU-SOT, 1962-1974. B.A., Denison Unversity; B.Th., Anderson University; Ph.D., Duke University; D.D., Rio Grande College.

NICHOLSON, Robert A. (1923-)

Faculty member, Anderson University, 1945 to 1990; Dean, A.U., 1958-1983, Vice-President for Academic Affairs and Dean, A.U., 1971-1983; President and member, governing board, A.U., 1983 to 1990; member, Commission on Christian Higher Education, 1958 to 1990. B.S., Anderson University; M.A., Ph.D., New York University. Autobiography *So I Said Yes!* (Anderson University Press, 2006).

OLT, George Russell (1895-1958)

Faculty member and Dean, Anderson University, 1925-1958; member, governing board, AU, 1925-1945. B.Ph., B.A., Lebanon University; B.A., Wilmington College; M.A., University of Cincinnati; L.H.D., Anderson University.

PAPPAS, Thomas N. (1936-)

Faculty member, Anderson University, 1962-1976; faculty member, Warner Pacific College, 1976-1978; Dean, WPC, 1978-1981. B.A., M.A., Wayne State University; Ph.D., Michigan State University.

PROVIDENCE, Clinton (1946-)

President, West Indies Theological College, 2000 to present. Dip. Th., West Indies Theological College; B.A., Warner Southern College; M.A. (cand.), Trinity Seminary.

RAMSEY, George H. (1922-)

Faculty member, Anderson University, 1947-1948; faculty member and President, Arlington College, 1961-1963; faculty member, AU, 1963-1984. B.S., Anderson University; B.D., Princeton Theological Seminary.

RATZLAFF, Leslie W. (1915-)

Faculty member, Warner Pacific College, 1956-1963; Dean, WPC, 1958-1963; administrator in advance of the beginning of Warner Southern College, 1966-1968; President, Warner Southern College, 1968-1969; Dean, WSC, 1968-1983. Ed.D. dissertation title: "The Implementation of Christian Goals in Christian Liberal Arts Colleges." B.A., B.Th., Anderson University; M.Div., Princeton Theological Seminary; M.A., Ed.D., Teachers College and Union Theological Seminary, Columbia University; L.H.D., Anderson University.

REARDON, Robert H. (1919-2007)

Assistant to the President, Anderson University, 1947-1952; Executive Vice-President, AU, 1952-1958, President, AU, 1958-1983. B.D. thesis titled: "The Doctrine of the Church and the Christian Life in the Church of God Reformation Movement." Author, *The Early Morning Light* (reflections on the first fifty years of the Church of God movement), 1979. B.A., Anderson University; B.D., Oberlin Graduate School of Theology; D.Min., Vanderbilt University; L.H.D., DePauw University; L.H.D., Anderson University. Biography by Barry L. Callen titled *Staying on Course* (2004).

RIGEL, W. Malcolm (1926-)

Member, governing board, Warner Southern College, 1964-1968; faculty member, Dean of Students, WSC, 1968-1979; associate faculty member, Anderson University School of Theology, 1979-1983; faculty member, WSC, 1983-1987. A.A., Vincennes University; B.A., Anderson University; M.A., University of South Florida; S.T.M., University of Dubuque Theological Seminary; S.T.D., Emory University.

RIGEL, William M., Jr. (1948-)

Faculty member, Warner Southern College, 1972 to the present. Dean, W.S.C., 1993 to the present. B.A., Anderson University. M.A., University of South Florida. Ph.D., Florida State University.

RODDY, Ronald N. (1943 -)

Staff, Mid-America Christian University, 1979-1992; Vice President for Academic Affairs, MACU, 1992 to present. B.A., University of Houston; B.S., Gulf-Coast Bible College; M. Ed., Our Lady of the Lake University; Ed. D., Oklahoma State University.

SAGO, Paul E. (1931-)

Vice-President for Financial Affairs, Anderson University, 1968-1976; President, Azusa Pacific University, 1976 to present. Ph.D. dissertation title: "Faculty and Administrative Concepts Relating to Shared Authority in Financial Decision-Making." B.S., Findlay College; M.S., St. Francis College; Ph.D., Walden University.

SARJU, Sawak (1938-)

Dean, Bay Ridge Christian College, 1974-1975. Diploma, West Indies Theological College; B.A., Pacific College; M.R.E., Mennonite Biblical Seminary; D.D., American Bible Institute.

SCHIECK, Gordon A. (1914-2003)

Dean, Gardner Bible College, 1951-1953; Acting President., GBC, 1953-1955; President, GBC, 1967-1974; Interim President, GBC, 1975-1977. B.A., Anderson University; M.A., Syracuse University.

SEBASTIAN, David L. (1948-)

Dean of Anderson University School of Theology, 1995 to present. B.A., Warner Southern College. M.A., Anderson University School of Theology. D. Min., Fuller Theological Seminary.

SHACKLETON, Frederick G. (1922-)

Faculty member, Anderson University, 1946-1950; faculty member, Warner Pacific College, 1950-1954; faculty member, Arlington College, 1954-1956; Dean, Arlington College, 1956-1968; faculty member, Azusa Pacific University, 1968 to present. B.A., Macalester College; M.A., Butler University; D.D., Western Evangelical Seminary.

SIMMONS, Stanford (1953-)

President, Bay Ridge Christian College, 2005 to the present. B.A., Northern Illinois University; M.A., University of the Pacific; Ed. D., University of San Francisco.

SMITH, Donald E. (1935-)

Faculty member, Mid-America Bible College, 1970-1973; Dean, MABC, 1970-1973. B.S., M.Ed., University of Illinois; Ed.D., Illinois State University.

SMITH, John W. V. (1914-1984)

Faculty member, Warner Pacific College, 1949-1952; faculty member, Anderson University School of Theology, 1952-1980, Associate Dean, AU-SOT, 1968-1983; visiting professor, Warner Southern College, 1969. Historian of the Church of God, 1957-1984, authoring in 1980 the comprehensive history of the Church of God titled *The Quest for Holiness and Unity*. Visiting professor, international Bible schools of the Church of God, 1983-1984. Ph.D. dissertation title: "The Approach of the Church of God (Anderson, Indiana) and Comparable Groups to the Problem of Christian Unity." B.A., Northwestern Oklahoma State College; M.A., University of Oklahoma; Ph.D., University of Southern California.

STAFFORD, Gilbert W. (1938-)

Faculty member, Anderson University School of Theology, 1976-2007; Associate Dean, AU-SOT, 1980-2007. Th.D. dissertation titled: "Experiential Salvation and Christian Unity in the Thought of Seven Theologians of the Church of God (Anderson, Indiana). B.A., Anderson University; M.Div., Andover Newton Theological School; Th.D., Boston University School of Theology.

WILLIAMS, Elbert (1945-)

Dean, Bay Ridge Christian College, 1977-1987; Executive Vice President, BRCC, 1983-1987. B.Th., Bay Ridge Christian College; M.S., Henderson State University.

WILLIAMS, Robert C. (1941-)

President, Bay Ridge Christian College, 1987-1991. Member, Commission on Christian Higher Education of the Church of God, 1984-1987. B.Th., Bay Ridge Christian College; M.Ed., Ed.D., University of Southern Mississippi.

WILSON, Joseph T. (1876-1954)

Principal and founder, Anderson Bible Training School (now Anderson University), 1917-1923, member, governing board, Anderson University, 1918-1946, chair, 1925-1931; President and founder, Warner Memorial University, 1929-1933. Graduate, Slippery Rock State Normal School; D.D., Anderson University.

WIUFF, Jarvis C. (1925-)

Dean, Gardner Bible College, 1962-1968. B.A., Anderson University.

YAMABE, Richard N. (1928-)

Dean, Gardner Bible College, 1957-1962 and 1968-1974. B.A., University of British Columbia; M.Div., Anderson University School of Theology.

Doctors of the Church

Historian Merle D. Strege devotes chapter twelve of his history of the Church of God movement (*I Saw the Church*, 2002) to "Doctors of the Church." He explains that the institutions of higher education of the Church of God have shaped the movement's theological landscape in significant ways. He highlights four individuals particularly prominent in this regard, four outstanding "doctors" of the church.

Earl L. Martin
1892-1961
Anderson University

Otto F. Linn
1887-1965
Warner Pacific College

Adam W. Miller
1896-1993
Anderson University

Albert F. Gray
1886-1969
Warner Pacific College

Index of Persons

T

U/V

W